The Nobel Reader

....

The NObel Reader

Short Fiction, Poetry, and Prose by Nobel Laureates in Literature

....

Edited by Jonathan Eisen and Stuart Troy

Clarkson N. Potter, INC./Publishers

Distributed by Crown Publishers, Inc., New York

Every effort has been made to locate the copyright holders of materials used in this book. Should there be any omissions or errors, we apologize and shall be pleased to make the appropriate acknowledgments in future editions. A detailed list of acknowledgments is located on pages 335–338.

Introduction and compilation copyright © 1987 by Jonathan Eisen and Stuart Troy

Published by Clarkson N. Potter, Inc., 225 Park Avenue South, New York, New York 10003 and represented in Canada by the Canadian MANDA Group.

CLARKSON N. POTTER, POTTER, and colophon are trademarks of Clarkson N. Potter, Inc.

Manufactured in the United States of America

Designed by Drenttel Doyle Partners

Library of Congress Cataloging-in-Publication Data

The Nobel reader.
1. Literature, Modern—20th century. 2. Nobel prizes. I. Eisen, Jonathan. II. Troy, Stuart.
PN6014.N57 1987   808.8'004   87-2448
ISBN 0-517-56351-7
10 9 8 7 6 5 4 3 2 1

First Edition

....

TO Alma S. Daniel and
Jessica Bess Troy,

for whom appearances were once important,

here appears a book.

—S. T.

....

TO Pam Krauss

for her engaged participation and patience.

Also to my relentless agent,

Ellen Levine,

for somewhat obscure

but nevertheless valid reasons.

—J. E.

....

CONTENTS

Preface ix

1901 René F. A. Sully Prudhomme ★ The Appointment 2

1907 Rudyard Kipling ★ Lispeth; Mandalay 4

1909 Selma Lagerlöf ★ The Peace of God 12

1913 Rabindranath Tagore ★ The Cabuliwallah 24

1917 Henrik Pontoppidan ★ Eagle's Flight 32

1923 William Butler Yeats ★ The Rose of the World;
Stream and Sun at Glendalough; Quarrel
in Old Age 37

1925 George Bernard Shaw ★ The Religion of the
Future 40

1929 Thomas Mann ★ The Infant Prodigy 48

1930 Sinclair Lewis ★ A Letter from the Queen 58

1932 John Galsworthy ★ The Consummation 76

1934 Luigi Pirandello ★ A Breath of Air 82

1936 Eugene O'Neill ★ Ile 90

1938 Pearl S. Buck ★ The Good Deed 106

1945 Gabriela Mistral ★ Drops of Gall; Rodin's Thinker .. 126

1946 Hermann Hesse ★ Inside and Outside 128

1947 André Gide ★ The Return of the Prodigal Son 140

Contents

1948   T. S. ELIOT ★ SONG; ON A PORTRAIT; AT GRADUATION
1905; SPLEEN 153

1949   WILLIAM FAULKNER ★ THRIFT 156

1950   BERTRAND RUSSELL ★ HAS RELIGION MADE USEFUL
CONTRIBUTIONS TO CIVILIZATION? 174

1951   PÄR LAGERKVIST ★ THE MYTH OF MANKIND 192

1954   ERNEST HEMINGWAY ★ INDIAN CAMP 198

1957   ALBERT CAMUS ★ THE RENEGADE 204

1958   BORIS PASTERNAK ★ THE NOBEL PRIZE 219

1961   IVO ANDRIĆ ★ THIRST 221

1962   JOHN STEINBECK ★ THE CHRYSANTHEMUMS 232

1966   S. Y. AGNON ★ THE KERCHIEF 244

1969   SAMUEL BECKETT ★ THE CALMATIVE 256

1970   ALEKSANDR SOLZHENITSYN ★ IN YESENIN COUNTRY;
THE ASHES OF A POET; THE OLD BUCKET;
A JOURNEY ALONG THE OKA; REFLECTIONS 270

1971   PABLO NERUDA ★ GENTLEMAN ALONE 280

1978   ISAAC BASHEVIS SINGER ★ SHORT FRIDAY 283

1982   GABRIEL GARCÍA MÁRQUEZ ★ EVA IS INSIDE HER CAT 295

1984   JAROSLAV SIEFERT ★ "YOU ARE ASKING ..."; ORANGEADE 306

1986   WOLE SOYINKA ★ THE MAN DIED 311

Afterword: Alfred Nobel's Literary Legacy 329

Acknowledgments 335

PREFACE

T HE ANTICIPATION AND EXCITEMENT
generated by the announcement of the Nobel laureate for literature
each year is matched only by major political and athletic events.
Each December 10 (the anniversary of Alfred Nobel's death) the
attention of the literary world focuses on Sweden, awaiting the news
that will be debated for months, in some cases for years, afterward.

All this with good reason, for the Nobel Prize for literature is the
most famous and (despite the politics and desire for balance involved in the decisions) arguably the most influential in the realm of
the arts. Controversy notwithstanding—and there is always controversy, whoever the recipient—the Nobel Prize has endured for
nearly a century as the ultimate literary award. Whether coveted or
rejected (some, like Jean-Paul Sartre, have refused the prize), the
fame and attention that accompany the prize often last a lifetime
and beyond.

The Nobel Reader is our attempt to bring together not just a representative selection of the winners since the prize's inception in
1901. We have also tried to select some of each author's most *interesting* work. We were looking for readability, timeless relevance, and
in some cases (as with the Eugene O'Neill selection) rarity.

PREFACE

We believe that there is historical continuity in these pages; we have endeavored to follow Nobel's original idea of honoring those writers whose concern for universal humanist goals carried them past art for art's sake without sacrificing their craft on the altar of ideology. We hope, too, that this anthology will give many hours of pleasure as well.

Jonathan Eisen
Stuart Troy

New York City

The Nobel Reader

René F. A. Sully Prudhomme

(1839–1907)

Prize awarded 1901 "in special recognition of his poetic composition, which gives evidence of lofty idealism, artistic perfection, and a rare combination of the qualities of both heart and intellect." ★ *Sully Prudhomme was just twenty-six when his first book of poetry,* **Stances et Poèmes,** *was published to critical acclaim. (A promising student of both law and science, Sully Prudhomme had turned to writing after his eyesight failed.) His poetry earned him a lifetime seat in the French Academy as well as popularity in France second only to that of Victor Hugo.*

Philosophically, Sully Prudhomme was a positivist. His poetry explored metaphysical and scientific themes in a formal, elegant style reminiscent of nineteenth-century writers. But his contemporary subject matter, foreshadowing that of the existentialists, made him a pivotal writer. Two long philosophical poems, **La Justice** *(1878) and* **Le Bonheur** *(1888), are considered his finest works. The tenderness and cool intellectualization of his poetry, his renown and philosophical subject matter, made Sully Prudhomme a strong selection for the first Nobel Prize for literature.*

2

THE APPOINTMENT

It's late; the astronomer in his lonely height,
Exploring all the dark, describes afar
Orbs that like distant islands of splendor are,
And mornings brightening in the infinite.

Like winnowed grain the worlds go by in flight,
Or swarm in glistening spaces nebular;
He summons one disheveled wandering star,—
Return ten centuries hence on such a night.

The star will come. It dare not by one hour
Cheat Science, or belie her calculation;
Men will have passed, but watchful in the tower
Man shall remain in sleepless contemplation;
And should all men have perished there in turn,
Truth in their place would watch that star's return.

(Translation by the Editors)

Rudyard Kipling

......

(1865–1936)

Prize awarded 1907 "in consideration of the power of observation, origi-nality of imagination, virility of ideas, and remarkable talent for narra-tion. . . ." ★ England's first Nobel Prize winner, Rudyard Kipling was born in India, the locale of his most memorable writings. Though Kipling was educated in England, he returned at twenty-six to India, where he worked as a journalist for a time. Kipling is best known for his short stories and poems celebrating the people and politics of the British empire's Eastern extension, among them "The White Man's Burden," "Mandalay," and "Gunga Din." His glorified depiction of the common British soldier in early poetry collections (Departmental Ditties, *1886) and volumes of stories* (Plain Tales from the Hills, *1887) earned him enormous popularity in his home country.* The Jungle Book *(1894),* Second Jungle Book *(1895),* Kim *(1901), and* Just So Stories for Little Children *(1902), written during the four years Kipling lived in Vermont, are enduring children's classics.*

With the decline of the idealistic view of colonialism and the widespread disillusionment following World War I, Kipling's popularity declined. But, due in part to the efforts of T. S. Eliot and George Orwell (himself once a colonial functionary in Burma), and to the timeless qualities of local color and humor, skillful imagery, and clear narrative style, Kipling's literary reputation has survived. His novels* The Light That Failed *(1891),* Captains Courageous *(1897),* The Man Who Would Be King *(1888), and* The Ballad of Gunga Din *(1890) have been successfully translated into film.*

4

LISPETH

Look, you have cast out Love! What Gods are these
  You bid me please?
The Three in One, the One in Three? Not so!
  To my own gods I go.
It may be they shall give me greater ease
Than your cold Christ and tangled Trinities.

.......THE CONVERT

SHE WAS THE DAUGHTER OF SONOO, A HILL-man of the Himalayas, and Jadéh his wife. One year their maize failed, and two bears spent the night in their only opium poppyfield just above the Sutlej Valley on the Kotgarh side; so, next season, they turned Christian, and brought their baby to the Mission to be baptized. The Kotgarh Chaplain christened her Elizabeth, and "Lispeth" is the Hill or *pahari* pronunciation.

Later, cholera came into the Kotgarh Valley and carried off Sonoo and Jadéh, and Lispeth became half servant, half companion, to the wife of the then Chaplain of Kotgarh. This was after the reign of the Moravian missionaries in that place, but before Kotgarh had quite forgotten her title of "Mistress of the Northern Hills."

Whether Christianity improved Lispeth, or whether the gods of her own people would have done as much for her under any circumstances, I do not know; but she grew very lovely. When a Hill-girl grows lovely, she is worth travelling fifty miles over bad ground to look upon. Lispeth had a Greek face—one of those faces people paint so often, and see so seldom. She was of a pale, ivory colour, and, for her race, extremely tall. Also, she possessed eyes that were wonderful; and, had she not been dressed in the abominable print-cloths affected by Missions, you would, meeting her on the hillside unexpectedly, have thought her the original Diana of the Romans going out to slay.

Lispeth took to Christianity readily, and did not abandon it when she reached womanhood, as do some Hill-girls. Her own people hated her because she had, they said, become a white woman and

5

washed herself daily; and the Chaplain's wife did not know what to do with her. One cannot ask a stately goddess, five feet ten in her shoes, to clean plates and dishes. She played with the Chaplain's children and took classes in the Sunday School, and read all the books in the house, and grew more and more beautiful, like the Princesses in fairy tales. The Chaplain's wife said that the girl ought to take service in Simla as a nurse or something "genteel." But Lispeth did not want to take service. She was very happy where she was.

When travellers—there were not many in those years—came in to Kotgarh, Lispeth used to lock herself into her own room for fear they might take her away to Simla, or out into the unknown world.

One day, a few months after she was seventeen years old, Lispeth went out for a walk. She did not walk in the manner of English ladies—a mile and a half out, with carriage-ride back again. She covered between twenty and thirty miles in her little constitutionals, all about and about, between Kotgarh and Narkanda. This time she came back at full dusk, stepping down the breakneck descent into Kotgarh with something heavy in her arms. The Chaplain's wife was dozing in the drawing-room when Lispeth came in breathing heavily and very exhausted with her burden. Lispeth put it down on the sofa, and said simply, "This is my husband. I found him on the Bagi Road. He has hurt himself. We will nurse him, and when he is well your husband shall marry him to me."

This was the first mention Lispeth had ever made of her matrimonial views, and the Chaplain's wife shrieked with horror. However, the man on the sofa needed attention first. He was a young Englishman, and his head had been cut to the bone by something jagged. Lispeth said she had found him down the hillside, and had brought him in. He was breathing queerly and was unconscious.

He was put to bed and tended by the Chaplain, who knew something of medicine; and Lispeth waited outside the door in case she could be useful. She explained to the Chaplain that this was the man she meant to marry; and the Chaplain and his wife lectured her severely on the impropriety of her conduct. Lispeth listened quietly, and repeated her first proposition. It takes a great deal of Christianity to wipe out uncivilised Eastern instincts, such as falling in love at first sight. Lispeth, having found the man she worshipped, did not see why she should keep silent as to her choice. She had no intention of being sent away, either. She was going to nurse that

Englishman until he was well enough to marry her. This was her programme.

After a fortnight of slight fever and inflammation, the Englishman recovered coherence and thanked the Chaplain and his wife, and Lispeth—especially Lispeth—for their kindness. He was a traveller in the East, he said—they never talked about "globe-trotters" in those days, when the P. & O. fleet was young and small—and had come from Dehra Dun to hunt for plants and butterflies among the Simla hills. No one at Simla, therefore, knew anything about him. He fancied that he must have fallen over the cliff while reaching out for a fern on a rotten tree-trunk, and that his coolies must have stolen his baggage and fled. He thought he would go back to Simla when he was a little stronger. He desired no more mountaineering.

He made small haste to go away, and recovered his strength slowly. Lispeth objected to being advised either by the Chaplain or his wife; therefore the latter spoke to the Englishman, and told him how matters stood in Lispeth's heart. He laughed a good deal, and said it was very pretty and romantic, but, as he was engaged to a girl at home, he fancied that nothing would happen. Certainly he would behave with discretion. He did that. Still he found it very pleasant to talk to Lispeth, and walk with Lispeth, and say nice things to her, and call her pet names while he was getting strong enough to go away. It meant nothing at all to him, and everything in the world to Lispeth. She was very happy while the fortnight lasted, because she had found a man to love.

Being a savage by birth, she took no trouble to hide her feelings, and the Englishman was amused. When he went away, Lispeth walked with him up the Hill as far as Narkanda, very troubled and very miserable. The Chaplain's wife, being a good Christian and disliking anything in the shape of fuss or scandal—Lispeth was beyond her management entirely—had told the Englishman to tell Lispeth that he was coming back to marry her. "She is but a child, you know, and, I fear, at heart a heathen," said the Chaplain's wife. So all the twelve miles up the Hill the Englishman, with his arm round Lispeth's waist, was assuring the girl that he would come back and marry her; and Lispeth made him promise over and over again. She wept on the Narkanda Ridge till he had passed out of sight along the Muttiani path.

Then she dried her tears and went in to Kotgarh again, and said to the Chaplain's wife, "He will come back and marry me. He has gone to his own people to tell them so." And the Chaplain's wife soothed Lispeth and said, "He will come back." At the end of two months Lispeth grew impatient, and was told that the Englishman had gone over the seas to England. She knew where England was, because she had read little geography primers; but, of course, she had no conception of the nature of the sea, being a Hill-girl. There was an old puzzle-map of the world in the house. Lispeth had played with it when she was a child. She unearthed it again, and put it together of evenings, and cried to herself, and tried to imagine where her Englishman was. As she had no ideas of distance or steamboats, her notions were somewhat wild. It would not have made the least difference had she been perfectly correct; for the Englishman had no intention of coming back to marry a Hill-girl. He forgot all about her by the time he was butterfly-hunting in Assam. He wrote a book on the East afterwards. Lispeth's name did not appear there.

At the end of three months Lispeth made daily pilgrimage to Narkanda to see if her Englishman was coming along the road. It gave her comfort, and the Chaplain's wife finding her happier thought that she was getting over her "barbarous and most indelicate folly." A little later the walks ceased to help Lispeth, and her temper grew very bad. The Chaplain's wife thought this a profitable time to let her know the real state of affairs—that the Englishman had only promised his love to keep her quiet—that he had never meant anything, and that it was wrong and improper of Lispeth to think of marriage with an Englishman, who was of a superior clay, besides being promised in marriage to a girl of his own people. Lispeth said that all this was clearly impossible because he had said he loved her, and the Chaplain's wife had, with her own lips, asserted that the Englishman was coming back.

"How can what he and you said be untrue?" asked Lispeth.

"We said it as an excuse to keep you quiet, child," said the Chaplain's wife.

"Then you have lied to me," said Lispeth, "you and he?"

The Chaplain's wife bowed her head, and said nothing. Lispeth was silent too for a little time; then she went out down the valley, and returned in the dress of a Hill-girl—infamously dirty, but without the nose-stud and ear-rings. She had her hair braided into the long pigtail, helped out with black thread, that Hill-women wear.

"I am going back to my own people," said she. "You have killed

Lispeth. There is only left old Jadéh's daughter—the daughter of a *pahari* and the servant of *Tarka Devi*. You are all liars, you English."

By the time that the Chaplain's wife had recovered from the shock of the announcement that Lispeth had 'verted to her mother's gods the girl had gone; and she never came back.

She took to her own unclean people savagely, as if to make up the arrears of the life she had stepped out of; and, in a little time, she married a woodcutter who beat her after the manner of *paharis*, and her beauty faded soon.

"There is no law whereby you can account for the vagaries of the heathen," said the Chaplain's wife, "and I believe that Lispeth was always at heart an infidel." Seeing she had been taken into the Church of England at the mature age of five weeks, this statement does not do credit to the Chaplain's wife.

Lispeth was a very old woman when she died. She had always a perfect command of English, and when she was sufficiently drunk could sometimes be induced to tell the story of her first love-affair.

It was hard then to realise that the bleared, wrinkled creature, exactly like a wisp of charred rag, could ever have been "Lispeth of the Kotgarh Mission."

MANDALAY

By the old Moulmein Pagoda, lookin' eastward to the sea,
There's a Burma girl a-settin', and I know she thinks o' me;
For the wind is in the palm-trees, and the temple-bells they say:
"Come you back, you British soldier; come you back to Mandalay!"
Come you back to Mandalay,
Where the old Flotilla lay:
Can't you 'ear their paddles chunkin' from Rangoon to Mandalay?
On the road to Mandalay,
Where the flyin'-fishes play,
An' the dawn comes up like thunder outer China 'crost the Bay!

'Er petticoat was yaller an' 'er little cap was green,
An' 'er name was Supi-yaw-lat—jes' the same as Theebaw's Queen,
An' I seed her first a-smokin' of a whackin' white cheroot,
An' a-wastin' Christian kisses on an 'eathen idol's foot:
Bloomin' idol made o' mud—
Wot they called the Great Gawd Budd—
Plucky lot she cared for idols when I kissed 'er where she stud!
On the road to Mandalay . . .

When the mist was on the rice-fields an' the sun was droppin' slow,
She'd git 'er little banjo an' she'd sing *"Kulla-lo-lo!"*
With 'er arm upon my shoulder an' 'er cheek agin my cheek
We useter watch the steamers an' the *hathis* pilin' teak.
Elephints a-pilin' teak
In the sludgy, squdgy creek,
Where the silence 'ung that 'eavy you was 'arf afraid to speak!
On the road to Mandalay . . .

But that's all shove be'ind me—long ago an' fur away,
An' there ain't no 'busses runnin' from the Bank to Mandalay;
An' I'm learnin' 'ere in London what the ten-year soldier tells:
"If you've 'eard the East a-callin', you won't never 'eed naught else."
No! you won't 'eed nothin' else
But them spicy garlic smells,

An' the sunshine an' the palm-trees an' the tinkly temple-bells;
On the road to Mandalay . . .

I am sick o' wastin' leather on these gritty pavin'-stones,
An' the blasted Henglish drizzle wakes the fever in my bones;
'Tho' I walks with fifty 'ousemaids outer Chelsea to the Strand,
An' they talks a lot o' lovin', but wot do they understand?
Beefy face an' grubby 'and—
Law! wot do they understand?
I've a neater, sweeter maiden in a cleaner, greener land!
On the road to Mandalay . . .

Ship me somewheres east of Suez, where the best is like the worst,
Where there aren't no Ten Commandments an' a man can raise a
    thirst;
For the temple-bells are callin', an' it's there that I would be—
By the old Moulmein Pagoda, looking lazy at the sea;
On the road to Mandalay,
Where the old Flotilla lay,
With our sick beneath the awnings when we went to Mandalay!
O the road to Mandalay,
Where the flyin'-fishes play,
An' the dawn comes up like thunder outer China 'crost the Bay!

selma Lagerlöf

(1858–1940)

Prize awarded 1909 "in appreciation of the lofty idealism, vivid imagination, and spiritual perception that characterize her writings." ★ *Selma Lagerlöf, the first woman to be awarded the Nobel Prize, achieved her earliest successes while working as a country school teacher. Folk tales and peasant themes often provided her inspiration; her first novel,* Gösta Berling's Saga *(1891), chronicled the legends remembered from her childhood. In Lagerlöf's powerfully evocative narratives, a clear sense of her personal Christian morality is evident. Although critics initially deprecated her unusual style and subject matter, the power and energy of her tales eventually won her both critical and popular acclaim.*

Lagerlöf's two-volume novel, Jerusalem *(1901–1902), which recounted the experiences of Swedish peasants who immigrated to the Holy Land and dedicated themselves to good works, was well received and marked the beginning of an outpouring of successful novels. With the appearance of* The Wonderful Adventures of Nils *(1906–1907), a children's book that is still highly regarded, Lagerlöf achieved international recognition as one of Sweden's greatest writers. Biblical and folkloric themes continued to inform her later work (*The Miracles of Antichrist, *1897), and her psychological insight is apparent in novels such as* The Tale of a Manor *(1899). Memories of my Childhood (1930) is a stirring autobiography. In 1914 Lagerlöf was elected to the Swedish Academy, the first woman ever to be so honored.*

THE PEACE OF GOD

ONCE UPON A TIME THERE WAS AN OLD farmhouse. It was Christmas Eve, the sky was heavy with snow, and the north wind was biting. It was just that time in the afternoon when everybody was busy finishing their work before they went to the bathhouse to have their Christmas bath. There they had made such a fire that the flames went right up the chimney, and sparks and soot were whirled about by the wind and fell down on the snow-decked roofs of the outhouses. And as the flames appeared above the chimney of the bathhouse and rose like a fiery pillar above the farm, everyone suddenly felt that Christmas was at hand. The girl who was scrubbing the entrance floor began to hum, although the water was freezing in the bucket beside her. The men in the woodshed who were cutting Christmas logs began to cut two at a time and swung their axes as merrily as if log cutting were a mere pastime.

An old woman came out of the pantry with a large pile of cakes in her arms. She went slowly across the yard into the large red-painted dwelling house, carried them carefully into the best room, and put them down on the long seat. Then she spread the tablecloth on the table and arranged the cakes in heaps, a large and a small cake in each heap. She was a singularly ugly old woman, with reddish hair, heavy drooping eyelids, and a peculiar strained look about the mouth and chin, as if the muscles were too short. But being Christmas Eve, there was such a joy and peace over her that one did not notice how ugly she was.

But there was one person on the farm who was not happy, and

13

that was the girl who was tying up the whisks made of birch twigs that were to be used for the baths. She sat near the fireplace, and had a whole armful of fine birch twigs lying beside her on the floor, but the withes with which she was to bind the twigs would not keep knotted. The best room had a narrow, low window, with small panes, and through them the light from the bathhouse shone into the room, playing on the floor and gilding the birch twigs. But the higher the fire burned, the more unhappy was the girl. She knew that the whisks would fall to pieces as soon as one touched them, and that she would never hear the last of it until the next Christmas fire was lighted.

Just as she sat there bemoaning herself, the person of whom she was most afraid came into the room. It was her master, Ingmar Ingmarson. He was sure to have been to the bathhouse to see if the stove was hot enough, and now he wanted to see how the whisks were getting on. He was old, was Ingmar Ingmarson, and he was fond of everything old, and just because people were beginning to leave off bathing in the bathhouses and being whipped with birch twigs, he made a great point of having it done on his farm, and having it done properly.

Ingmar Ingmarson wore an old coat of sheepskin, skin trousers, and shoes smeared over with pitch. He was dirty and unshaven, slow in all his movements, and came in so softly that one might very well have mistaken him for a beggar. His features resembled his wife's features, and his ugliness resembled his wife's ugliness, for they were relations, and from the time the girl first began to notice anything, she had learned to feel a wholesome reverence for anybody who looked like that; for it was a great thing to belong to the old family of the Ingmars, which had always been the first in the village. But the highest to which a man could attain was to be Ingmar Ingmarson himself and be the richest, the wisest, and the mightiest in the whole parish.

Ingmar Ingmarson went up to the girl, took one of the whisks, and swung it in the air. It immediately fell to pieces; one of the twigs landed on the Christmas table, another on the big four-poster.

"I say, my girl," said old Ingmar, laughing, "do you think one uses that kind of whisk when one takes a bath at the Ingmars', or are you very tender, my girl?"

When the girl saw that her master did not take it more seriously than that, she took heart and answered that she could certainly make whisks that would not go to pieces if she could get proper withes to bind them with.

"Then I suppose I must try to get some for you, my girl," said old Ingmar, for he was in a real Christmas humor.

He went out of the room, stepped over the girl who was scouring the floor, and remained standing on the doorstep, to see if there were anyone about whom he could send to the birch wood for some withes. The farmhands were still busy cutting Yule logs; his son came out of the barn with the Christmas sheaf; his two sons-in-law were putting the carts into the shed so that the yard could be tidy for the Christmas festival. None of them had time to leave their work.

The old man then quietly made up his mind to go himself. He went across the yard as if he were going into the cowshed, looked cautiously around to make sure no one noticed him, and stole along outside the barn where there was a fairly good road to the wood. The old man thought it was better not to let anyone know where he was going, for either his son or his sons-in-law might then have begged him to remain at home, and old people like to have their own way.

He went down the road, across the fields, through the small pine forest into the birch wood. Here he left the road and waded in the snow to find some young birches.

About the same time the wind at last accomplished what it had been busy with the whole day: it tore the snow from the clouds and now came rushing through the wood with a long train of snow after it.

Ingmar Ingmarson had just stooped down and cut off a birch twig when the wind came tearing along laden with snow. Just as the old man was getting up, the wind blew a whole heap of snow in his face. His eyes were full of snow, and the wind whirled so violently around him that he was obliged to turn around once or twice.

The whole misfortune, no doubt, arose from Ingmar Ingmarson being so old. In his young days a snowstorm would certainly not have made him dizzy. But now everything danced around him as if he had joined in a Christmas polka, and when he wanted to go home he went in the wrong direction. He went straight into the large pine forest behind the birch wood instead of going toward the fields.

It soon grew dark, and the storm continued to howl and whirl

15

around him among the young trees on the outskirts of the forest. The old man saw quite well that he was walking among fir trees, but he did not understand that this was wrong, for there were also fir trees on the other side of the birch wood nearest the farm. But by and by he got so far into the forest that everything was quiet and still—one could not feel the storm, and the trees were high with thick stems—then he found out that he had mistaken the road and would turn back.

He became excited and upset at the thought that he *could* lose his way, and as he stood there in the midst of the pathless wood, he was not sufficiently clear-headed to know in which direction to turn. He went first to the one side and then to the other. At last it occurred to him to retrace his way in his own footprints, but darkness came on, and he could no longer follow them. The trees around him grew higher and higher. Whichever way he went, it was evident to him that he got farther and farther into the forest.

It was like witchcraft and sorcery, he thought, that he should be running about the woods like this all evening and be too late for the bathing. He turned his cap and re-bound his garter, but his head was no clearer. It had become quite dark, and he began to think that he would have to remain the whole night in the woods.

He leaned against a tree, stood still for a little, and tried to collect his thoughts. He knew this forest so well, and had walked in it so much, that he ought to know every single tree. As a boy he had gone there and tended sheep. He had gone there and laid snares for the birds. In his young days he had helped to fell trees there. He had seen old trees cut down and new ones grow up. At last he thought he had an idea where he was and fancied if he went that and that way, he must come upon the right road; but all the same, he only went deeper and deeper into the forest.

Once he felt smooth, firm ground under his feet and knew that he had at last come to some road. He tried now to follow this, for a road, he thought, was bound to lead to some place or other. But then the road ended at an open space in the forest, and there the snowstorm had it all its own way; there was neither road nor path, only drifts and loose snow. Then the old man's courage failed him; he felt like some poor creature destined to die a lonely death in the wilderness.

He began to grow tired of dragging himself through the snow, and time after time he sat down on a stone to rest; but as soon as he sat down he felt he was on the point of falling asleep, and he knew he would be frozen to death if he did fall asleep. Therefore he tried to walk and walk; that was the only thing that could save him. But all at once he could not resist the inclination to sit down. He thought if he could only rest, it did not matter if it did cost him his life.

It was so delightful to sit down that the thought of death did not in the least frighten him. He felt a kind of happiness at the thought that when he was dead the account of his whole life would be read aloud in the church. He thought of how beautifully the old dean had spoken about his father, and how something equally beautiful would be sure to be said about him. The dean would say that he had owned the oldest farm in the district, and he would speak about the honor it was to belong to such a distinguished family, and then something would be said about responsibility. Of course there was responsibility in the matter; that he had always known. One must endure to the very last when one was an Ingmar.

The thought rushed through him that it was not befitting for him to be found frozen to death in the wild forest. He would not have that handed down to posterity; and he stood up again and began to walk. He had been sitting so long that masses of snow fell from his fur coat when he moved. But soon he sat down again and began to dream.

The thought of death now came quite gently to him. He thought about the whole of the funeral and all the honor they would show his dead body. He could see the table laid for the great funeral feast in the large room on the first floor: the dean and his wife in the seats of honor; the justice of the peace, with the white frill spread over his narrow chest; the major's wife in full dress, with a low silk bodice and her neck covered with pearls and gold. He saw all the best rooms draped in white—white sheets before the windows, white over the furniture; branches of fir strewn the whole way from the entrance hall to the church; house cleaning and butchering, brewing and baking for a fortnight before the funeral; the corpse on a bier in the inmost room; smoke from the newly lighted fires in the rooms; the whole house crowded with guests; singing over the body while the lid of the coffin was being screwed on; silver plates on the coffin; twenty loads of wood burned in a fortnight; the whole village busy cooking food to take to the funeral; all the tall hats newly ironed; all the corn brandy from the autumn drunk up during the funeral feast; all the roads crowded with people as at fair time.

17

Again the old man started up. He had heard them sitting and talking about him during the feast.

"But how did he manage to go and get frozen to death?" asked the justice of the peace. "What could he have been doing in the large forest?"

And the captain would say that it was probably from Christmas ale and corn brandy. And that roused him again. The Ingmars had never been drunkards. It should never be said of him that he was muddled in his last moments. And he began again to walk and walk; but he was so tired that he could scarcely stand on his legs. It was quite clear to him now that he had got far into the forest, for there were no paths anywhere but many large rocks, of which he knew there were none lower down. His foot caught between two stones, so that he had difficulty in getting it out, and he stood and moaned. He was quite done for.

Suddenly he fell over a heap of fagots. He fell softly onto the snow and branches, so he was not hurt, but he did not take the trouble to get up again. He had no other desire in the world than to sleep. He pushed the fagots to one side and crept under them as if they were a rug; but when he pushed himself under the branches, he felt that underneath there was something warm and soft. This must be a bear, he thought.

He felt the animal move and heard it sniff; but he lay still. The bear might eat him if it liked, he thought. He had not strength enough to move a single step to get out of its way.

But it seemed as if the bear did not want to harm anyone who sought its protection on such a night as this. It moved a little farther into its lair, as if to make room for its visitor, and directly afterward it slept again with even, snorting breath.

In the meantime there was but scanty Christmas joy in the old farm of the Ingmars. The whole of Christmas Eve they were looking for Ingmar Ingmarson. First they went all over the dwelling house and all the outhouses. They searched high and low from loft to cellar. Then they went to the neighboring farms and inquired for Ingmar Ingmarson.

As they did not find him, his sons and his sons-in-law went into the fields and roads. They used the torches that should have lighted the way for people going to early service on Christmas morning in the search for him. The terrible snowstorm had hidden all traces, and the howling of the wind drowned the sound of their voices when they called and shouted. They were out and about until long after midnight, but then they saw that it was useless to continue the search, that they must wait until daylight to find the old man.

At the first pale streak of dawn everybody was up at Ingmar's farm, and the men stood about the yard ready to set out for the wood. But before they started, the old housewife came and called them into the best room. She told them to sit down on the long benches; she herself sat down by the Christmas table with the Bible in front of her and began to read. She tried her best to find something suitable for the occasion and chose the story of the man who was traveling from Jerusalem to Jericho and fell among thieves.

She read slowly and monotonously about the unfortunate man who was succored by the good Samaritan. Her sons and sons-in-law, her daughters and daughters-in-law, sat around her on the benches. They all resembled her and each other, big and clumsy with plain, old-fashioned faces, for they all belonged to the old race of the Ingmars. They all had reddish hair, freckled skin, and light blue eyes with white eyelashes. They might be different enough from each other in some ways, but they all had a stern look about the mouth, dull eyes, and heavy movements, as if everything were a trouble to them. But one could see that they all, every one of them, belonged to the first people in the neighborhood, and that they knew themselves to be better than other people.

All the sons and daughters of the house of Ingmar sighed deeply during the reading of the Bible. They wondered if some good Samaritan had found the master of the house and taken care of him, for all the Ingmars felt as if they had lost part of their own soul when a misfortune happened to anyone belonging to the family.

The old woman read and read and came to the question "Who was neighbor unto him that fell amongst thieves?" But before she had read the answer the door opened and old Ingmar came into the room.

"Mother, here is Father," said one of the daughters; and the answer, that the man's neighbor was he who had shown mercy unto him, was never read.

Later in the day the housewife sat again in the same place and read her Bible. She was alone; the women had gone to church, and

19

the men were bear hunting in the forest. As soon as Ingmar Ingmarson had eaten and drunk, he took his sons with him and went out to the forest; for it is every man's duty to kill a bear wherever and whenever he comes across one. It does not do to spare a bear, for sooner or later it will get a taste for flesh, and then it will spare neither man nor beast.

But after they were gone a great feeling of fear came over the old housewife, and she began to read her Bible. She read the lesson for the day, which was also the text for the pastor's sermon; but she did not get further than this: "Peace on earth, goodwill toward men." She remained sitting and staring at these words with her dull eyes, now and again sighing deeply. She did not read any further, but she repeated time after time in her slow, drawling voice, "Peace on earth, goodwill toward men."

The eldest son came into the room just as she was going to repeat the words afresh.

"Mother," he said softly.

She heard him but did not take her eyes from the book while she asked:

"Are you not with the others in the forest?"

"Yes," said he, still more softly, "I have been there."

"Come to the table," she said, "so that I can see you."

He came nearer, but when she looked at him she saw that he was trembling. He had to press his hands hard against the edge of the table in order to keep them still.

"Have you got the bear?" she asked again.

He could not answer; he only shook his head.

The old woman got up and did what she had not done since her son was a child. She went up to him, laid her hand on his arm, and drew him to the bench. She sat down beside him and took his hand in hers.

"Tell me now what has happened, my boy."

The young man recognized the caress that had comforted him in bygone days when he had been in trouble and unhappy, and he was so overcome that he began to weep.

"I suppose it is something about Father?" she said.

"It is worse than that," the son sobbed.

"Worse than that?"

The young man cried more and more violently; he did not know how to control his voice. At last he lifted his rough hand, with the broad fingers, and pointed to what she had just read—"Peace on earth . . ."

"Is it anything about that?" she asked.

"Yes," he answered.

"Is it anything about the peace of Christmas?"

"Yes."

"You wished to do an evil deed this morning?"

"Yes."

"And God has punished us?"

"God has punished us."

So at last she was told how it had happened. They had with some trouble found the lair of the bear, and when they had got near enough to see the heap of fagots, they stopped in order to load their guns. But before they were ready the bear rushed out of its lair straight against them. It went neither to the right nor to the left but straight for old Ingmar Ingmarson and struck him a blow on the top of the head that felled him to the ground as if he had been struck by lightning. It did not attack any of the others but rushed past them into the forest.

In the afternoon Ingmar Ingmarson's wife and son drove to the dean's house to announce his death. The son was spokesman, and the old housewife sat and listened with a face as immovable as a stone figure.

The dean sat in his easy chair near his writing table. He had entered the death in the register. He had done it rather slowly; he wanted time to consider what he should say to the widow and the son, for this was, indeed, an unusual case. The son had told him frankly how it had all happened, but the dean was anxious to know how they themselves looked at it. They were peculiar people, the Ingmars.

When the dean had closed the book, the son said:

"We wanted to tell you, sir, that we do not wish any account of Father's life to be read in church."

The dean pushed his spectacles over his forehead and looked searchingly at the old woman. She sat just as immovable as before. She only crumpled a little the handkerchief that she held in her hand.

"We wish to have him buried on a weekday," continued the son.

"Indeed!" said the dean.

21

He could hardly believe his own ears. Old Ingmar Ingmarson to be buried without anyone taking any notice of it! The congregation not to stand on railings and mounds in order to see the display when he was being carried to the grave!

"There will not be any funeral feast. We have let the neighbors know that they need not think of preparing anything for the funeral."

"Indeed, indeed!" said the dean again.

He could think of nothing else to say. He knew quite well what it meant for such people to forgo the funeral feast. He had seen both widows and fatherless comforted by giving a splendid funeral feast.

"There will be no funeral procession, only I and my brothers."

The dean looked almost appealingly at the old woman. Could she really be a party to all this? He asked himself if it could be her wishes to which the son had given expression. She was sitting there and allowing herself to be robbed of what must be dearer to her than gold and silver.

"We will not have the bells rung, or any silver plates on the coffin. Mother and I wish it to be done in this way, but we tell you all this, sir, in order to hear, sir, if you think we are wronging Father."

Now the old woman spoke:

"We should like to hear if Your Reverence thinks we are doing Father a wrong."

The dean remained silent, and the old woman continued, more eagerly:

"I must tell Your Reverence that if my husband had sinned against the king or the authorities, or if I had been obliged to cut him down from the gallows, he should all the same have had an honorable funeral, as his father before him, for the Ingmars are not afraid of anyone, and they need not go out of their way for anybody. But at Christmas God has made peace between man and beast, and the poor beast kept God's commandment, whilst we broke it, and therefore we now suffer God's punishment; and it is not becoming for us to show any ostentatious display."

22

The dean rose and went up to the old woman.

"What you say is right," he said, "and you shall follow the dictates of your own conscience." And involuntarily he added, perhaps most to himself: "The Ingmars are a grand family."

The old woman straightened herself a little at these words. At that moment the dean saw in her the symbol of her whole race. He understood what it was that had made these heavy, silent people, century after century, the leaders of the whole parish.

"It behooves the Ingmars to set the people a good example," she said. "It behooves us to show that we humble ourselves before God."

Rabindranath Tagore

(1861–1941)

Prize awarded 1913 "because of his profoundly sensitive, fresh, and beautiful verse, by which, with consummate skill, he has made his poetic thought . . . a part of the literature of the West." ★ *The variety and quantity of Tagore's literary output—twenty-one volumes of poetry in his last twenty-five years—are equaled only by his contributions in education and art: Tagore founded Visva-Bharati University and was a prominent painter. After briefly studying law in England, he returned to India to manage his father's enormous estate, living close to the poor tenants. The humble nobility of character and widespread suffering he observed not only moved Tagore to support Indian nationalism, but became the core of much of his poignant short fiction. Ancient Sanskrit scriptures and sacred Hindu writings were also potent influences.*

Tagore published several song books before the appearance of his first poetry collection, Manasi *(1890), in which he introduced Western forms, such as the ode, to the Bengali reader. The poetry incorporated his progressive, humanistic social and political values. He went on to write more than fifty plays, dozens of novels and story collections, and one hundred books of poetry. The diversity of Tagore's work made it accessible to and beloved by all strata of Indian society, and his influence on Western culture (he translated much of his own work into English) was profound as well. Images of the Ganges permeate his poetry, which enjoyed some success outside his homeland. Less well known are Tagore's novels, of which the most widely read is* Gora *(1910). In 1919, in response to the Amritsar massacre, he renounced the knighthood he'd received four years earlier. He traveled widely throughout Europe, Asia, and America (sometimes accompanied by his goat), and his correspondence with such notables as George Bernard Shaw and Albert Einstein makes for stimulating and amusing reading.*

24

THE CABULIWALLAH

(The Fruitseller from Cabul)

MINI, MY FIVE-YEAR-OLD DAUGH-
ter, cannot live without chattering. I really believe that in all her life
she has not wasted one minute in silence. Her mother is often vexed
at this and would stop her prattle, but I do not. To see Mini quiet
is unnatural, and I cannot bear it for long. Because of this, our
conversations are always lively.

One morning, for instance, when I was in the midst of the seventeenth chapter of my new novel, Mini stole into the room and,
putting her hand into mine, said: "Father! Ramdayal the door-
keeper calls a crow a krow! He doesn't know anything, does he?"

Before I could explain the language differences in this country,
she was on the trace of another subject. "What do you think, Father? Shola says there is an elephant in the clouds, blowing water
out of his trunk, and that is why it rains!"

The child had seated herself at my feet near the table and was
playing softly, drumming on her knees. I was hard at work on my
seventeenth chapter, where Pratap Singh, the hero, had just caught
Kanchanlata, the heroine, in his arms, and was about to escape with
her by the third-story window of the castle, when all of a sudden
Mini left her play and ran to the window, crying: "A Cabuliwallah!
A Cabuliwallah!" Sure enough, in the street below was a Cabuliwallah passing slowly along. He wore the loose, soiled clothing of his
people and a tall turban; there was a bag on his back, and he carried
boxes of grapes in his hand.

I cannot tell what my daughter's feelings were at the sight of this
man, but she began to call him loudly. Ah, I thought, he will come

in, and my seventeenth chapter will never be finished! At this exact moment the Cabuliwallah turned and looked up at the child. When she saw this she was overcome by terror, fled to her mother's protection, and disappeared. She had a blind belief that inside the bag that the big man carried were two or three children like herself. Meanwhile, the peddler entered my doorway and greeted me with a smiling face.

So precarious was the position of my hero and my heroine that my first impulse was to stop and buy something, especially since Mini had called to the man. I made some small purchases, and a conversation began about Abdurrahman, the Russians, the English, and the Frontier Policy.

As he was about to leave, he asked: "And where is the little girl, sir?"

I, thinking that Mini must get rid of her false fear, had her brought out. She stood by my chair, watching the Cabuliwallah and his bag. He offered her nuts and raisins, but she would not be tempted and only clung closer to me, with all her doubts increased. This was their first meeting.

One morning, however, not many days later, as I was leaving the house, I was startled to find Mini seated on a bench near the door, laughing and talking with the great Cabuliwallah at her feet. In all her life, it appeared, my small daughter had never found so patient a listener, except for her father. Already the corner of her little sari was stuffed with almonds and raisins, gifts from her visitor. "Why did you give her those?" I said, and taking out an eight-anna piece, handed it to him. The man accepted the money without delay and slipped it into his pocket.

Alas, on my return an hour later, I found the unfortunate coin had made twice its own worth of trouble! The Cabuliwallah had given it to Mini, and her mother, seeing the bright round object, had pounced on the child with: "Where did you get that eight-anna piece?"

"The Cabuliwallah gave it to me," said Mini cheerfully.

"The Cabuliwallah gave it to you!" cried her mother, much shocked. "Oh, Mini! How could you take it from him?"

Entering at this moment, I saved her from impending disaster and proceeded to make my own inquiries. I found that it was not the first or the second time the two had met. The Cabuliwallah had overcome the child's first terror by a judicious bribery of nuts and almonds, and the two were now great friends.

They had many quaint jokes that afforded them a great deal of amusement. Seated in front of him, and looking with all her tiny dignity on his gigantic frame, Mini would ripple her face with laughter and begin, "Oh, Cabuliwallah! Cabuliwallah! What have you got in your bag?"

He would reply in the nasal accents of a mountaineer: "An elephant!" Not much cause for merriment, perhaps, but how they both enjoyed their joke! And for me, this child's talk with a grown-up man always had in it something strangely fascinating.

Then the Cabuliwallah, not to be caught behind, would take his turn with: "Well, little one, and when are you going to the father-in-law's house?"

Now most small Bengali maidens have heard long ago about the father-in-law's house, but we, being a little modern, had kept these things from our child, and at this question Mini must have been a trifle bewildered. But she would not show it and with instant composure replied: "Are you going there?"

Among men of the Cabuliwallah class, however, it is well known that the words "father-in-law's house" have a double meaning. It is a euphemism for jail, the place where we are well cared for at no expense. The sturdy peddler would take my daughter's question in this sense. "Ah," he would say, shaking his fist at an invisible policeman, "I will thrash my father-in-law!" Hearing this, and picturing the poor, uncomfortable relative, Mini would go into peals of laughter, joined by her formidable friend.

These were autumn mornings, the time of year when kings of old went forth to conquest; and I, never stirring from my little corner in Calcutta, would let my mind wander over the whole world. At the very name of another country, my heart would go out to it, and at the sight of a foreigner in the streets, I would fall to weaving a network of dreams: the mountains, the glens, the forests of his distant homeland with a cottage in its setting, and the free and independent life of far-away wilds. Perhaps these scenes of travel pass in my imagination all the more vividly because I lead a vegetable existence such that a call to travel would fall upon me like a thunderbolt. In the presence of this Cabuliwallah I was immediately transported to the foot of mountains, with narrow defiles twisting in

Rabindranath Tagore

camels bearing merchandise, and the company of turbaned merchants carrying queer old firearms and some of their spears down toward the plains. I could see—but at this point Mini's mother would intervene, imploring me to "beware of that man."

Unfortunately Mini's mother is a very timid lady. Whenever she hears a noise in the street or sees people coming toward the house, she always jumps to the conclusion that they are either thieves, drunkards, snakes, tigers, malaria, cockroaches, caterpillars, or an English sailor. Even after all these years of experience, she is not able to overcome her terror. Thus she was full of doubts about the Cabuliwallah and used to beg me to keep a watchful eye on him.

I tried to gently laugh her fear away, but then she would turn on me seriously and ask solemn questions.

Were children never kidnapped?

Was it, then, not true that there was slavery in Cabul?

Was it so very absurd that this big man should be able to carry off a tiny child?

I told her that, though not impossible, it was highly improbable. But this was not enough, and her dread persisted. As her suspicion was unfounded, however, it did not seem right to forbid the man to come to the house, and his familiarity went unchecked.

Once a year, in the middle of January, Rahmun the Cabuliwallah was in the habit of returning to his country, and as the time approached he would be very busy going from house to house collecting his debts. This year, however, he always found time to come and see Mini. It would have seemed to an outsider that there was some conspiracy between them, for when he could not come in the morning, he would appear in the evening.

Even to me it was a little startling now and then to suddenly surprise this tall, loose-garmented man of bags in the corner of a dark room; but when Mini would run in, smiling, with her "Oh, Cabuliwallah! Cabuliwallah!" and the two friends so far apart in age would subside into their old laughter and their old jokes, I felt reassured.

28   One morning, a few days before he had made up his mind to go, I was correcting my proof sheets in my study. It was chilly weather. Through the window the rays of the sun touched my feet, and the slight warmth was very welcome. It was almost eight o'clock, and the early pedestrians were returning home with their heads covered. All at once I heard an uproar in the street and, looking out, saw

Rahmun bound and being led away between two policemen, followed by a crowd of curious boys. There were bloodstains on the clothes of the Cabuliwallah, and one of the policemen carried a knife. Hurrying out, I stopped them and inquired what it all meant. Partly from one, partly from another, I gathered that a certain neighbor had owed the peddler something for a Rampuri shawl but had falsely denied having bought it, and that in the course of the quarrel Rahmun had struck him. Now, in the heat of his excitement, the prisoner began calling his enemy all sorts of names.

Suddenly, from a verandah of my house, my little Mini appeared with her usual exclamation: "Oh, Cabuliwallah! Cabuliwallah!"

Rahmun's face lighted up as he turned to her. He had no bag under his arm today, so she could not discuss the elephant with him. She therefore at once proceeded to the next question: "Are you going to the father-in-law's house?"

Rahmun laughed and said: "Just where I am going, little one!" Then, seeing that the reply did not amuse the child, he held up his fettered hands. "Ah," he said, "I would have thrashed that old father-in-law, but my hands are bound!"

On a charge of murderous assault, Rahmun was sentenced to many years of imprisonment.

Time passed, and he was forgotten. The accustomed work in the accustomed place was ours, and the thought of the once free mountaineer spending his years in prison seldom occurred to us. Even my light-hearted Mini, I am ashamed to say, forgot her old friend. New companions filled her life. As she grew older she spent more of her time with girls, so much in fact that she came no more to her father's room. I was scarcely on speaking terms with her.

Many years passed. It was autumn once again, and we had made arrangements for Mini's marriage; it was to take place during the Puja holidays. With the goddess Durga returning to her seasonal home in Mount Kailas, the light of our home was also to depart, leaving our house in shadows.

The morning was bright. After the rains, there was a sense of cleanness in the air, and the rays of the sun looked like pure gold, so bright that they radiated even to the sordid brick walls of our Calcutta lanes. Since early dawn, the wedding pipes had been sounding, and at each beat my own heart throbbed. The wailing tune, "Bhairavi," seemed to intensify my pain at the approaching separation. My Mini was to be married tonight.

From early morning, noise and bustle pervaded the house. In the courtyard the canopy had to be slung on its bamboo poles; the tinkling chandeliers should be hung in each room and verandah; there was great hurry and excitement. I was sitting in my study, looking through the accounts, when someone entered, saluting respectfully, and stood before me. It was Rahmun the Cabuliwallah, and at first I did not recognize him. He had no bag, nor the long hair, nor the same vigor that he used to have. But he smiled, and I knew him again.

"When did you come, Rahmun?" I asked him.

"Last evening," he said, "I was released from jail."

The words struck harsh upon my ears. I had never talked with anyone who had wounded his fellow man, and my heart shrank when I realized this, for I felt that the day would have been omened had he not turned up.

"There are ceremonies going on," I said, "and I am busy. Could you perhaps come another day?"

At once he turned to go; but as he reached the door he hesitated and said: "May I not see the little one, sir, for a moment?" It was his belief that Mini was still the same. He had pictured her running to him as she used to do, calling, "Oh, Cabuliwallah! Cabuliwallah!" He had imagined that they would laugh and talk together, just as in the past. In fact, in memory of those former days he had brought, carefully wrapped up in paper, a few almonds and raisins and grapes, somehow obtained from a countryman—his own little fund was gone.

I said again: "There is a ceremony in the house, and you will not be able to see anyone today."

The man's face fell. He looked wistfully at me for a moment, said, "Good morning," and went out.

I felt a little sorry, and would have called him back, but saw that he was returning of his own accord. He came close up to me, holding out his offerings, and said: "I brought these few things, sir, for the little one. Will you give them to her?"

I took them and was going to pay him, but he caught my hand and said: "You are very kind, sir! Keep me in your recollection; do not offer me money! You have a little girl; I too have one like her in my own home. I thought of my own, and brought fruits to your child, not to make a profit for myself."

Saying this, he put his hand inside his big loose robe and brought out a small, dirty piece of paper. With great care he unfolded this and smoothed it out with both hands on my table. It bore the impression of a little hand, not a photograph, not a drawing. The impression of an ink-smeared hand laid flat on the paper. This touch of his own little daughter had been always on his heart, as he had come year after year to Calcutta to sell his wares in the streets.

Tears came to my eyes. I forgot that he was a poor Cabuli fruitseller, while I was—but no, was I more than he? He was also a father.

That impression of the hand of his little Parbati in her distant mountain home reminded me of my own little Mini, and I immediately sent for her from the inner apartment. Many excuses were raised, but I would not listen. Clad in the red silk of her wedding day, with the sandal paste on her forehead and adorned as a young bride, Mini came and stood bashfully before me.

The Cabuliwallah was staggered at the sight of her. There was no hope of reviving their old friendship. At last he smiled and said: "Little one, are you going to your father-in-law's house?"

But Mini now understood the meaning of the word "father-in-law," and she could not reply to him as in the past. She flushed at the question and stood before him with her bride's face looking down.

I remembered the day when the Cabuliwallah and my Mini first met, and I felt sad. When she had gone, Rahmun heaved a deep sigh and sat down on the floor. The idea had suddenly come to him that his daughter also must have grown up during this long time, and that he would have to make friends with her all over again. Surely he would not find her as he used to know her; besides, what might have happened to her in these eight years?

The marriage pipes sounded, and the mild autumn sun streamed around us. But Rahmun sat in the little Calcutta lane and saw before him the barren mountains of Afghanistan.

I took out a bank note and gave it to him, saying: "Go back to your own daughter, Rahmun, in your own country, and may the happiness of your meeting bring good fortune to my child!"

After giving this gift, I had to eliminate some of the festivities. I could not have the electric lights, nor the military band, and the ladies of the house were saddened. But to me the wedding feast was brighter because of the thought that in a distant land a long-lost father met again with his only child.

Henrik Pontoppidan

(1857–1943)

Prize awarded 1917 "for his authentic descriptions of present-day life in Denmark." ★ Pontoppidan was a principal contributor to the renaissance of modern Danish literature, producing novels and short stories that accurately and thoroughly depicted all classes of Danish society. His writing reflected the same critical and enlightened nationalism felt by many other late-nineteenth-century Scandinavians, including Alfred Nobel himself.

The son of a puritanical Protestant minister, Pontoppidan frequently addressed the problems of the clergy, as in The Promised Land *(1892) and the three-volume* Lykke-Per *(1898–1905). He was a product of the Romantic tradition and an accomplished lyricist who, like Kierkegaard, strongly opposed reflexive morality. His prose is easy and direct, his descriptions and characterizations memorable.* Staekkede Vinger, *his first collection of stories, appeared in 1881, and his productive career spanned half a century after that. Pontoppidan's early books dealing with country and town life (*Landsbybilled, *1883;* Fra Hytterne, *1887; and* Skyer, *1890) reflect indignation at social injustice and show an already well-developed sense of irony, laying the foundation for the bleak visions of* Lucky Peter *(1898–1904) and* Kingdom of the Dead *(1912–1916), which depict the failures of Danish society.*

Pontoppidan shared his Nobel Prize with fellow Dane novelist Karl Gjellerup. "Eagle's Flight," an allegory, is an interesting departure from his usual naturalistic style.

EAGLE'S FLIGHT

THIS IS THE STORY OF A YOUNG EAGLE THAT in its yellow-beaked infancy was found by some boys and taken to the old parsonage, where kind people cared for it and became so attached to it that they kept it there. Like the Ugly Duckling of the fairy tale, it grew up among quacking ducks and cackling hens and bleating sheep, and so well did it thrive in these surroundings that it grew large and broad and, as the minister said, "actually acquired a belly."

It was usually perched on an old fence near the pigsty, where it sat and waited for the maid to bring garbage from the kitchen. As soon as old Dorothy came in view, it would throw itself on the pavement and waddle toward the filled trough with the burlesque sack-race stride peculiar to the kings of the ether when moving on earth.

Once in a while, especially on windy days or before a thunder-storm, a vague longing, like a dim homesickness, might awaken in the bosom of the captive prince of the air. Then it would sit for days with its beak buried in the dirty plumage of its breast and would refuse to stir or eat. Then suddenly it would spread its wings as if embracing the air and start boldly toward the sky—but its flight was always brief. Its wings were well clipped, and after fluttering clumsily for a moment it would fall to the ground, where, perplexed, it would take a few sidewise hops and with craned neck run and hide in some dark corner, as if ashamed.

When it had lived in this way for a couple of years, it happened that the old minister was taken ill and died. In the following con-

33

fusion the royal bird, which had been given the plebeian name of Claus, was for a while forgotten. As usual it waggled around peacefully and a little timidly among the other birds of the poultry yard, being used to cuffings from the minister's daughters when once in a while it resolved to assert its innate superiority over the small fry.

But when one day a fresh south wind blew spring and warmth over the country, the strange thing happened that the eagle suddenly found itself upon the ridge of the big barn, without any idea of how this had come to pass. As so often before, it had been perched on the fence, dreaming dejectedly, and then in a sudden vague yearning for liberty had spread its wings for flight. But instead of dropping down on the pavement as usual, it had been lifted into the air so swiftly that, frightened, it had hurried to the nearest foothold.

Now it was sitting up there on the high roof, quite dazed by the course of events. Never before had it seen the world from such a lofty place. Eagerly it turned its head, now one way, now the other; then, irresistibly drawn by the drifting clouds and the azure of the sky, it spread its wings anew and soared upward, at first carefully and tentatively, soon with greater boldness and assurance, until at last with a wild scream of joy it swung itself high up in the air and made a great circle. In a flash it knew what it meant to be an eagle.

Villages, forests, sunny lakes passed under it. The eagle rose higher and higher toward the blue sky, dizzy from the wide horizon and the strength of its wings.

But suddenly it stopped. The empty vastness all around frightened it, and it began to search for a resting place.

By good luck it reached a projecting rock high above the river valley. But looking around, still a little dizzy, in search of the parsonage and the ridge of the barn, it received a new shock. All around, wherever it glanced, spread a strange and unknown country. Not one familiar spot, not one refuge, was there as far as the eye could see.

Above its head rose rock upon rock—steep bare stone walls without a single shelter from the wind. In the west, beyond the open country, the sun was just setting in scarlet evening clouds that boded storm and dark nights.

A crushing sense of loneliness seized the young royal bird as the yellowish mists of dusk enveloped the valley far beneath. Depressed, it gazed after a flock of crows that with shrill cries were passing it on the way home to their nests, down there near the cozy human dwellings. With closely folded wings, and its beak plunged into its breast feathers, it sat solitary and still on the silent, desolate rock.

Suddenly a whir of wings is heard overhead. A white-breasted female eagle is circling above it under the red evening sky.

For a while the young eagle remains where it is, craning its neck and pondering on this strange sight. But all at once its indecision is swept away. With a mighty rushing of its stretched wings it soars upward and in a moment is close to its mate.

Now begins a wild chase over the mountains, the she-eagle always ahead and above, Claus doing his best to overtake her, though heavier and panting.

Soon they are among the high mountains. The sun is still illuminating the loftiest peaks, but they sail over the mountaintops, into the growing darkness. Far beneath is heard the somber rustling of huge forests and the hollow boom of the rivers in the deep gorges.

Will she never sit down? he thinks, frightened by this sinister unknown roaring. He is almost exhausted, and his wings feel tired and heavy.

Higher and higher soars his beloved, farther and farther above the crimson peaks, calling, coaxing him to follow.

They have reached a vast stone desert, a chaos of gigantic blocks tumbled upon each other like the ruins of an overthrown tower of Babel. Suddenly the view before them opens. High above the drifting clouds spreads like a vision the unearthly realm of perpetual snow, unsoiled by swarming life, the home of the eagle and the great stillness. The last rays of day seem to be resting in quiet slumber on the white snow. Behind it rises the dark blue sky covered with calm stars.

Terrified, Claus stops his flight and settles on a rock. He sits there trembling with cold and discomfort, gazing at this white spectral land, these large stars that twinkle at him through the darkness like so many evil cat's eyes. Sadly his thoughts turn back anew to the home he left behind. He recalls his warm place on the fence and the cozy poultry yard where his small friends are now sitting on their perches, sleeping peacefully with their heads under their wings. He thinks of the chubby little pigs, which are now lying in a heap close to their mother, dreaming and sucking at the same time, and of fat old Dorothy, who will come from the kitchen with the steaming food, when the church bells announce the rising of the sun.

The call of the female comes down through the frosty air. But Claus spreads his wings noiselessly and steals back, first irresolutely, fluttering from block to block, but soon swiftly, eagerly, chased by his terror, his anxiety, his sweet longing—home—home—home!

Not until next morning did the poor bird reach the parsonage after his headstrong flight. For some moments it remained hovering over its beloved home, as if wanting to make sure that everything down there was as usual.

Then it descended slowly.

But a disaster was to take place. The hired man, who happened to notice it and had not heard of the disappearance of Claus, ran quickly to the house for his gun and took his stand behind a tree, to give fire when the supposed poultry thief should be near enough.

The shot fell.

A few feathers fluttered in the air, and the dead eagle fell like a stone straight down on the dunghill.

It avails but little to have come from an eagle's egg, if one is raised in the poultry yard.

william Butler Yeats

(1865–1939)

Prize awarded 1923 "for his always inspired poetry, which in a highly artistic form gives expression to the spirit of a whole nation." ★ *Ireland's greatest lyric poet, William Butler Yeats was born in Dublin. His grandfather and great-grandfather were both rectors in the Protestant Church of Ireland, but Yeats's father, a painter, broke away from the church. As a boy, Yeats studied in London, developing an interest in Celtic legend and the occult that would become a constant theme in his poetry and prose writing.*

Yeats always made conscious use of symbolism, and his early poems are permeated with his unrequited love for Maud Gonne, a beautiful Irish patriot. (When Yeats married in 1917, however, it was to Georgie Hyde-Lees, an Englishwoman with whom he had a son and a daughter.) Yeats's strong nationalist sentiments are also evident in many of these works, including The Wanderings of Oisin *(1889). Yeats was active in the Irish theater as both playwright and producer, co-founding the Irish Literary Theatre, which produced his* The Countess Cathleen *(1892) and* The Hour Glass *(1903).*

*In 1923, the year he won the Nobel Prize, Yeats became one of the first senators of the Irish Free State. He was profoundly concerned about the destruction of modern civilization, but his poetry also examines the internal conflicts within the mind itself. While the poetry of his middle years showed a more satirical, realistic bent (*The Green Helmet and Other Poems, *1910), in* A Vision *(1926) he explored the relation between imagination, history, and the occult.* The Winding Stair *(1929) is widely considered to be his finest work.*

37

THE ROSE OF THE WORLD

Who dreamed that beauty passes like a dream?
For these red lips, with all their mournful pride,
Mournful that no new wonder may betide,
Troy passed away in one high funeral gleam,
And Usna's children died.

We and the labouring world are passing by:
Amid men's souls, that waver and give place
Like the pale waters in their wintry race,
Under the passing stars, foam of the sky,
Lives on this lonely face.

Bow down, archangels, in your dim abode:
Before you were, or any hearts to beat,
Weary and kind one lingered by His seat;
He made the world to be a grassy road
Before her wandering feet.

STREAM AND SUN AT
GLENDALOUGH

Through intricate motions ran
Stream and gliding sun
And all my heart seemed gay:
Some stupid thing that I had done
Made my attention stray.

Repentance keeps my heart impure;
But what am I that dare
Fancy that I can
Better conduct myself or have more
Sense than a common man?

What motion of the sun or stream
Or eyelid shot the gleam
That pierced my body through?
What made me live like these that seem
Self-born, born anew?

QUARREL IN OLD AGE

Where had her sweetness gone?
What fanatics invent
In this blind bitter town,
Fantasy or incident
Nor worth thinking of,
Put her in a rage.
I had forgiven enough
That had forgiven old age.

All lives that has lived;
So much is certain;
Old sages were not deceived:
Somewhere beyond the curtain
Of distorting days
Lives that lonely thing
That shone before these eyes
Targeted, trod like Spring.

39

George Bernard Shaw

(1856–1950)

Prize awarded 1925 "for his work, which is marked by both idealism and humanity, his stimulating satire often being infused with a singular poetic beauty." ★ *Shaw was born in Dublin and left school at fourteen to work in a real estate office. He left for London at twenty, to be supported by his parents for the next nine years while he wrote novels* (An Unsocial Socialist *and* Cashel Byron's Profession) *and became an active Socialist. Eventually he established himself as a journalist, a music and drama critic, and an essayist. At the age of forty he wrote the first of his more than fifty-two plays, which combined outrageous wit with social themes.* Widowers' Houses, *targeting landlord abuses, was first produced in 1893.* Mrs. Warren's Profession, *which examined the economic realities of prostitution, was written in 1893 but censored until 1902.* The Philanderer *(1893) dealt with feminism;* John Bull's Other Island *(1904) with the Irish problem;* Major Barbara *(1905) with capitalism;* Androcles and the Lion *(1912) with religion. A prominent Fabian Socialist, Shaw attacked in his entertaining and pointed manner all of the middle-class values from matrimony to meat eating.* The Intelligent Woman's Guide to Socialism and Capitalism *(1928) remains a relevant text in socioeconomic thought. Shaw used lengthy prefaces to his plays, beginning with* Arms and the Man *(1894), about a pacifist misfit, and especially in* Man and Superman *(1903) and* Saint Joan *(1923), to expound his ideas on parenthood, education, women's rights, poverty, fashion, politics, and class.* The Devil's Disciple *(1897),* Caesar and Cleopatra *(1899),* Pygmalion *(1912),* Heartbreak House *(1917),* Back to Methuselah *(1922), and many other Shaw plays are read and produced; and all of them, "pleasant and unpleasant" (as he divided them in an 1898 collection) serve to uphold his reputation as a major playwright of the highest rank.*

THE RELIGION OF THE FUTURE

HERETIC IS LIKE A MAN WITH A mechanical genius who begins tinkering with a bicycle or a motor car and makes it something different from what the manufacturer has made it. Such a man is a heretic in mechanics; he has a mind and a genius which enables him to choose for himself. If he has a bad motor car he makes a good one of it—he makes it to suit himself. The Heretic is a sort of person who, no matter what religion is supplied at the shop—by which I mean the nearest church—he will tinker at it until he makes it what he thinks it should be. The Heretic is really a man with homemade religion, and if a man can make a religion for himself at home we need not bother about him—he will make his religion to suit himself. What we want to trouble about is the great mass of people who take religion as they find it—as they get it at the shop. What the Heretics have to do is to prepare a ready-made religion for the next generation for the people who have to accept religion as it comes. It is of the most enormous importance for any community what ready-made article they are supplying in their schools and churches, as a religion, to the community. Therefore, when I am dealing with the religion of the future, remember that I am not dealing with what the Heretics of the next generation will be talking about. They will be discussing and criticizing whatever the religion is, and the great mass of the people will be outside and will have a ready-made religion and will obey laws founded on that religion, many of them founded more or less on the idea that certain courses of conduct are more or less displeasing to whatever force might be moving the world—the

41

mainspring which at present we call God, and might call other names in future—at any rate the driving force.

Now if we want to get any system of this kind we must really get some sort of God whom we can understand. It is no use falling back on the old evasion and saying that God is beyond our comprehension. The man who says he believes in God and does not understand God had much better turn a good, practical atheist at once. Better atheist than agnostic: an agnostic is only an atheist without the courage of his opinions. The actual, practical use we can make of our God is that we can establish laws and morality which we suppose to be the will of God, and if we do not understand God's purpose we cannot do anything of the kind. Therefore we find a large number of people in the country not understanding God who are practically atheists. It is surprising how little we hear of the name of God outside of our places of worship. We hardly ever hear the name of God mentioned in a court of justice, except, perhaps, when a witness is going through the preliminary form of committing perjury, or when the judge has put on the black cap and is sentencing some unhappy wretch to death. In Parliament we never hear about it at all. I do not know whether you ever hear about it in Cambridge, but you will notice that the mention of God has gone completely out of fashion, and that if the name of God is mentioned it is in a perfunctory sort of way, and seems to come as a sort of shock if the person mentioning it does so in the way of taking the current conception of God seriously.

Here in England we have no fundamental religion of our own. Western Europe, of all places in the world, you will say, is, prima facie, the place for the birthplace of a modern religion, yet we have never produced one. We use a sort of Oriental religion as the nucleus of our religion—a lot of legends that we must get rid of. The man who believes the story of the Gadarene swine will believe anything, and we must leave him out as a critical force. Also the man who believes the story of Elisha and the bears will worship anything. But we must not leave such people out of account as a practical fact in the universe, because these are the people for whom we want to found a religion.

Religion virtually went out with the Middle Ages. If we read through Shakespeare's plays we find a man of very great power and imagination, who evidently had no well-considered views of any kind, who produced a mass of plays in which he set forth his own

42

knowledge of humanity in a very wonderful way, and practically left religion out of account. Then we strike the beginning of a commercial age, an age of people who went to church but who gradually began leaving religion more and more out of their lives and practical affairs. There are many people who are made more religious if they have a God who produces frightful calamities. If we study the proceedings of African and, I have no doubt, European kings, we shall find the same thing. In order, however, not to be personal, I shall keep to the African potentates as much as possible. [*Laughter*] In Africa they had found it generally necessary, when building their palaces, to bury several people alive and to commit a great number of cruel and horrible murders. This was to create an impression on the tribe and show their majesty and greatness.

In Mahometan religion, Mahomet found it necessary to describe the Judgment Day in most revolting and disgusting terms—to introduce intimidation into religion in order to impress the wild and warlike Arabs. The man of genius finds it difficult to make people understand him. I know this, for I am by profession a man of genius. [*Laughter and Applause*] The difference between a man of genius and the ordinary man is that the man of genius perceives the importance of things. There are a great number of people who do not understand the vital truths of religion, and so the man of genius has to amuse and frighten them with more or less dreadful things.

We have hitherto been governed by a system of idolatry. We made idols of people and resorted to some sort of stage management. Men and women capable of giving orders were taken to the head of affairs—sometimes they took themselves [*Laughter*], and we gave them crowns or gold lace on their collars, or a certain kind of hat, and sat them on a particular kind of chair. Those people generally were a sort of secondhand idol: they said, "I am the agent of the will of another idol. I understand his will and hand it on to you." We generally had to give them such a different income from our own that their way of life would be entirely removed from that of the multitude. They had to wash their faces oftener, live in a different kind of house, and it was out of the question that their sons and daughters should marry the son or daughter of a common man. In democracy we are trying to get human nature up to a point at which idolatry no longer appeals to us. We see that in revolutions, like the French Revolution, democracy went first to the cathedrals and knocked off the heads of the idols of stone. Nothing happened.

43

No crash of thunder stunned the universe, the veil of the temple remained intact. Then the people went to the palaces and cut off the heads of the idols of flesh and blood. Still nothing happened. Cutting off King Charles's head was a sort of vivisection experiment—a much more justifiable experiment than many that take place today, because we learned something from it. But if Cromwell had not died when he did, if he had lived five or even two years longer, he would have been compelled to put the crown on his own head and make himself King Oliver. It was an entire failure trying to make people obey laws in England because they were intelligent laws. The people said they must have a king. And so they took Charles II and made him king. But democracy is progressing. Take myself, for example, a democrat to the teeth. It is no use trying these kings and gods on *me:* I refuse to be imposed on. And, indeed, with my utter lack of the bump of veneration (a phrenologist told me long ago that my bump was a 'ole), I like and respect kings and judges and bishops as men, but they might just as well give up the robes and aprons as far as I am concerned. I do not value their opinions on politics or law or religion any more than if they were plain Mr. Smith.

We are gradually getting more and more rid of our idols, and in the future we shall have to put before the people religions that are practical systems, which on the whole we can perceive work out in practice, instead of resulting in flagrant contradictions as they do at present. People, however, go from one extreme to the other, and when they do so they are apt to throw out the good things with the bad ones, and so they make little progress. The old-fashioned atheist revolted against the idea of an omnipotent being being the God of cancer, epilepsy and war, as well as of the good that happened. They could not believe that a God of love could allow such things. And so they seized with avidity upon the idea of natural selection put forward by Charles Darwin. Darwin was not the originator of the idea of evolution—that was long before his time—but he made us familiar with that particular form of evolution known as natural selection. That idea was seized upon with a feeling of relief—relief that the old idea of God was banished from the world. This feeling of relief was so great that for the time it was overlooked what a horrible void had been created in the universe. Natural selection left us in a world which was very largely full of horrors, apparently accounted for by the fact that it as a whole happened by accident.

But if there is no purpose or design in the universe the sooner we all cut our throats the better, for it is not much of a place to live in.

Most of the natural selection men of the nineteenth century were very brilliant, but they were cowards. We want to get back to men with some belief in the purpose of the universe, with determination to identify themselves with it and with the courage that comes from that. As for my own position, I am, and always have been, a mystic. I believe that the universe is being driven by a force that we might call the life-force. I see it as performing the miracle of creation, that it has got into the minds of men as what they call their will. Thus we see people who clearly are carrying out a will not exclusively their own.

To attempt to represent this particular will or power as God—in the former meaning of the word—is now entirely hopeless; nobody can believe that. In the old days the Christian apologists got out of the difficulty of God as the God of cancer and epilepsy, and all the worst powers that were in one, by believing in God and the devil. They said that when a man did wrong he was possessed by the devil, and when he did right that he was possessed by the grace of God. It was, in fact, the conception of "old Nick." It was a conception of enormous value, for the devil was always represented as a person who could do nothing by himself, and that he had to tempt people to do wrong. I implore you to believe that, because it helps you a great deal. People always used to assume that the only way in which the devil could carry out his will was by inspiring or tempting people to do what he wanted them to do. Temptation and inspiration mean the same thing exactly as firmness and obstinacy mean the same thing, only people use the one word when they want to be complimentary and the other when they want to be abusive. Let me therefore ask you to think of God in a somewhat similar nature, as something not possessing hands and brains such as ours, and having therefore to use ours, as having brought us into existence in order to use us, and not being able to work in any other way. If we conceive God as working in that way and having a tremendous struggle with a great, whirling mass of matter, civilization means our molding this mass to our own purposes and will, and in doing that really molding it to the will of God. If we accept that conception we can see the limitations of our God and can even pity him. In this way you can imagine that something—the life-force—through trial and error, beginning in a very blind and feeble way at first, first

45

laboriously achieving motion, making a little bit of slime to move and then going on through the whole story of evolution, building up and up until at last man was reached.

Contrast this position with that of the Christian apologists, and their God, who has to be excused the responsibility of cancer and epilepsy, excused, too, for humanity and the present audience. You require a lot of apology as a visit to the looking glass, coupled with reflections on your life during the past week, would speedily show. The only consolation is that *up-to-date* God has been able to produce nothing better.

We must believe in the will to good—it is impossible to regard man as willing his own destruction. But in that striving after good that will is liable to make mistakes and to let loose instead something that is destructive. We may regard the typhoid bacillus as one of the failures of the life-force that we call God, but that same force is trying through our brains to discover some method of destroying that malign influence. If you get that conception, you will be able to give an answer to those people who ask for an explanation of the origin of evil. Evil things are things that are made with the object of their doing good, but turn out wrong, and therefore have to be destroyed. This is the most important conception for the religion of the future, because it gives us what we are at present and gives us courage and self-respect. And it is ours to work for something better, to talk less about the religion of love (love is an improper subject) and more about the religion of life, and of work, to create a world that shall know a happiness that need not be the happiness of drunkenness—a world of which we need not be ashamed. The world must consist of people who are happy and at the same time sober. At the present the happiness of the world is as the happiness of drunken people. I don't mean that everybody who is happy is like the man who is locked up for being drunk, but ordinary men or women, even in the politest society, at present are not happy and do not respect themselves and do not exult in their existence until they have had at least a cup of tea. [*Laughter*] We have all sorts of factitious aids to life. We are trying to fight off the consciousness of ourselves because we do not see the consciousness of a mission, and finally the consciousness of a magnificent destiny.

We are all experiments in the direction of making God. What God is doing is making himself, getting from being a mere powerless will or force. This force has implanted into our minds the ideal

46

of God. We are not very successful attempts at God so far, but I believe that if we can drive into the heads of men the full consciousness of moral responsibility that comes to men with the knowledge that there never will be a God unless we make one—that we are the instruments through which that ideal is trying to make itself a reality—we can work towards that ideal until we get to be supermen, and then super-supermen, and then a world of organisms who have achieved and realized God. We could then dispense with idolatry, intimidation, stimulants, and the nonsense of civilization, and be a really happy body with splendid hopes and a very general conception of the world we live in. In the meantime those of you who have exceptional, expensive educations should make it your business to give such ideals to the great mass of people. If you adopt a religion of this kind, with some future in it, I believe that you can at last get the masses to listen, because experience would never contradict it. You will not have people saying that Christianity will not work out in business; you will get a religion that will work in business, and I believe that instead of its being a lower religion than Christianity, it will be a higher one. Also it will fulfill the condition which I set out at starting: it will be a Western religion, not an Oriental one. Make the best religion you can, and no longer go about in the rags and tatters of the East, and then, when the different races of the earth have worked out their own conceptions of religion, let those religions all meet and criticize each other, and end, perhaps, in only one religion, and an inconceivably better religion than we now have any conception of. [Applause]

Thomas Mann

(1875–1955)

Prize awarded in 1929 "principally for his great novel Buddenbrooks, *which
has won steadily increased recognition as one of the classic works of contemporary literature."* ★ *Mann, who lived in Munich for much of his life, remains
(with Goethe) the most widely read German author in the world. In addition to
his novels, he wrote illuminating essays on Goethe, Freud, Nietzsche, Chekhov,
and Tolstoy. His first novels and stories (reflecting perhaps his own mercantile
parentage) examined the artist and his difficult relationship to bourgeois society*
(Buddenbrooks, *1901;* Tonio Kröger, *1914;* Tristran, *1903;* Death in
Venice, *1912), espousing a nationalism and a romanticism marked by that
"perilous sympathy, enchantment, and temptation to which the European soul
has been inclined." He slowly repudiated this attitude over the twelve years he
spent writing* The Magic Mountain *(1924).*

*In reaction to the rise of nazism, Mann began to advocate the principles of
democracy and humanitarianism. His anti-Fascist outlook found expression in*
Mario and the Magician *(1929) and in speeches and radio broadcasts during
World War II. He left Germany in 1933 for Switzerland and in 1938 came to
the United States, where he wrote the rest of his works. The four-part* Joseph
and His Brothers *(1934) depicts the evolution of a people blindly living myths
into a people able to direct events freely through responsible and humane action.
In* Dr. Faustus *(1948), the fall of the protagonist poignantly reflects the moral
and physical fall of Germany. Although there is humor in his work, Mann draws
his characters with an irony and distance that belies the fervent concern he had
for mankind.*

THE INFANT PRODIGY

THE INFANT PRODIGY ENTERS—THE EN-
tire hall grows silent.

It grows silent, and then the people begin to clap, because somewhere a born ruler of men and leader of the herd has started the
applause. They have as yet heard nothing, but they clap their hands,
for a mighty advertising campaign has paved the way for the infant
prodigy, and the people are already under a spell, whether they are
aware of it or not.

The infant prodigy emerges from behind a magnificent screen,
which is embroidered all over with garlands in the Empire style and
large, fabulous flowers. He hurriedly climbs the steps to the platform and walks into the applause as into a bath, shivering a bit,
touched by a slight shudder, and yet as into a friendly element. The
boy goes to the edge of the platform, smiles as though he were
about to be photographed, and thanks the audience with a small,
shy, charming, and very girlish bow.

He is dressed entirely in white silk, which does not fail of its effect
upon the audience. He wears a small white silk jacket of fantastic
cut, with a sash beneath it, and even his shoes are of white silk. But
the bare legs contrast sharply with the white silk knickers, for they
are quite brown; the boy is a Greek.

His name is Bibi Saccellaphylaccas. This is really his name. No
one knows of what Christian name "Bibi" may be an abbreviation or
pet form, none save the impresario, and he regards it as a business
secret. Bibi's hair is smooth and black and hangs down to his shoulders. Yet it is parted sideways and held back from the small, brown,

bulging forehead by means of a small silk bow. He has the most innocent, childlike face in the world, with an unformed little nose and an unsophisticated mouth; only that part of his face which lies below the coal-black, mouselike eyes is already a little weary and clearly expressive of two traits of character. He looks as though he were nine years old, but he is only eight as yet and is announced as only seven. People do not know themselves whether they really believe this. Perhaps they know better and nevertheless believe it, as they are so often wont to do. A bit of falsehood, they think, belongs to beauty. What, they think, would become of recreation and edification after the day's work if they did not come with a bit of goodwill, and let two and two make five? And they are quite right, with that collective mind of theirs!

The infant prodigy bows until the rustle of greetings has laid itself; then he goes to the grand piano, and the people throw a final glance at the program. The first number is *"Marche solennelle,"* then *Rêverie,* and then *"Le Hibou et les moineaux"*—all by Bibi Saccellaphylaccas. The entire program is by him—these are his own compositions. He cannot, to be sure, write them down, but he has them all safe in his small, uncommon head, and they must be accorded artistic significance, as the posters prepared by the impresario attest in a sober, matter-of-fact style. It appears that the impresario has wrested this concession from his critical nature in severe struggles.

The infant prodigy sits down upon the revolving stool and angles for the pedals with his little legs. These pedals are raised much higher than usual by means of an ingenious contrivance, so that Bibi may reach them. The grand piano is his own, and he takes it everywhere with him. It rests upon wooden blocks, and its polish is rather damaged by its being transported so frequently, but all that merely makes the thing more interesting.

Bibi puts his silky white feet upon the pedals; the expression of his little face grows pointed and arch; he looks straight before him and raises his right hand. It is a naïve, brown, childish little hand, but the wrist is strong and not at all childish, for it reveals well-developed joints.

Bibi puts on this mien for his audience, for he knows that he must entertain it a little. But he himself, for his part, takes a quiet pleasure in the affair, a pleasure that he could not describe to anyone. It is this nervous joy, this secret thrill of bliss, which creeps through him whenever he sits down in front of the open piano—and he will never lose this feeling. Again the keys offer themselves to his fingers, these seven black-and-white octaves, among which he has so often lost himself in adventures and profoundy exciting experiences and which nevertheless appear again as pure and untouched as a drawing slate that has been wiped off. It is music, the world of music, that lies before him! It lies outspread before him like a tempting sea, and he is able to plunge in and swim about blissfully, allow himself to be borne hither and thither, let himself go down in a storm and yet keep the mastery in his hands, govern and dispose of it all— He holds his right hand aloft.

There is a breathless stillness in the hall. It is this tension before the first chord—how will it begin? It begins thus: Bibi fetches the first tone out of the piano with his forefinger, an unexpectedly powerful tone in the middle register, resembling a trumpet blast. Others align themselves to this, and the introduction begins—the muscles of the audience relax.

The hall is a very ornate one, situated in a first-class fashionable hotel, with paintings showing much rosy flesh upon the walls, with luxuriant pillars, mirrors with heavily decorated frames, and a vast number, a perfect solar system, of electric bulbs, which sprout forth everywhere in clusters and fill the room with a thin, golden, celestial radiance, far brighter than day. No chair is empty; yes, people are standing even in the side aisles and at the back of the hall. In front, where the price is twelve marks (for the impresario is devoted to the principle of awe-inspiring prices), we find the members of high society; for there is a lively interest in the infant prodigy in these lofty circles. Many uniforms are visible and a great deal of good taste in the matter of evening toilets. There are even a number of children there, who let their legs dangle in a well-bred manner from their chairs and who regard their small, gifted, and silky white colleague with shining eyes.

In front to the left sits the mother of the infant prodigy, a very corpulent dame with a powdered double chin and a plume in her hair, and at her side is the impresario, a gentleman of Oriental type with large golden buttons in his far-protruding cuffs. The princess is seated in the middle of the first row. She is a small, wrinkled, dried-up old princess, but she patronizes the arts, insofar as they are refined. She is seated in a deep fauteuil of plush, and Persian rugs are spread before her. She holds her hands folded upon her striped gray dress of silk, close beneath her breast, inclines her head to one side, and affords a picture of aristocratic peace as she contemplates the infant prodigy in action. Her lady-in-waiting sits beside her, dressed in a costume of striped green silk. But she is for all that only a lady-in-waiting and must not even lean back in her chair.

Bibi comes to a close with a great flourish. With what force this urchin handles the piano! One can scarcely believe one's ears. The theme of the march, a swinging, enthusiastic melody, breaks forth once more in a passage of full harmony, broadly and boastfully, and at every chord Bibi throws back the upper part of his body, as though he were marching triumphantly in a festival procession. He then closes grandly, slips in a crouching attitude sidewise from his stool, and waits smiling for the applause.

And the applause bursts forth, unanimous, touched, enraptured. Just see the dainty hips of the child as he makes his girlish bow! Clap! Clap! Wait, I'll take off my gloves! Bravo, little Saccophylax, or whatever your name may be! Why, he is a perfect little devil of a fellow!

Bibi must come forth thrice from behind the screen before the people are satisfied. A few stragglers, tardy arrivals, come crowding in from behind and find place with great difficulty in this full hall. And then the concert proceeds.

Bibi lets his *Rêverie* flow liquidly—it is entirely composed of arpeggios, over which from time to time a bit of melody lifts itself with feeble wings; and then he plays "*Le Hibou et les moineaux.*" This piece is a great success and exerts a stirring effect upon the audience. It is a real child's piece and marvelously fanciful. The bass notes show us the owl sitting and dolefully opening and shutting his veiled eyes; then in the treble the sparrows flutter, pertly yet timorously, as they tease him. Four times Bibi is called out with jubilation after this piece. An employee of the hotel in a brass-buttoned livery carries three huge wreaths of laurel up to the platform and holds them in front of him, from the side, while Bibi bows his thanks. Even the princess participates in the applause by gently touching her flat hands against each other, even though no sound ensues.

How well this small, accomplished wight knows how to draw out the applause! He keeps them waiting from his place behind the screen, lingers a little upon the steps of the platform, regards the colored satin bows of the wreaths with childish pleasure, even though they have long since begun to bore him, bows charmingly and hesitatingly, and leaves the people time to work off their enthusiasm, so that none of the precious noise of their palms is lost. *"Le Hibou"* is my strong card, he thinks, for he has learned this term from the impresario. Then comes *Fantaisie*, which is really much better, especially the place in C sharp. But you have gone mad about this *hibou*, you public, although it is the first thing and the stupidest which I have ever made. And he bows graciously.

He then plays *Méditation* and then *Etude*—it is a most comprehensive program. *Méditation* goes much like *Rêverie*, which is no reflection upon it, and in *Etude* Bibi shows all his technical dexterity, which is slightly inferior to his power of invention. And then comes *Fantaisie*. It is his favorite piece. He always plays it a bit differently, treats it in a free manner, and at times surprises himself by new turns and conceits, when he is in good form.

He sits and plays, very small and shining white in front of the great black piano, lone and erect upon the platform over that blurred mass of humanity, which has only one heavy soul, to be moved with difficulty, a soul upon which he must operate with his own, lone and lifted above the multitude. His soft black hair, together with the white silk bow, has fallen across his forehead; his strong, bony, trained wrists are in action, and one sees the muscles of his brown, childish cheeks strain and quiver.

At times there come to him seconds of forgetfulness and solitude, during which his strange, mouselike eyes, with their dull circles, glide sideways from the audience toward the frescoed wall of the hall at his side, through which they peer, in order to lose themselves in adventurous distances filled with a vague life. And then a glance from the corners of his eyes darts back into the hall, and he is again one with his hearers.

Complaint and jubilation, a soaring aloft, and a profound plunge—my *Fantaisie*! thinks Bibi quite tenderly. Now listen, here comes the part which goes into C sharp! And he lets the pedals play as it goes into C sharp. Are they aware of it? In faith, not in the least, they are aware of nothing! And so he casts his eyes up prettily toward the ceiling, so that they may at least have something to look at.

The people sit there in long rows and look at the infant prodigy. And they think all manner of thoughts with their collective brain. An old gentleman with a white beard, a seal ring on his forefinger and a knotty growth on his bald pate, an excrescence, if you will,

53

thinks to himself: One ought really to be ashamed of oneself. One has never been able to get beyond playing "Three Hunters from the Palatinate," and here one sits as an old graybeard and has miracles performed for one by this midget. But one must not forget that this gift is a divine one. God bestows his gifts as He will; there is no help for that, and it is no shame to be an ordinary human being. It is somewhat as with the child Jesus. One may bow before a child without being ashamed. How comforting to feel this! He does not dare to think: How sweet it is! "Sweet" would be unworthy of a robust old gentleman. But he feels it! He feels it for all that!

Art, thinks the businessman with the parrotlike nose. Of course! Art brings a bit of a gleam into life, a little tinkle, a touch of white silk. And the deal furthermore is not a bad one. There are at least fifty seats at twelve marks apiece sold; that alone makes six hundred marks—and then all the incidentals. Deducting the rent of the hall, and the cost of lighting and the programs, there will be a balance of at least a thousand marks. Not at all to be despised.

Well, that was Chopin that he just played, thinks the piano teacher, a lady with a pointed nose, of about that age when hopes begin to go to sleep and the intelligence acquires an additional sharpness. One might say that the boy is not very direct. I shall say afterward that he is not very direct. That sounds well. The way he holds his hands is, moreover, very undisciplined. One should be able to lay a coin upon the back of the hand—I should give him a bit of the ruler.

A young girl, who looks very waxen-faced, and who is of an age in which there are certain tensions inducing delicious thoughts, thinks to herself: What is it that he is playing there? Why, it is passion, passion, that he is playing! But he is a mere child! Were he to kiss me, it would seem as though my little brother kissed me—it would not be a kiss at all. Can it be that there is a passion that is disconnected from all earthy things, pure passion, something that is only passionate child's play? Well, if I should say that aloud, they would dose me with cod-liver oil. That is the way of the world.

An officer leans against a pillar. He surveys the successful Bibi and thinks: You are somebody and I am somebody, each in his own way. He draws his heels together and pays the infant prodigy that homage which he pays to all existent powers.

The critic, however, an aging man in a seedy black coat and turned-up, mud-spattered trousers, occupies his free seat, and thinks: Just look at this Bibi, this urchin! As an individual he has still some distance to go, but as a type he is quite finished—it is the type of the artist. He carries in him the majesty of the artist as well as his lack of dignity, his charlatanism and his sacred spark, his contempt and his secret rapture. But I must not write that—it is really too good. Ah, yes, believe me, I might have become an artist myself if I had not seen through it all so clearly.

The infant prodigy has finished, and a veritable tempest of applause breaks loose. He is forced to appear again and again from behind his screen. The man with the brass buttons comes with new garlands in tow, four laurel wreaths, a lyre made of violets, a bouquet of roses. His two arms do not suffice to hand all these tributes to the infant prodigy; the impresario himself ascends the platform to help him. He hangs a laurel wreath around Bibi's neck; he strokes his black hair tenderly. And suddenly, as though he were overcome by emotion, he bends low and bestows a kiss upon the infant prodigy, a sounding kiss, full upon the mouth. This causes the tempest to increase to a hurricane. This kiss acts like a galvanic shock upon the audience; it shoots through the crowd and thrills every nerve. The people are borne away by a mad desire for noise. Loud bravos mingle with the wild tumult of hands. Several of Bibi's small and matter-of-fact comrades down there wave their handkerchiefs. But the critic thinks: Of course, that kiss from the impresario was bound to come. An old and effective trick. Yes, by heavens! If one only didn't see through it all so plainly!

And then the concert of the infant prodigy draws to a close. It began at half-past seven and is over by half-past eight. The platform is filled with garlands, and two small flowerpots are standing upon the lamp brackets of the grand piano. Bibi plays his *"Rhapsodie grecque"* as his final number, and this passes at the close into the Greek national hymn. Those of Bibi's countrymen who happen to be present would like to join in and sing this, if this concert were not such a fashionable one. They compensate themselves at the close by making a tremendous noise, a hot-blooded row, a national demonstration. But the aging critic thinks: Of course, that national hymn was bound to come. One plays the whole affair into another sphere, no means of rousing enthusiasm is left untried. I'll write that such things are inartistic. But perhaps it is artistic after all. What is the artist? A clown. Criticism is the highest of all functions. But I can-

55

not write that. And then he removes himself with his bespattered trousers.

After nine or ten calls the overheated infant prodigy no longer retires behind his screen but goes down to his mamma and to the impresario in the hall. The people are standing among the disarranged chairs and applauding and pushing forward in order to have a look at Bibi close at hand. A few also wish to have a look at the princess; two close-packed groups form in front of the platform, around the infant prodigy and the princess, and it is difficult to say which of the two is really receiving. But then the lady-in-waiting is commanded to go to Bibi; she tugs and smoothes his silken jacket a bit, to make him presentable for court, leads him by the arm in front of the princess, and earnestly indicates to him that he should kiss the hand of Her Royal Highness.

"How do you do it, my child?" asks the princess. "Does it come to you by itself, when you sit down?"

"*Oui, madame,*" Bibi replies. But inwardly he thinks: Oh, you stupid old princess!

Then he turns away with a shy rudeness and goes back to his own people.

Outside there is great confusion at the cloakrooms. One holds up one's check; with open arms one receives furs, shawls, and galoshes across the table. The piano teacher is standing there among her acquaintances and criticizing. "He is not very direct," says she aloud, and looks about her.

A young aristocratic lady is standing in front of one of the tall mirrors against the wall, and her two brothers, both lieutenants, are helping her with her cloak and her fur overshoes. She is wonderfully pretty, with her steel-blue eyes and her clear, thoroughbred face, a perfect little aristocrat. Done with her dressing, she stands waiting for her brothers.

"Adolf, don't stand in front of the mirror so long!" she says to one of them in a low, angry voice, for he finds it difficult to tear himself away from the image of his handsome but fatuous face. Well, if that does not beat everything! Surely Lieutenant Adolf has the right to button his overcoat in front of a mirror without her leave! Then they go out, and outside in the street, where the arc lamps shimmer turbidly through the whirling snow, Lieutenant Adolf begins to cut up a bit—turns up his coat collar, shoves his hands into the slanting pockets of his overcoat, and begins to execute a short cakewalk upon the snow, for it is very cold.

A child! thinks a girl with unkempt hair who walks with dangling arms behind them, in the company of a solemn-looking youth. A most lovable child! In there everything was full of reverence. . . . Then with a loud, monotonous voice she says: "We are all infant prodigies, we creators!"

Well, thinks the old gentleman who has never been able to get beyond "Three Hunters from the Palatinate" and whose excrescence is now covered by a top hat, what does she mean? A kind of Pythia, it seems to me.

But the solemn-looking youth, who understands her every word, nods slowly.

Then they are silent, and the girl with unkempt hair follows that aristocratic sister and her brothers with her eyes. She despises them, yet she follows them with her eyes until they have vanished around the corner.

sinclair Lewis

(1885–1951)

Prize awarded 1930 "for his vigorous and graphic art of description and his

ability to create, with wit and humor, new types of characters." ★ *Sinclair Lewis*

was the first American recipient of the Nobel Prize for literature, a novelist best

known for his portrayals of the American middle class. He was born in Min-

nesota and educated at Yale. Lewis's early work was neither distinguished nor

successful: Our Mr. Wrenn *(1914) and four other novels sentimental and*

weakly constructed. Nonetheless, they revealed a Dickensian talent for social

criticism, and by 1915 Lewis was selling stories to the Saturday Evening Post

and earning his living as a writer.

With Main Street *(1920), a satirical novel that captured the stifling men-*

tality of small-town life, Lewis won critical praise and a large readership. Over

the next decade he wrote four more highly regarded novels: Babbitt *(1922),*

about a successful provincial businessman; Arrowsmith *(1925);* Elmer Gan-

try *(1927), set in the milieu of religious revivalism; and* Dodsworth *(1929),*

which portrayed a middle-aged midwestern industrialist and his wife in Europe.

The novels that followed made less of an impact. Although he created some

memorable characters, Lewis's importance is not so much literary as sociological.

"Babbitt" and "Main Street" have been incorporated into our language as

symbols of oppressive, bourgeois aspects of American culture.

A Letter from the Queen

DOCTOR SELIG WAS AN ADVENTURER. He did not look it, certainly. He was an amiable young bachelor with thin hair. He was instructor in history and economics in Erasmus College, and he had to sit on a foolish little platform and try to coax some fifty young men and women, who were interested only in cuddling and four-door sedans, to become hysterical about the law of diminishing returns.

But at night, in his decorous boarding house, he sometimes smoked a pipe, which was viewed as obscene in the religious shades of Erasmus, and he was boldly writing a book which was to make him famous.

Of course everyone is writing a book. But Selig's was different. It was profound. How good it was can be seen from the fact that with only three-quarters of it done, it already had fifteen hundred footnotes—such lively comments as *"Vid.* J.A.S.H.S. VIII, 234 *et seq."* A real book, nothing flippant or commercialized.

It was called *The Influence of American Diplomacy on the Internal Policies of Paneuropa.*

"Paneuropa," Selig felt, was a nice and scholarly way of saying "Europe."

It would really have been an interesting book if Doctor Selig had not believed that all literature is excellent in proportion as it is hard to read. He had touched a world romantic and little known. Hidden in old documents, like discovering in a desert an oasis where girls laugh and fountains chatter and the market place is noisy, he found the story of Franklin, who in his mousy fur cap was the Don Juan of

59

Paris, of Adams fighting the British government to prevent their recognizing the Confederacy, of Benjamin Thompson, the Massachusetts Yankee who in 1791 was chief counselor of Bavaria, with the title of Count Rumford.

Selig was moved by these men who made the young America more admired than she is today. And he was moved and, in a most unscholarly way, he became a little angry as he reviewed the story of Senator Ryder.

He knew, of course, that Lafayette Ryder had prevented war between England and America in the first reign of Grover Cleveland; he knew that Ryder had been Secretary of State, and Ambassador to France, courted by Paris for his wisdom, his manners, his wit; that as Senator he had fathered (and mothered and wet-nursed) the Ryder-Hanklin Bill, which had saved our wheat markets; and that his two books, *Possibilities of Disarmament* and *The Anglo-American Empire*, were not merely glib propaganda for peace, but such inspired documents as would have prevented the Boer War, the Spanish-American War, the Great War, if there had been in his Victorian world a dozen men with minds like his. This Selig knew, but he could not remember when Ryder had died.

Then he discovered with aghast astonishment that Senator Ryder was not dead, but still alive at ninety-two, forgotten by the country he had helped to build.

Yes, Selig felt bitterly, we honor our great men in America—sometimes for as much as two months after the particular act of greatness that tickles us. But this is a democracy. We mustn't let anyone suppose that because we have given him an (undesired) parade up Broadway and a (furiously resented) soaking of publicity on March first, he may expect to be taken seriously on May second.

The Admiral Dewey whom the press for a week labeled as a combination of Nelson, Napoleon, and Chevalier Bayard, they later nagged to his grave. If a dramatist has a success one season, then may the gods help him, because for the rest of his life everyone will attend his plays only in the hope that he will fail.

60 But sometimes the great glad-hearted hordes of boosters do not brag down the idol in the hope of finding clay feet, but just forget him with the vast, contemptuous, heavy indifference of a hundred and twenty million people.

So felt Doctor Selig, angrily, and he planned for the end of his book a passionate resurrection of Senator Ryder. He had a shy hope that his book would appear before the Senator's death, to make him happy.

Reading the Senator's speeches, studying his pictures in magazine files, he felt that he knew him intimately. He could see, as though the Senator were in the room, that tall ease, the contrast of long thin nose, gay eyes, vast globular brow that made Ryder seem a combination of Puritan, clown, and benevolent scholar.

Selig longed to write to him and ask—oh, a thousand things that only he could explain; the proposals of Lionel Sackville-West regarding Colombia; what Queen Victoria really had said in that famous but unpublished letter to President Harrison about the Newfoundland fisheries. Why couldn't he write to him?

No! The man was ninety-two, and Selig had too much reverence to disturb him, along with a wholesome suspicion that his letter would be kicked out by the man who had once told Gladstone to go to the devil.

So forgotten was the Senator that Selig could not, at first, find where he lived. *Who's Who* gave no address. Selig's superior, Professor Munk, who was believed to know everything in the world except the whereabouts of his last season's straw hat, bleated, "My dear chap, Ryder is dwelling in some cemetery! He passed beyond, if I remember, in 1901."

The mild Doctor Selig almost did homicide upon a venerable midwestern historian.

At last, in a bulletin issued by the Anti-Prohibition League, Selig found among the list of directors: "Lafayette Ryder (form. U.S. Sen., Sec'y State), West Wickley, Vermont." Though the Senator's residence could make no difference to him, that night Selig was so excited that he smoked an extra pipe of tobacco.

He was planning his coming summer vacation, during which he hoped to finish his book. The presence of the Senator drew him toward Vermont, and in an educational magazine he found the advertisement: "Sky Peaks, near Wickley, Vt., woodland nook with peace and a library—congenial and intellectual company and writers—tennis, handball, riding—nightly Sing around Old-time Bonfire—fur. bung. low rates."

That was what he wanted: a nook and a library and lots of low rates, along with nearness to his idol. He booked a fur. bung. for the summer, and he carried his suitcase to the station on the beautiful day when the young fiends who through the year had tormented him with unanswerable questions streaked off to all parts of the world and for three tremendous months permitted him to be a private human being.

When he reached Vermont, Selig found Sky Peaks an old farm, redecorated in a distressingly tea-roomy fashion. His single bungalow, formerly an honest corncrib, was now painted robin's-egg blue with yellow trimmings and christened "Shelley." But the camp was on an upland, and air sweet from hayfield and spruce grove healed his lungs, spotted with classroom dust.

At his first dinner at Sky Peaks, he demanded of the host, one Mr. Iddle, "Doesn't Senator Ryder live somewhere near here?"

"Oh, yes, up on the mountain, about four miles south."

"Hope I catch a glimpse of him some day."

"I'll run you over to see him any time you'd like."

"Oh, I couldn't do that! Couldn't intrude!"

"Nonsense! Of course he's old, but he takes quite an interest in the countryside. Fact, I bought this place from him and— Don't forget the Sing tonight."

At eight that evening Iddle came to drag Selig from the security of his corncrib just as he was getting the relations of the Locarno Pact and the Versailles Treaty beautifully coordinated.

It was that kind of Sing: "The Long, Long Trail" and "All God's Chillun Got Shoes." (God's Chillun also possessed coats, pants, vests, flivvers, and watermelons, interminably.) Beside Selig at the campfire sat a young woman with eyes, a nose, a sweater, and an athletic skirt, none of them very good or particularly bad. He would not have noticed her, but she picked on him:

"They tell me you're in Erasmus, Doctor Selig."

"Um."

"Real attention to character. And after all, what benefit is there in developing the intellect if the character isn't developed to keep pace with it? You see, I'm in educational work myself—oh, of course nothing like being on a college faculty, but I teach history in the Lincoln High School at Schenectady—my name is Selma Swanson. We must have some good talks about teaching history, mustn't we!"

"Um!" said Selig, and escaped, though it was not till he was safely in his corncrib that he said aloud, "We must *not*!"

For three months he was not going to be a teacher, or heed the horrors of character-building. He was going to be a great scholar. Even Senator Ryder might be excited to know how powerful an intellect was soothing itself to sleep in a corncrib four miles away!

He was grinding hard next afternoon when his host, Iddle, stormed in with: "I've got to run in to Wickley Center. Go right near old Ryder's. Come on. I'll introduce you to him."

"Oh, no, honestly!"

"Don't be silly: I imagine he's lonely. Come on!"

Before Selig could make up his mind to get out of Iddle's tempestuous flivver and walk back, they were driving up a mountain road and past marble gateposts into an estate. Through a damp grove of birches and maples they came out on meadows dominated by an old brick house with a huge porch facing the checkered valley. They stopped with a dash at the porch, and on it Selig saw an old man sunk in a canvas deck chair and covered with a shawl. In the shadow the light seemed to concentrate on his bald head, like a sphere of polished vellum, and on long bloodless hands lying as in death on shawl-draped knees. In his eyes there was no life nor desire for it.

Iddle leaped out, bellowing, "Afternoon, Senator! Lovely day, isn't it? I've brought a man to call on you. This is Mr. Selig of—uh—one of our colleges. I'll be back in an hour."

He seized Selig's arm—he was abominably strong—and almost pulled him out of the car. Selig's mind was one wretched puddle of confusion. Before he could dredge any definite thought out of it, Iddle had rattled away, and Selig stood below the porch, hypnotized by the stare of Senator Ryder—too old for hate or anger, but not too old for slow contempt.

Not one word Ryder said.

Selig cried, like a schoolboy unjustly accused:

"Honestly, Senator, the last thing I wanted to do was to intrude on you. I thought Iddle would just introduce us and take me away. I suppose he meant well. And perhaps subconsciously I did want to intrude! I know your *Possibilities of Disarmament* and *Anglo-American Empire* so well—"

The Senator stirred like an antediluvian owl awakening at twilight. His eyes came to life. One expected him to croak, like a cynical old bird, but his still voice was fastidious:

63

"I didn't suppose anyone had looked into my books since 1910."
Painful yet gracious was the gesture with which he waved Selig to a
chair. "You are a teacher?"

"Instructor in a small Ohio college. Economics and history. I'm
writing a monograph on our diplomacy, and naturally— There are
so many things that only you could explain!"

"Because I'm so old?"

"No! Because you've had so much knowledge and courage—
perhaps they're the same thing! Every day, literally, in working on
my book I've wished I could consult you. For instance— Tell me,
sir, didn't Secretary of State Olney really want war with England
over Venezuela? Wasn't he trying to be a tin hero?"

"No!" The old man threw off his shawl. It was somehow a little
shocking to find him not in an ancient robe laced with gold, but in
a crisp linen summer suit with a smart bow tie. He sat up, alert, his
voice harsher. "No! He was a patriot. Sturdy. Honest. Willing to be
conciliatory but not flinching. Miss Tully!"

At the Senator's cry, out of the wide fanlighted door of the
house slid a trained nurse. Her uniform was so starched that it
almost clattered, but she was a peony sort of young woman, the
sort who would insist on brightly mothering any male, of any
age, whether or not he desired to be mothered. She glared at
the intruding Selig; she shook her finger at Senator Ryder, and
simpered:

"Now I do hope you aren't tiring yourself, else I shall have to be
ever so stern and make you go to bed. The doctor said—"

"Damn the doctor! Tell Mrs. Tinkham to bring me down the file
of letters from Richard Olney, Washington, for 1895—O-l-n-e-y—
and hustle it!'"

Miss Tully gone, the Senator growled, "Got no more use for a
nurse than a cat for two tails! It's that muttonheaded doctor, the old
fool! He's seventy-five years old, and he hasn't had a thought since
1888. Doctors!"

He delivered an address on the art of medicine with such vigorous blasphemy that Selig shrank in horrified admiration. And the
Senator didn't abate the blazing crimson of his oration at the entrance of his secretary, Mrs. Tinkham, a small, narrow, bleached,
virginal widow.

Selig expected her to leap off the porch and commit suicide in terror. She didn't. She waited, she yawned gently, she handed the Senator a manila envelope, and gently she vanished.

The Senator grinned. "She'll pray at me tonight! She daren't while you're here. There! I feel better. Good cussing is a therapeutic agent that has been forgotten in these degenerate days. I could teach you more about cussing than about diplomacy—to which cussing is a most valuable aid. Now here is a letter that Secretary Olney wrote me about the significance of his correspondence with England."

It was a page of history. Selig handled it with more reverence than he had given to any material object in his life.

He exclaimed, "Oh, yes, you used—of course I've never seen the rest of this letter, and I can't tell you, sir, how excited I am to see it. But didn't you use this first paragraph—it must be about on page 276 of your *Anglo-American Empire?*"

"I believe I did. It's not my favorite reading!"

"You know, of course, that it was reprinted from your book in the *Journal of the American Society of Historical Sources* last year?"

"Was it?" The old man seemed vastly pleased. He beamed at Selig as at a young but tested friend. He chuckled, "Well, I suppose I appreciate now how King Tut felt when they remembered him and dug him up. . . . Miss Tully! Hey! Miss Tully, will you be so good as to tell Martens to bring us whisky and soda, with two glasses? Eh? Now you look here, young woman; we'll fight out the whole question of my senile viciousness after our guest has gone. Two glasses, I said! . . . Now about Secretary Olney. The fact of the case was . . ."

Two hours later, Senator Ryder was still talking and in that two hours he had given Selig such unrecorded information as the researcher could not have found in two years of study.

Selig had for two hours walked with presidents and ambassadors; he had the dinner conversation of foreign ministers, conversations so private, so world-affecting, that they never had been set down, even in letters. The Senator had revealed his friendship with King Edward, and the predictions about the future World War the King had made over a glass of mineral water.

The mild college instructor, who till this afternoon had never spoken to anyone more important than the president of a prairie college, was exalted with a feeling that he had become the confidant

65

of kings and field marshals, of Anatole France and Lord Haldane, of Sarah Bernardt and George Meredith.

He had always known but till now he had never understood that in private these great personages were plain human beings, like Doctor Wilbur Selig of Erasmus. It made him feel close to King Edward to hear (though the Senator may have exaggerated) that the King could not pronounce his own name without a German accent; it made him feel a man of the world to learn the details of a certain not very elevating party at which an English duke and a German prince and a Portuguese king, accompanied by questionable ladies, had in bibulous intimacy sung to Senator Ryder's leadership the lyric, "How Dry I Am."

During that two hours, there had been ten minutes when he had been entirely off in a Conan Doyle spirit world. His notion of prodigious alcoholic dissipation was a bottle of home-brewed beer once a month. He had tried to mix himself a light whisky and soda—he noted, with some anxiety about the proper drinking-manners in diplomatic society, that he took approximately one-third as much whisky as the Senator.

But while the old man rolled his drink in his mouth and shook his bald head rapturously and showed no effect, Selig was suddenly lifted six million miles above the earth, through pink-gray clouds shot with lightning, and at that altitude he floated dizzily while below him the Senator discoursed on the relations of Cuban sugar to Colorado beets.

And once Iddle blatted into sight, in his dirty flivver, suggested taking him away, and was blessedly dismissed by the Senator's curt, "Doctor Selig is staying here for dinner. I'll send him back in my car."

Dinner . . . Selig, though he rarely read fiction, had read in some novel about "candle-flames, stilled in the twilight and reflected in the long stretch of waxed mahogany as in a clouded mirror—candles and roses and old silver." He had read, too, about stag horns and heraldic shields and the swords of old warriors.

Now, actually, the Senator's dining room had neither stag horn nor heraldic shield nor sword, and if there were still candle-flames, there was no mahogany to reflect them, but instead a silver stretch

66

of damask. It was a long room, simple, with old portraits against white panels. Yet Selig felt that he was transported into all the romance he had ever read.

The dinner was countrylike. By now, Selig expected peacocks' tongues and caviar; he got steak and cantaloupe and corn pudding. But there were four glasses at each plate, and along with water, which was the familiar drink at Erasmus, he had, and timidly, tasted sherry, Burgundy, and champagne.

If Wilbur Selig of Iowa and Erasmus had known anything, it was that champagne was peculiarly wicked, associated with light ladies, lewd talk, and losses at roulette invariably terminating in suicide. Yet it was just as he was nibbling at his very first glass of champagne that Senator Ryder began to talk of his delight in the rise of Anglo-Catholicism.

No. It was none of it real.

If he was exhilarated that he had been kept for dinner, he was ecstatic when the Senator said, "Would you care to come for dinner again day after tomorrow? Good. I'll send Martens for you at seven-thirty. Don't dress."

In a dream phantasmagoria he started home, driven by Martens, the Senator's chauffeur-butler, with unnumbered things that had puzzled him in writing his book made clear.

When he arrived at the Sky Peaks camp, the guests were still sitting about the dull campfire.

"My!" said Miss Selma Swanson, teacher of history. "Mr. Iddle says you've spent the whole evening with Senator Ryder. Mr. Iddle says he's a grand person—used to be a great politician."

"Oh, he was kind enough to help me about some confused problems," murmured Selig.

But as he went to bed—in a reformed corncrib—he exulted, "I bet I could become quite a good friend of the Senator! Wouldn't that be wonderful!"

Lafayette Ryder, when his visitor—a man named Selig or Selim—was gone, sat at the long dining table with a cigarette and a distressingly empty cognac glass. He was meditating, "Nice eager young chap. Provincial. But mannerly. I wonder if there really are a few people who know that Lafe Ryder once existed?"

He rang, and the crisply coy Miss Tully, the nurse, waltzed into the dining room, bubbling, "So we're all ready to go to bed now, Senator!"

"We are not! I didn't ring for you; I rang for Martens."

"He's driving your guest."

"Humph! Send in cook. I want some more brandy."

"Oh, now, Daddy Ryder! You aren't going to be naughty, are you?"

"I am! And who the deuce ever told you to call me 'Daddy'? Daddy!"

"You did. Last year."

"I don't—this year. Bring me the brandy bottle."

"If I do, will you go to bed then?"

"I will not!"

"But the doctor—"

"The doctor is a misbegotten hound with a face like a fish. And other things. I feel cheerful tonight. I shall sit up late. Till All Hours."

They compromised on eleven-thirty instead of All Hours, and one glass of brandy instead of the bottle. But, vexed at having thus compromised—as so often, in ninety-odd years, he had been vexed at having compromised with Empires—the Senator was (said Miss Tully) very naughty in his bath.

"I swear," said Miss Tully afterward, to Mrs. Tinkham, the secretary, "if he didn't pay so well, I'd leave that horrid old man tomorrow. Just because he was a politician or something, once, to think he can sass a trained nurse!"

"You would not!" said Mrs. Tinkham. "But he *is* naughty."

And they did not know that, supposedly safe in his four-poster bed, the old man was lying awake, smoking a cigarette and reflecting:

"The gods have always been much better to me than I have deserved. Just when I thought I was submerged in flood of women and doctors, along comes a man for companion, a young man who seems to be a potential scholar, and who might preserve for the world what I tried to do. Oh, stop pitying yourself, Lafe Ryder! . . . I wish I could sleep."

Senator Ryder reflected, the next morning, that he had probably counted too much on young Selig. But when Selig came again for dinner, the Senator was gratified to see how quickly he was already fitting into a house probably more elaborate than any he had known. And quite easily he told of what the Senator accounted his uncivilized farm boyhood, his life in a state university.

"So much the better that he is naïve, not one of these third-secretary cubs who think they're cosmopolitan because they went to Groton," considered the Senator. "I must do something for him."

Again he lay awake that night, and suddenly he had what seemed to him an inspired idea.

"I'll give young Selig a lift. All this money and no one but hang-jawed relatives to give it to! Give him a year of freedom. Pay him—he probably earns twenty-five hundred a year; pay him five thousand and expenses to arrange my files. If he makes good, I'd let him publish my papers after I pass out. The letters from John Hay, from Blaine, from Choate! No set of unpublished documents like it in America! It would *make* the boy!"

Mrs. Tinkham would object. Be jealous. She might quit. Splendid! "Lafe, you arrant old coward, you've been trying to get rid of that woman without hurting her feelings for three years! At that, she'll probably marry you on your dying bed!"

He chuckled, a wicked, low, delighted sound, the old man alone in darkness.

"Yes, and if he shows the quality I think he has, leave him a little money to carry on with while he edits the letters. Leave him—let's see."

It was supposed among Senator Ryder's lip-licking relatives and necessitous hangers-on that he had left of the Ryder fortune perhaps two hundred thousand dollars. Only his broker and he knew that he had by secret investment increased it to a million, these ten years of dark, invalid life.

He lay planning a new will. The present one left half his fortune to his university, a quarter to the town of Wickley for a community center, the rest to nephews and nieces, with ten thousand each for the Tully, the Tinkham, Martens, and the much-badgered doctor, with a grave proviso that the doctor should never again dictate to any patient how much he should smoke.

Now to Doctor Selig, asleep and not even dream-warned in his absurd corncrib, was presented the sum of twenty-five thousand dollars, the blessings of an old man, and a store of historical documents which could not be priced in coin.

69

In the morning, with a headache, and very strong with Miss Tully about the taste of the aspirin—he suggested that she had dipped it in arsenic—the Senator reduced Selig to five thousand, but that night it went back to twenty-five.

How pleased the young man would be.

Doctor Wilbur Selig, on the first night when he had unexpectedly been bidden to stay for dinner with Senator Ryder, was as stirred as by— What *would* most stir Doctor Wilbur Selig? A great play? A raise in salary? An Erasmus football victory?

At the second dinner, with the house and the hero less novel to him, he was calmly happy, and zealous about getting information. The third dinner, a week after, was agreeable enough, but he paid rather more attention to the squab in casserole than to the Senator's revelations about the Baring panic, and he was a little annoyed that the Senator insisted (so selfishly) on his staying till midnight, instead of going home to bed at a reasonable hour like ten—with, perhaps, before retiring, a few minutes of chat with that awfully nice bright girl, Miss Selma Swanson.

And through that third dinner he found himself reluctantly critical of the Senator's morals.

Hang it, here was a man of good family, who had had a chance to see all that was noblest and best in the world, and why did he feel he had to use such bad language, why did he drink so much? Selig wasn't (he proudly reminded himself) the least bit narrow-minded. But an old man like this ought to be thinking of missing his peace; ought to be ashamed of cursing like a stableboy.

He reproved himself next morning. "He's been mighty nice to me. He's a good old coot—at heart. And of course a great statesman."

But he snapped back to irritation when he had a telephone call from Martens, the chauffeur: "Senator Ryder would like you to come over for tea this afternoon. He has something to show you."

"All right, I'll be over."

70 Selig was curt about it, and he raged, "Now, by thunder, of all the thoughtless, selfish old codgers! As if I didn't have anything to do but dance attendance on him and amuse him! And here I'd planned to finish a chapter this afternoon! 'Course he does give me some inside information, but still—as if I needed all the tittle-tattle of

embassies for my book! Got all the stuff I need now. And how am I to get over there? The selfish old hound never thinks of that! Does he suppose I can afford a car to go over? I'll have to walk! Got half a mind not to go!"

The sulkiness with which he came to tea softened when the Senator began to talk about the Queen Victoria letter.

Historians knew that during the presidency of Benjamin Harrison, when there was hostility between America and Britain over the seizure by both sides of fishing boats, Queen Victoria had written in her own hand to President Harrison. It was believed that she deplored her royal inability to appeal directly to Parliament, and suggested his first taking the difficulty up with Congress. But precisely what was in this unofficial letter, apparently no one knew.

This afternoon Senator Ryder said placidly, "I happen to have the original of the letter in my possession."

"*What?*"

"Perhaps some day I'll give you a glimpse of it. I think I have the right to let you quote it."

Selig was electrified. It would be a sensation—*he* would be a sensation! He could see his book, and himself, on the front pages. But the Senator passed on to a trivial, quite improper anecdote about a certain Brazilian ambassador and a Washington milliner, and Selig was irritable again. Darn it, it was indecent for a man of over ninety to think of such things! And why the deuce was he so skittish and secretive about his old letter? If he was going to show it, why not do it?

So perhaps Doctor Selig of Erasmus was not quite so gracious as a Doctor Selig of Erasmus should have been when, at parting, the old man drew from under his shawl a worn blue-gray pamphlet, and piped:

"I'm going to give you this, if you'd like it. There's only six copies left in the world, I believe. It's the third one of my books—privately printed and not ordinarily listed with the others. It has, I imagine, a few things in it the historians don't know; the real story of the Paris commune."

"Oh, thanks," Selig said brusquely and, to himself, in the Senator's car, he pointed out that it showed what an egotistic old codger Ryder was to suppose that just because he'd written something, it must be a blooming treasure!

71

He glanced into the book. It seemed to have information. But he wasn't stirred, for it was out of line with what he had decided were the subjects of value to Doctor Selig and, therefore, of general interest.

After tea, now, it was too late for work before dinner, and he had Ryder's chauffeur set him down at Tredwell's General Store, which had become for members of the Sky Peaks camp a combination of department store, post office, and café, where they drank wild toasts in lemon pop.

Miss Selma Swanson was there, and Selig laughingly treated her to chewing gum, Attaboy Peanut Candy Rolls, and seven fishhooks. They had such a lively time discussing that funny Miss Elkington up at the camp.

When he started off, with Miss Swanson, he left the Senator's book behind him in the store. He did not miss it till he had gone to bed.

Two days afterward, the Senator's chauffeur again telephoned an invitation to tea for that afternoon, but this time Selig snapped, "Sorry! Tell the Senator I unfortunately shan't be able to come!"

"Just a moment, please," said the chauffeur. "The Senator wishes to know if you care to come to dinner tomorrow evening—eight—he'll send for you."

"Well— Yes, tell him I'll be glad to come."

After all, dinner here at Sky Peaks was pretty bad, and he'd get away early in the evening.

He rejoiced in having his afternoon free for work. But the confounded insistence of the Senator had so bothered him that he banged a book on his table and strolled outside.

The members of the camp were playing One Old Cat, with Selma Swanson, very jolly in knickerbockers, as cheerleader. They yelped at Selig to join them and, after a stately refusal or two, he did. He had a good time. Afterward he pretended to wrestle with Miss Swanson—she had the supplest waist and, seen close up, the moistest eyes. So he was glad that he had not wasted his afternoon listening to that old bore.

72

The next afternoon, at six, a splendid chapter done, he went off for a climb up Mount Poverty with Miss Swanson. The late sun was so rich on pasture, pine clumps, and distant meadows, and Miss Swanson was so lively in tweed skirt and brogues—but the stockings were silk—that he regretted having promised to be at the Senator's at eight.

"But of course I always keep my promises," he reflected proudly.

They sat on a flat rock perched above the valley, and he observed in rather a classroom tone, "How remarkable that light is—the way it picks out that farmhouse roof, and then the shadow of those maples on the grass. Did you ever realize that it's less the shape of things than the light that gives a landscape beauty?"

"No, I don't think I ever did. That's so. It's the light! My, how observant you are!"

"Oh, no, I'm not. I'm afraid I'm just a bookworm."

"Oh, you are not! Of course you're tremendously scholarly—my, I've learned so much about study from you—but then, you're so active—you were just a circus playing One Old Cat yesterday. I do admire an all-around man."

At seven-thirty, holding her firm hand, he was saying, "But really, there's so much that I lack that— But you do think I'm right about it's being so much manlier not to drink like that old man? By the way, we must start back."

At a quarter to eight, after he had kissed her and apologized and kissed her, he remarked, "Still, he can wait a while—won't make any difference."

At eight: "Golly, it's so late! Had no idea. Well, I better not go at all now. I'll just phone him this evening and say I got balled up on the date. Look! Let's go down to the lake and dine on the wharf at the boathouse, just you and I."

"Oh, that would be grand!" said Miss Selma Swanson.

Lafayette Ryder sat on the porch that, along with his dining room and bedroom, had become his entire world, and waited for the kind young friend who was giving back to him the world he had once known. His lawyer was coming from New York in three days, and there was the matter of the codicil to his will. But—the Senator stirred impatiently—this money matter was grubby; he had for Selig something rarer than money—a gift for a scholar.

He looked at it and smiled. It was a double sheet of thick bond, with "Windsor Castle" engraved at the top. Above this address was written in a thin hand: "To my friend L. Ryder, to use if he ever sees fit. Benj. Harrison."

73

The letter began, "To His Excellency, the President," and it was signed, "Victoria R." In a few lines between inscription and signature there was a new history of the great Victoria of the Nineteenth Century. . . . Dynamite does not come in large packages.

The old man tucked the letter into a pocket down beneath the rosy shawl that reached up to his gray face.

Miss Tully rustled out, to beg, "Daddy, you won't take more than one cocktail tonight? The doctor says it's so bad for you!"

"Heh! Maybe I will and maybe I won't! What time is it?"

"A quarter to eight."

"Doctor Selig will be here at eight. If Martens doesn't have the cocktails out on the porch three minutes after he gets back, I'll skin him. And you needn't go looking for the cigarettes in my room, either! I've hidden them in a brand-new place, and I'll probably sit up and smoke till dawn. Fact; doubt if I shall go to bed at all. Doubt if I'll take my bath."

He chuckled as Miss Tully wailed. "You're so naughty!"

The Senator need not have asked the time. He had groped down under the shawl and looked at his watch every five minutes since seven. He inwardly glared at himself for his foolishness in anticipating his young friend, but—all the old ones were gone.

That was the devilishness of living so many years. Gone, so long. People wrote idiotic letters to him, still, begging for his autograph, for money, but who save this fine young Selig had come to him? . . . So long now!

At eight, he stirred, not this time like a drowsy old owl, but like an eagle, its lean head thrusting forth from its pile of hunched feathers, ready to soar. He listened for the car.

At ten minutes past, he swore, competently. Confound that Martens!

At twenty past, the car swept up the driveway. Out of it stepped only Martens, touching his cap, murmuring, "Very sorry, sir. Mr. Selig was not at the camp."

"Then why the devil didn't you wait?"

"I did, sir, as long as I dared."

"Poor fellow! He may have been lost on the mountain. We must start a search!"

"Very sorry, sir, but if I may say so, as I was driving back past the foot of the Mount Poverty trail, I saw Mr. Selig with a young woman, sir, and they were talking and laughing and going away from the camp, sir. I'm afraid—"

"Very well. That will do."

"I'll serve dinner at once, sir. Do you wish your cocktail out here?"

"I won't have one. Send Miss Tully."

When the nurse had fluttered to him, she cried out with alarm. Senator Ryder was sunk down into his shawl. She bent over him to hear his whisper:

"If it doesn't keep you from your dinner, my dear, I think I'd like to be helped up to bed. I don't care for anything to eat. I feel tired."

While she was anxiously stripping the shawl from him, he looked long, as one seeing it for the last time, at the darkening valley. But as she helped him up, he suddenly became active. He snatched from his pocket a stiff double sheet of paper and tore it into fragments which he fiercely scattered over the porch with one sweep of his long arm.

Then he collapsed over her shoulder.

John Galsworthy

(1867–1933)

Prize awarded 1932 "for his distinguished art of narration, which takes its highest form in The Forsyte Saga." ★ Galworthy is best known today for his lengthy series of novels known as The Forsyte Saga (1922) and the post–World War I sequel, A Modern Comedy (1929)—three trilogies in all. They chronicle a large, upper-middle-class English clan, similar in many ways to Galsworthy's own family.

Galsworthy studied at Oxford, but his youthful travels left him unwilling to practice law, his intended profession. A chance meeting with Joseph Conrad, who became his lifelong friend, may have contributed to his decision to become a writer.

Galsworthy's first books, From the Four Winds (1897) and Jocelyn (1898), were published at his own expense. He did not advocate modernism; his novels and plays were conventional in form and naturalistic in content, but his narratives were lively. He was an ardent humanist who created vehicles for social commentary, especially in his plays. The Silver Box (1906), for example, dramatized the law's inequitable treatment of rich and poor. Strife (1909) dealt with the exploitation of workers. Justice (1910) was actually effective in instigating prison reform.

Galsworthy's sincere sense of social justice, along with a perceptive irony (compensating for a lack of subtlety or insight into character), made his works a model of socially responsible Edwardian art.

THE CONSUMMATION

ABOUT 1889 THERE LIVED IN LONDON a man named Harrison, of an amiable and perverse disposition. One morning, at Charing Cross Station, a lady in whom he was interested said to him:

"But Mr. Harrison, why don't you *write*? You are just the person!"

Harrison saw that he was, and at the end of two years had produced eleven short stories, with two of which he was not particularly pleased, but as he naturally did not like to waste them, he put them with the others and sent them all to a publisher. In the course of time he received from the publisher a letter saying that for a certain consideration or commission he would be prepared to undertake the risk of publishing these stories upon Harrison's incurring all the expenses. This pleased Harrison who, feeling that no time should be wasted in making his "work" public, wrote desiring the publisher to put the matter in hand. The publisher replied to this with an estimate and an agreement, to which Harrison responded with a cheque. The publisher answered at once with a polite letter, suggesting that for Harrison's advantage a certain additional sum should be spent on advertisements. Harrison saw the point of this directly, and replied with another cheque—knowing that between gentlemen there could be no question of money.

In due time the book appeared. It was called *In the Track of the Stars,* by Cuthbert Harrison; and within a fortnight Harrison began to receive reviews. He read them with extraordinary pleasure, for they were full of discriminating flattery. One asked if he were a "Lancelot in disguise." Two Liberal papers described the stories as masterpieces; one compared them to the best things in Poe and de Maupassant; and another called him a second Rudyard Kipling. He was greatly encouraged, but, being by nature modest, he merely wrote to the publisher inquiring what he thought of a second edition. His publisher replied with an estimate, mentioning casually that he had already sold about four hundred copies. Harrison referred to his cheque book and saw that the first edition had been a thousand copies. He replied, therefore, that he would wait. He waited, and at the end of six months wrote again. The publisher replied that he had now sold four hundred and three copies, but that, as Mr. Harrison had at present an unknown name, he did not advise a second edition: there was no market for short stories. These had, however, been so well received that he recommended Mr. Harrison to write a long story. The book was without doubt a success, so far as a book of short stories could ever be a success. . . . He sent Harrison a small cheque, and a large number of reviews which Harrison had already received.

Harrison decided not to have a second edition, but to rest upon his *succès d'estime*. All his relations were extremely pleased, and almost immediately he started writing his long story. Now it happened that among Harrison's friends was a man of genius, who sent Harrison a letter.

"I had no idea," he said, "that you could write like this; of course, my dear fellow, the stories are not 'done'; there is no doubt about it, they are *not* 'done.' But you have plenty of time; you are young, and I see that you can do things. Come down here and let us have a talk about what you are at now."

On receiving this Harrison wasted no time, but went down. The man of genius, over a jug of claret-cup, on a summer's afternoon, pointed out how the stories were not "done."

"They show a feeling for outside drama," said he, "but there is none of the real drama of psychology."

Harrison showed him his reviews. He left the man of genius on the following day with a certain sensation of soreness. In the course of a few weeks, however, the soreness wore off, and the words of the man of genius began to bear fruit, and at the end of two months Harrison wrote:

"You are quite right—the stories were not 'done.' I think, however, that I am now on the right path."

At the end of another year, after submitting it once or twice to the man of genius, he finished his second book, and called it *John Endacott*. About this time he left off alluding to his "work" and began to call his writings "stuff."

He sent it to the publisher with the request that he would consider its publication on a royalty. In rather more than the ordinary course of time the publisher replied, that in his opinion (a lay one) *John Endacott* didn't quite fulfil the remarkable promise of Mr. Harrison's first book; and, to show Harrison his perfect honesty, he enclosed an extract from the "reader's" opinion, which stated that Mr. Harrison had "fallen between the stools of art and the British public." Much against the publisher's personal feelings, therefore, the publisher considered that he could only undertake the risk in the then bad condition of trade—if Mr. Harrison would guarantee the expenses.

Harrison hardened his heart, and replied that he was not prepared to guarantee the expenses. Upon which the publisher returned his manuscript, saying that in his opinion (a lay one) Mr. Harrison was taking the wrong turning, which he (the publisher) greatly regretted, for he had much appreciated the pleasant relations which had always existed between them.

Harrison sent the book to a younger publisher, who accepted it on a postponed royalty. It appeared.

At the end of three weeks Harrison began to receive reviews. They were mixed. One complained that there was not enough plot; another, fortunately by the same post, that there was too much plot. The general tendency was to regret that the author of *In the Track of the Stars* had not fulfilled the hopes raised by his first book, in which he had shown such promise of completely hitting the public taste. This might have depressed Harrison had he not received a letter from the man of genius couched in these terms:

"My dear fellow, I am more pleased than I can say. I am now more than ever convinced that you can do things."

Harrison at once began a third book.

Owing to the unfortunate postponement of his royalty, he did not receive anything from his second book. The publisher sold three hundred copies. During the period (eighteen months) that he was writing his third book the man of genius introduced Harrison to a critic, with the words: "You may rely on his judgment; the beggar is infallible."

While to the critic he said: "I tell you, this fellow can do things."

79

The critic was good to Harrison, who, as before said, was of an amiable disposition.

When he had finished his third book he dedicated it to the man of genius and called it *Summer*.

"My dear fellow," wrote the man of genius, when he received his copy, "*it is good!* There is no more to be said about it; it *is* good! I read it with indescribable pleasure."

On the same day Harrison received a letter from the critic which contained the following; "Yes, it's undoubtedly an advance. It's not quite Art, but it's a great advance!"

Harrison was considerably encouraged. The same publisher brought out the book, and sold quite two hundred copies; but he wrote rather dolefully to Harrison, saying that the public demand seemed "almost exhausted." Recognising the fact that comparisons are odious, Harrison refrained from comparing the sale of the book with that of *In the Track of the Stars,* in which he had shown such promise of "completely hitting the public taste." Indeed, about this time he began to have dreams of abandoning the sources of his private income and living the true literary life. He had not many reviews, and began his fourth book.

He was two years writing this "work," which he called *A Lost Man* and dedicated to the critic. He sent a presentation copy to the man of genius, from whom he received an almost immediate reply:

"My dear fellow, it is amazing, really amazing, how you progress! Who would ever imagine you were the same man that wrote *In the Track of the Stars?* yet I pique myself on the fact that even in your first book I spotted that you could do things. Ah!—I wish I could write like you! *A Lost Man* is wonderfully good."

The man of genius was quite sincere in these remarks, which he wrote after perusing the first six chapters. He never, indeed, actually finished reading the book—he felt so tired, as if Harrison had exhausted him—but he always alluded to it as "wonderfully good," just as if he really had finished it.

Harrison sent another copy to the critic, who wrote a genuinely warm letter, saying that he, Harrison, had "achieved" it at last. "This," he said, "is *art*. I doubt if you will ever do anything better than this. . . . I crown you."

Harrison at once commenced his fifth book.

He was more than three years upon this new "work," and called it *A Pilgrimage*. There was a good deal of difficulty in getting it published. Two days after it appeared, however, the critic wrote to Harrison: "I cannot tell you," he said, "how very good I think your new book. It is perhaps stronger than *A Lost Man,* perhaps more original. If anything it is too—I have not finished it yet, but I've written off at once to let you know."

As a matter of fact, he never finished the book. He could not— it was too—! "It's wonderfully good," he said, however, to his wife, and he made *her* read it.

Meanwhile, the man of genius wired saying; "Am going to write to you about your book. Positively am, but have lumbago and cannot hold pen."

Harrison never received any letter, but the critic received one saying: "Can you read it? *I* can't. Altogether over 'done.' "

Harrison was elated. His new publisher was not. He wrote in a peevish strain, saying there was *absolutely no sale.* Mr. Harrison must take care what he was doing or he would exhaust his public, and enclosing a solitary review, which said amongst other things: "This book may be very fine art, too fine altogether. *We* found it dull."

Harrison went abroad, and began his sixth book. He named it *The Consummation,* and worked at it in hermitlike solitude; in it, for the first time, he satisfied himself. He wrote it, as it were, with his heart's blood, with an almost bitter delight. And he often smiled to himself as he thought how with his first book he had so nearly hit the public taste; and how of his fourth the critic had said: "This is *art.* I doubt if you will ever do anything better than this." How far away they seemed! Ah! *this* book was indeed the "consummation" devoutly to be wished.

In the course of time he returned to England and took a cottage at Hampstead, and there he finished the book. The day after it was finished he took the manuscript and, going to a secluded spot on the top of the Heath, lay down on the grass to read it quietly through. He read three chapters, and, putting the remainder down, sat with his head buried in his hands.

"Yes," he thought, "I *have* done it at last. *It is good,* wonderfully good!" and for two hours he sat like that, with his head in his hands. He had indeed exhausted his public. It was *too* good—*he could not read it himself!*

Returning to his cottage, he placed the manuscript in a drawer. He never wrote another word.

81

Luigi Pirandello

(1867–1936)

Prize awarded 1934 "for his bold and ingenious revival of dramatic and scenic art." ★ *So important were the thematic, philosophical, and structural contributions of this author, particularly of his plays, that the word "Pirandellian" has passed into general usage. It has come to stand for the "relativity" of human experience: a reality that may shift at any moment.*

At twenty-three Pirandello began writing short stories (some three hundred of them) and novels dealing with the arbitrariness of perception (even self-perception), the unshared realities of individuals, and the unsubstantial quality of personality (Love Without Love, *1894;* The Jests of Life and Death, *1902–1903;* The Outcast, *1893). Peopled largely by the common folk of his native Sicily, his work captures and reflects the southern Italian locale and folklore. During World War I, he began to write for the theater, and he gained international recognition. Among the most renowned of his plays are* Right You Are If You Think You Are *(1922),* Six Characters in Search of an Author *(1921), and* King Henry IV *(1922), which present psychological and philosophical problems with dark humor.*

Before exposure to Freud's ideas, Pirandello had an understanding of the subconscious that informed his work—even before Proust. Pirandello had a profound ability to combine his preoccupation with psychosocial relativity and the delusions human beings cling to with a sympathetic manner that reveals intense compassion rather than disdain.

82

A BREATH OF AIR

PARKLING EYES, BLOND HAIR, BARE LITTLE arms and legs, childish laughter escaping in muffled giggles—that imp of a Tina darted across the room to open the glass doors of the balcony.

She had started to turn the knob when a hoarse growl, like that of a wild beast surprised in his lair, quickly stopped her. Petrified with fear, she turned around to stare into the room.

Everything was dark.

The balcony shutters were open only a crack. Although her eyes were still blinded by the lighted corridor from which she had come, she was keenly aware of her grandfather's presence in the darkness, a huge mound propped up in his big chair heaped with cushions, gray-checked shawls, and rough, shaggy blankets, all smelling of stuffy old age stagnating in paralysis.

His immovable bulk did not frighten her so much as the fact that she had forgotten him there in the dark and had disobeyed her parents' strict order never to go into his room without first knocking and asking permission. What was it she was supposed to say? "May I come in, Grandpapa?" Then she must enter very, very quietly, on tiptoe, without making a sound!

The first impulsive laugh was quickly stifled by a gasp verging on a sob. The trembling child tiptoed toward the door not realizing that the old man, accustomed to the dark, could see her.

"Here!" he commanded harshly, just as she was about to step over the threshold.

She caught her breath and hesitantly tiptoed back toward him.

83

Now that she too began to see in the darkness, the wicked look in her grandfather's piercing eyes made her quickly lower her own.

Those eyes, alert with inexorable terror and silent hate, showed between puffy, inflamed bags that reminded her of the sticky body of a tarantula. Already held captive by death, the old man's huge frame seemed to have banished his soul, which now rallied only in his eyes.

He could still move his left hand a little. After staring at it a long time with those implacable eyes, willing animation into it, he at least succeeded in lifting it ever so slightly above the covers. After a fraction of a second it fell back again, inert. He persevered in this exercise because that flicker of movement was all the life left to him—"life" understood as movement in which others participated at will and in which he, too, could still take this infinitesimal part.

"Why . . . the balcony?" he faltered, his sluggish tongue struggling with words.

Still trembling, the child did not answer. The old man immediately sensed something different in her. She trembled with fear every time her mother or father bade her approach him, yet this time it was not the same. She had been startled by his harsh, unexpected command, but there was something else that sent a thrill through her whole body.

"What's the matter?" he asked.

"Nothing," she replied, hardly daring to raise her eyes.

The old man still detected something unusual in the child's voice, even in the way she breathed.

"What is the matter?" he repeated resentfully.

She burst into tears and threw herself on the floor. She screamed and struggled with such convulsive violence that the old man was increasingly irritated, for here too he sensed a difference.

"Heavens, Tina, what's the matter?" cried her mother, running into the room. "What's come over you? Now, now, hush! Come to Mama. Why did you come in here? . . . What's that? Bad! Who is bad? . . . Ah! Grandpa! No, *you* are bad. Grandpa loves you. What happened?"

84

The old man, to whom the last question had been addressed, stared fiercely at the smile on his daughter-in-law's red lips, then at the lovely strand of golden hair the child pulled from her mother's head in her struggle to drag her from the room.

"Oww! My hair . . . Oh! Tina, you'll pull it all out. Mama's poor hair! Bad little girl! Look!" she said, opening the small hand and drawing the hairs, one by one, through the little fingers, repeating, "See . . . see . . ."

The child stared down at her fingers with tears in her eyes. She suddenly believed she had really pulled out all her mother's hair. But seeing nothing in her hand, and hearing her mother's happy laugh, she started to cry again, tugging at her mother to leave the room.

The old man breathed heavily. He was nettled by the question, which had rekindled his hatred.

"What's the matter with all of them?" he said to himself.

Their eyes, their voices—even his daughter-in-law's laugh, and the way she drew those hairs, one by one, through the child's little fingers—had something unusual about them. No, neither of them behaved the same as on other days. What was it all about?

His resentment soared when he lowered his eyes and saw a golden hair resting on the blanket over his knees. Wafted there by her carefree laugh, it had settled on his dead legs. He tried doggedly to urge his hand along little by little toward the hair that mocked him so bitterly. When his son came in, as was his custom before leaving the house to go to work, he found the old man exhausted from the effort he had been making in vain for half an hour.

"Good morning, Papa!"

The old man looked up, his eyes dilating with fear and surprise. His son, too?

Understanding his look to mean that the child had annoyed him, the son hastened to say, "Tina is a little devil! Did she disturb you? Listen, she's still crying because I scolded her. So long, Papa. I'm in a hurry. See you later. Nerina will come in to you shortly."

The old man's eyes followed him all the way to the door.

Yes, his son, too! Never before had he used that tone. "Good morning, Papa!" Why? What had he expected? Were they all in league against him? What had happened? First the child came in all a-flutter, then the mother laughed because her hair was pulled, and now his son with his cheerful "Good morning, Papa!"

Something had happened or was going to happen today, and they all wanted to keep it from him. What could it be?

They had taken the world for themselves, his son and daughter-in-law and grandchild—*his* world that he had created and into which he had placed them. Not only that, but they had also appropriated time—as if he no longer existed in time! As if time were not his also—was he not to see, nor breathe, nor think in it? He still breathed, and he saw everything—more than all of them put together.

A stream of impressions and memories ran riot in his mind, like lightning flashing in a storm. La Plata, the pampas, the salt marshes of lost rivers, innumerable pawing herds bleating, whinnying, lowing. Out there, he had built a fortune from nothing in forty-five years, always keeping his eye on the main chance, forever hatching schemes with patient cunning. Beginning as a herdsman, he had gone on to become a small-holdings settler, then an employee of big railroad contractors, and finally a contractor and builder on his own. He had come back to Italy after the first fifteen years and married, but immediately after the birth of his only son he had gone back there alone. His wife died without his having seen her again, and his son, raised by his mother's relatives, had grown up without knowing him.

Four years ago he had returned, a sick man near death, his body horribly distended by dropsy, suffering from hardening of the arteries, ruined kidneys, and a bad heart. But although his days and even his hours were numbered, he didn't stop. He bought land in Rome and started building, having himself transported to and from the site in a wheelchair, enormously swollen but rugged as a rock. Every fifteen days or so they would drain quarts of fluid from his belly, and then he'd be right back in the thick of things again. That is, until two years ago when he was felled by a stroke of apoplexy— but not quite finished off. No, he had not been granted the good fortune to die in harness. For two years now he'd been completely paralyzed, smoldering in resentful anticipation of the end and hating his son, who was so unlike himself, a stranger to him. His son had voluntarily liquidated the whole business, about which he knew nothing, and had prudently invested the paternal fortune, but he had chosen to continue his own modest legal practice—as if refusing to give the old man any satisfaction, thus avenging his mother and himself for their long abandonment.

86

He detested the son. They had nothing in common, either of thought or feeling. Yes, he detested his daughter-in-law too, and that child! He despised them all because they had excluded him from their life, refusing to tell him what had happened today to change all three of them.

Big tears slipped from his eyes. He let himself go and cried like a baby, forgetting the tower of strength he had been for so many years.

Nerina, the servant, paid no attention to his tears when she came in a little later to take care of him. The old man was so full of water that it did no harm if a little of it spilled out of his eyes. With this thought, she carelessly dried his face and took up a bowl of milk.

"Eat, eat," she told him, dipping a biscuit into the warm milk and holding it to his mouth.

He ate, peering stealthily up at her. She sighed, he thought, but not because she was tired or bored. He suddenly raised his eyes and stared at her. There! She was about to sigh again but smothered it. Instead of ignoring his gaze, she huffed and shrugged her shoulders as if she were cross. Then, for no reason at all, she blushed! What was the matter with *her*? They all had something strange about them today. What could it be?

He refused to eat any more.

"What's the matter with you?" he demanded testily.

"Me? What's the matter with me?" she repeated, surprised.

"Yes, you—everybody. What is it? What's happened?" he asked.

"Nothing . . . I don't know. What do you mean?"

"Sighs!" he mumbled.

"Did I sigh? Not at all! Well, if I did, maybe I did it unconsciously. I really have no reason to sigh," she said, and laughed merrily.

"Why do you laugh like that?"

"Laugh? I laughed because you said I sighed," she told him, laughing all the more.

"Oh, go away," the old man snapped.

Later, when the doctor arrived for his regular visit and they all gathered in the room—his son, daughter-in-law, and their little girl—the suspicion he had nursed all day, even in his sleep, that they were hiding something from him became a certainty.

They were all in on the secret. They talked of other things in his presence just to put him off, but the understanding between them showed clearly in their glances. They had never before looked at one another in just this way. Their gestures, their voices, their very smiles, did not match their words. And what about all that animated discussion about wigs? It seemed that wigs were coming into fashion again!

"Green, if you please, green, or mauve!" cried his daughter-in-law, turning pink with mock indignation, so feigned indeed that she couldn't help laughing outright.

Her mouth laughed of its own accord, and her hand rose instinctively to caress her hair—as if her hair needed that caress!

"I understand, I quite understand," the doctor said, his full-moon face wreathed in smiles. "When one has hair like yours, dear lady, it would be a crime to hide it under a wig."

The old man could hardly restrain his anger. He would have liked to bellow and drive them all out of the room. The doctor, accompanied by the daughter-in-law holding her little girl by the hand, was hardly through the door when his rage exploded against his son, left alone with him in the room. He shot the same questions at him as he had put in vain to the child and to the servant girl.

"What's the matter with all of you? Why are you all behaving like this today? What's happened? What are you trying to hide from me?"

"Nothing at all, Papa. What is there to hide?" his son replied in surprise and dismay. "We're all just about the same as usual, I think."

"It's not true! There's something different. I see it! I feel it in all of you! You think I don't see anything or feel anything because I'm like *this!*" he said thickly, trying to turn his head to the wall.

"But, Papa, I really can't think what you see new or different in us today. Nothing has happened. Believe me. I swear and double-swear it! Now, you must be calm."

The old man was somewhat mollified by his son's evident sincerity, but he was not yet fully convinced. He had no doubt whatsoever that something was up. He saw it; he felt it in all of them. What could it be?

When he was alone in the room, the reply came suddenly, silently, from the balcony. The knob, half turned by the child that morning, was released now in the early evening by a breath of air, and the door onto the balcony swung open.

He did not notice it at first, but then he smelled a delicious perfume invading the room that came from the garden. He looked up and saw a strip of moonlight lying across the floor, a trace of luminous brilliance piercing the dark shadows.

"Ah, so that's it," he said, sighing.

The others could not see it. They could not even feel it in themselves because they were still part of life. But he who was almost dead, he had seen and felt it there among them. So that was why the child had trembled this morning. That was why his daughter-in-law had laughed and taken such delight in her golden hair. And that was why the servant girl sighed. That was why they had all behaved differently, without even knowing it.

Spring had come.

Eugene O'Neill

(1888–1953)

Prize awarded 1936 "for the power, honesty, and deep-felt emotions of his dramatic works, which embody an original concept of tragedy." ★ Eugene O'Neill began writing plays at the age of twenty-four. In 1916 he met the group that founded the Provincetown Players, which produced ten of his early one-act plays, bringing him his first critical and popular acceptance. The son of James O'Neill, a successful touring actor, he spent a turbulent childhood in hotel rooms, on trains, and backstage—a life that resulted in his mother's drug addiction. After a year at Princeton, he shipped to and lived as a derelict on waterfronts around the world, submerged himself in alcohol, and attempted suicide before ending up in a sanitarium. There, he experienced what he was to call his "rebirth" and began to write plays. Many of O'Neill's plays, especially the earlier one-acts, are drawn from these adventures, including Beyond the Horizon (1919), his first full-length work produced in New York, which won him the first of three Pulitzer Prizes.

A realist, O'Neill uses extended inner monologue (Strange Interlude, 1927) and expressionist devices such as masks (The Great God Brown, 1926) as instruments for penetrating psychological portraits. Primarily a tragedian, he studiously emulated Greek fatalism in drama (most obviously in Mourning Becomes Electra, 1931), informing his work with an intensely personal sense of tragedy. Characteristic is the autobiographical Long Day's Journey into Night (produced in 1956), which deals with sibling rivalry, guilt, addiction to drink and drugs, sexuality, and the emotional distancing of others. O'Neill is credited with bringing a European maturity to the predominantly light, romantic American stage. Interestingly, he was awarded the Nobel Prize over the other major nominee in 1936, Sigmund Freud, whose influence on O'Neill's insightful dramas is apparent.

90

I L E

C H A R A C T E R S

BEN, *the cabin boy.*
THE STEWARD.
CAPTAIN KEENEY.
SLOCUM, *second mate.*
MRS. KEENEY.
JOE, *a harpooner.*
    Members of the Crew of the
    Atlantic Queen.

. . . .

S C E N E

CAPTAIN KEENEY'S *cabin on board the steam whaling ship* Atlantic Queen—*a small, square compartment about eight feet high, with a skylight in the center looking out on the poop deck. On the left (the stern of the ship) a long bench with rough cushions is built in against the wall. In front of the bench a table. Over the bench, several curtained port-holes.*

In the rear left, a door leading to the captain's sleeping quarters. To the right of the door a small organ, looking as it were brand new, is placed against the wall.

On the right, to the rear, a marble-topped sideboard. On the sideboard, a woman's sewing basket. Farther forward, a doorway leading to the companion-way, and past the officers' quarters to the main deck.

In the center of the room, a stove. From the middle of the ceiling a hanging lamp is suspended. The walls of the cabin are painted white.

There is no rolling of the ship, and the light which comes through the sky-light is sickly and faint, indicating one of those gray days of calm when ocean and sky are alike dead. The silence is unbroken except for the measured tread of someone walking up and down on the poop deck overhead.

It is nearing two bells—one o'clock—in the afternoon of a day in the year 1895.

At the rise of the curtain there is a moment of intense silence. Then THE

STEWARD *enters and commences to clear the table of the few dishes which still remain on it after the Captain's dinner. He is an old grizzled man, dressed in dungaree pants, a sweater, and a woolen cap with ear flaps. His manner is sullen and angry. He stops stacking up the plates and casts a quick glance upward at the skylight, then tiptoes over to the closed door in rear and listens with his ear pressed to the crack. What he hears makes his face darken, and he mutters a furious curse. There is a noise from the doorway on the right, and he darts back to the table.*

BEN *enters. He is an overgrown, gawky boy with a long, pinched face. He is dressed in sweater, fur cap, etc. His teeth are chattering with the cold, and he hurries to the stove, where he stands for a moment shivering, blowing on his hands, slapping them against his sides, on the verge of crying.*

THE STEWARD (*in relieved tones—seeing who it was*)—Oh, 'tis you, is it? What're ye shiverin' 'bout? Stay by the stove where ye belong, and ye'll find no need of chatterin'.

BEN—It's c-c-cold. (*Trying to control his chattering teeth—derisively*) Who d'ye think it were—the Old Man?

THE STEWARD (*makes a threatening move—BEN shrinks away*)—None o' your lip, young un, or I'll learn ye. (*More kindly*) Where was it ye've been all o' the time—the fo'c'stle?

BEN—Yes.

THE STEWARD—Let the Old Man see ye up for'ard monkeyshinin' with the hands, and ye'll get a hidin' ye'll not forget in a hurry.

BEN—Aw, he don't see nothin'. (*A trace of awe in his tones—he glances upward.*) He jest walks up and down like he didn't notice nobody—and stares at the ice to the no'the'ard.

THE STEWARD (*the same tone of awe creeping into his voice*)—He's always starin' at the ice. (*In a sudden rage, shaking his fist at the skylight*) Ice, ice, ice! Damn him and damn the ice! Holdin' us in for nigh on a year—nothin' to see but ice—stuck in it like a fly in molasses!

BEN (*apprehensively*)—Ssshh! He'll hear ye.

THE STEWARD (*raging*)—Aye, damn, and damn the Arctic seas, and damn this rotten whalin' ship of his, and damn me for a fool to ever ship on it! (*Subsiding, as if realizing the uselessness of this outburst—shaking his head—slowly, with deep conviction.*) He's a hard man—as hard a man as ever sailed the seas.

BEN (*solemnly*)—Aye.

THE STEWARD—The two years we all signed up for are done this day! Two years o' this dog's life, and no luck in the fishin', and the hands half-starved with the food runnin' low, rotten as it is; and not a sign of him turnin' back for home! (*Bitterly*) Home! I begin to doubt if I'll set foot on land again. (*Excitedly*) What is it he thinks he's goin' to do? Keep us all up here after our time is worked out, till the last man of us is starved to death or frozen? We've grub enough hardly to last out the voyage back if we started now. What are the men goin' to do 'bout it? Did you hear any talk in the fo'c's'tle?

BEN (*going over to him—in a half whisper*)—They said if he don't put back south for home today they're goin' to mutiny.

THE STEWARD (*with grim satisfaction*)—Mutiny? Aye, 'tis the only thing they can do; and serve him right after the manner he's treated them—'s if they weren't no better nor dogs.

BEN—The ice is all broke up to s'uth'ard. They's clear water 'sfar's you can see. He ain't got no excuse for not turnin' back for home, the men says.

THE STEWARD (*bitterly*)—He won't look nowheres but no'the'ard, where they's only the ice to see. He don't want to see no clear water. All he thinks on is gettin' the ile—'s if it was our fault he ain't had good luck with the whales. (*Shaking his head*) I think the man's mighty nigh losin' his senses.

BEN (*awed*)—D'you really think he's crazy?

THE STEWARD—Aye, it's the punishment o' God on him. Did ye ever hear of a man who wasn't crazy do the things he does? (*Pointing to the door in rear*) Who but a man that's mad would take this woman—and as sweet a woman as ever was—on a rotten whalin' ship to the Arctic seas to be locked in by the ice for nigh on a year, and maybe lose her senses forever?—for it's sure she'll never be the same again.

BEN (*sadly*)—She useter be awful nice to me before—(*His eyes grow wide and frightened*)—she got like she is.

THE STEWARD—Aye, she was good to all of us. 'Twould have been hell on board without her; for he's a hard man—a hard, hard man—a driver, if there ever was one. (*With a grim laugh*) I hope he's satisfied now—drivin' her on till she's near lost her mind. And who could blame her? 'Tis a God's wonder we're not a ship full of crazed people—with the ice all the time, and the quiet so thick you're afraid to hear your own voice.

BEN (*with a frightened glance toward the door on right*)—She don't never speak to me no more—jest looks at me 's if she didn't know me.

93

THE STEWARD—She don't know no one—but him. She talks to him—when she does talk—right enough.

BEN—She does nothin' all day long now but sit and sew—and then she cries to herself without makin' no noise. I've seen her.

THE STEWARD—Aye, I could hear her through the door a while back.

BEN (*tiptoes over to the door and listens*)—She's cryin' now.

THE STEWARD (*furiously—shaking his fist*)—God send his soul to hell for the devil he is! (*There is the noise of someone coming slowly down the companionway stairs.* THE STEWARD *hurries to his stacked-up dishes. He is so nervous from fright that he knocks off the top one, which falls and breaks on the floor. He stands aghast, trembling with dread.* BEN *is violently rubbing off the organ with a piece of cloth which he has snatched from his pocket.* CAPTAIN KEENEY *appears in the doorway on right and comes into the cabin, removing his fur cap as he does so. He is a man of about forty, around five ten in height, but looking much shorter on account of the enormous proportions of his shoulders and chest. His face is massive and deeply lined, with gray-blue eyes of a bleak hardness, and a tightly clenched, thin-lipped mouth. His thick hair is long and gray. He is dressed in a heavy blue jacket and blue pants stuffed into his sea boots. He is followed into the cabin by the* SECOND MATE, *a rangy six-footer with a lean, weatherbeaten face.* THE MATE *is dressed about the same as* THE CAPTAIN. *He is a man of thirty or so.*)

KEENEY (*comes toward* THE STEWARD *with a stern look on his face.* THE STEWARD *is visibly frightened, and the stack of dishes rattles in his trembling hands.* KEENEY *draws back his fist and* THE STEWARD *shrinks away. The fist is gradually lowered and* KEENEY *speaks slowly*)—'Twould be like hitting a worm. It is nigh two bells, Mr. Steward, and this truck not cleared yet.

THE STEWARD (*stammering*)—Y-y-yes, sir.

KEENEY—Instead of doin' your rightful work ye've been below here gossipin' old women's talk with that boy. (*To* BEN, *fiercely*) Get out o' this, you! Clean up the chart room. (BEN *darts past* THE MATE *to the open doorway.*) Pick up that dish, Mr. Steward!

THE STEWARD (*doing so with difficulty*)—Yes, sir.

KEENEY—The next dish you break, Mr. Steward, you take a bath in the Bering Sea at the end of a rope.

THE STEWARD (*trembling*)—Yes, sir. (*He hurries out.* THE SECOND MATE *walks slowly over to* THE CAPTAIN.)

MATE—I warn't 'specially anxious the man at the wheel should

94

catch what I wanted to say to you, sir. That's why I asked you to come below.

KEENEY (*impatiently*)—Speak your say, Mr. Slocum.

MATE (*unconsciously lowering his voice*)—I'm afeared there'll be trouble with the hands, by the look o'things. They'll likely turn ugly, every blessed one o' them, if you don't put back. The two years they signed up for is up today.

KEENEY—And d'you think you're tellin' me something new, Mr. Slocum? I've felt it in the air this long time past. D'you think I've not seen their ugly looks and the grudgin' way they worked? (*The door in rear is opened and* MRS. KEENEY *stands in the doorway. She is a slight, sweet-faced little woman, primly dressed in black. Her eyes are red from weeping, and her face drawn and pale. She takes in the cabin with a frightened glance, and stands as if fixed to the spot by some nameless dread, clasping and unclasping her hands nervously. The two men turn and look at her.*)

KEENEY (*with rough tenderness*)—Well, Annie?

MRS. KEENEY (*as if awakening from a dream*)—David, I— (*She is silent.* THE MATE *starts for the doorway.*)

KEENEY (*turning to him—sharply*)—Wait!

MATE—Yes, sir.

KEENEY—D'you want anything, Annie?

MRS. KEENEY (*after a pause, during which she seems to be endeavoring to collect her thoughts*)—I thought maybe—I'd go up on deck, David, to get a breath of fresh air. (*She stands humbly awaiting his permission. He and* THE MATE *exchange a significant glance.*)

KEENEY—It's too cold, Annie. You'd best stay below. There's nothing to look at on deck—but ice.

MRS. KEENEY (*monotonously*)— I know—ice, ice, ice! But there's nothing to see down here but these walls. (*She makes a gesture of loathing.*)

KEENEY—You can play the organ, Annie.

MRS. KEENEY (*dully*)—I hate the organ. It puts me in mind of home.

KEENEY (*a touch of resentment in his voice*)—I got it jest for you!

MRS. KEENEY (*dully*)—I know. (*She turns away from them and walks slowly to the bench on left. She lifts up one of the curtains and looks through a port-hole, then utters an exclamation of joy.*) Ah, water! Clear water! As far as I can see! How good it looks after all these months of ice! (*She turns round to them, her face transfigured with joy.*) Ah, now I must go up on deck and look at it, David!

KEENEY (*frowning*)—Best not today, Annie. Best wait for a day when the sun shines.

95

MRS. KEENEY (*desperately*)—But the sun never shines in this terrible place.

KEENEY (*a tone of command in his voice*)—Best not today, Annie.

MRS. KEENEY (*crumbling before this command—abjectly*)—Very well, David. (*She stands there, staring straight before her as if in a daze. The two men look at her uneasily.*)

KEENEY (*sharply*)—Annie!

MRS. KEENEY (*dully*)—Yes, David.

KEENEY—Me and Mr. Slocum has business to talk about—ship's business.

MRS. KEENEY—Very well, David. (*She goes slowly out, rear; and leaves the door three-quarters shut behind her.*)

KEENEY—Best not have her on deck if they's goin' to be any trouble.

MATE—Yes, sir.

KEENEY—And trouble they's goin' to be. I feel it in my bones. (*Takes a revolver from the pocket of his coat and examines it.*) Got your'n?

MATE—Yes, sir.

KEENEY—Not that we'll have to use 'em—not if I know their breed of dog—jest to frighten 'em up a bit. (*Grimly*) I ain't never been forced to use one yit; and trouble I've had by land and by sea s'long as I kin remember, and will have till my dyin' day, I reckon.

MATE (*hesitatingly*)—Then you ain't goin'—to turn back?

KEENEY—Turn back! Mr. Slocum, did you ever hear o' me pointin' s'uth for home with only a measly four hundred barrel of ile in the hold?

MATE (*hastily*)—But the grub's gettin' low.

KEENEY—They's enough to last a long time yit, if they're careful with it; and they's plenty of water.

MATE—They say it's not fit to eat—what's left; and the two years they signed on fur is up today. They might make trouble for you in the courts when we git home.

KEENEY—Let them make what law trouble they kin! I don't give a damn 'bout the money. I've got to git the ile! (*Glancing sharply at* THE MATE) *You* ain't turnin' no sea lawyer, be you, Mr. Slocum?

96   MATE (*flushing*)—Not by a hell of a sight, sir.

KEENEY—What do the fools want to go home fur now? Their share o' the four hundred barrel wouldn't keep them in chewin' terbacco.

MATE (*slowly*)—They wants to git back to their old folks an' things, I s'pose.

KEENEY (*looking at him searchingly*)—'N you want to turn back, too.

(THE MATE *looks down confusedly before his sharp gaze.*) Don't lie, Mr. Slocum. It's writ down plain in your eyes. (*With grim sarcasm*) I hope, Mr. Slocum, you ain't agoin' to jine the men agin me.

MATE (*indignantly*)—That ain't fair, sir, to say sich things.

KEENEY (*with satisfaction*)—I warn't much afeard o' that, Tom. You been with me nigh on ten year, and I've learned ye whalin'. No man kin say I ain't a good master, if I be a hard one.

MATE—I warn't thinkin' of myself, sir—'bout turnin' home, I mean. (*Desperately*) But Mrs. Keeney, sir—seems like she ain't jest satisfied up here, ailin'-like—what with the cold an' bad luck an' the ice an' all.

KEENEY (*his face clouding—rebukingly, but not severely*)—That's my business, Mr. Slocum. I'll thank you to steer a clear course o' that. (*A pause.*) The ice'll break up soon to no'the'ard. I could see it startin' today. And when it goes and we git some sun, Annie'll pick up. (*Another pause—then he bursts forth*) It ain't the damned money what's keepin' me up in the northern seas, Tom. But I can't go back to Homeport with a measly four hundred barrel of ile. I'd die fust. I ain't never come back home in all my days without a full ship. Ain't that true?

MATE—Yes, sir; but this voyage you been icebound, an'—

KEENEY (*scornfully*)—And d'you s'pose any of 'em would believe that—any o' them skippers I've beaten voyage after voyage? Can't you hear 'em laughin' and sneerin'—Tibbots 'n' Harris 'n' Simms and the rest—and all o' Homeport makin' fun o' me? "Dave Keeney, what boasts he's the best whalin' skipper out o' Homeport, comin' back with a measly four hundred barrel of ile!" (*The thought of this drives him into a frenzy, and he smashes his fist down on the marble top of the sideboard.*) I got to git the ile, I tell you! How could I figure on this ice? It's never been so bad before in the thirty year I been a-comin' here. And now it's breakin' up. In a couple o' days it'll be all gone. And they's whale here, plenty of 'em. I know they is, and I ain't never gone wrong yit. I got to git the ile! I got to git it in spite of all hell, and by God, I ain't a-goin' home till I do git it! (*There is the sound of subdued sobbing from the door in rear. The two men stand silent for a moment, listening. Then* KEENEY *goes over to the door and looks in. He hesitates for a moment as if he were going to enter—then closes the door softly.* JOE, *the harpooner, an enormous six-footer with a battered, ugly face, enters from right and stands waiting for* THE CAPTAIN *to notice him.*)

KEENEY (*turning and seeing him*)—Don't be standin' there like a hawk, Harpooner. Speak up!

97

JOE (*confusedly*)—We want—the men, sir—they wants to send a depitation aft to have a word with you.

KEENEY (*furiously*)—Tell 'em to go to— (*Checks himself and continues grimly*)—Tell 'em to come. I'll see 'em.

JOE—Aye, aye, sir. (*He goes out.*)

KEENEY (*with a grim smile*)—Here it comes, the trouble you spoke of, Mr. Slocum, and we'll make short shift of it. It's better to crush such things at the start than let them make headway.

MATE (*worriedly*)—Shall I wake up the First and Fourth, sir? We might need their help.

KEENEY—No, let them sleep. I'm well able to handle this alone, Mr. Slocum. (*There is the shuffling of footsteps from outside and five of the crew crowd into the cabin, led by* JOE. *All dressed alike—sweaters, sea boots, etc. They glance uneasily at* THE CAPTAIN, *twirling their fur caps in their hands.*)

KEENEY (*after a pause*)—Well? Who's to speak fur ye?

JOE (*stepping forward with an air of bravado*)—I be.

KEENEY (*eyeing him up and down coldly*)—So you be. Then speak your say and be quick about it.

JOE (*trying not to wilt before* THE CAPTAIN's *glance, and avoiding his eyes*)—The time we signed up for is done today.

KEENEY (*icily*)—You're tellin' me nothin' I don't know.

JOE—You ain't p'intin' fur home yit, far 'swe kin see.

KEENEY—No, and I ain't agoin' to till this ship is full of ile.

JOE—You can't go no further no'th with the ice before ye.

KEENEY—The ice is breaking up.

JOE (*after a slight pause, during which the others mumble angrily to one another*)—The grub we're gittin' now is rotten.

KEENEY—It's good enough fur ye. Better men than ye are have eaten worse. (*There is a chorus of angry exclamations from the crowd.*)

JOE (*encouraged by this support*)—We ain't agoin' to work no more 'less you puts back for home.

KEENEY (*fiercely*)—You ain't, ain't you?

JOE—No; and the law courts'll say we was right.

KEENEY—To hell with your law courts! We're at sea now, and I'm the law on this ship! (*Edging up toward the harpooner.*) And every mother's son of you what don't obey orders goes in irons. (*There are more angry exclamations from the crew.* MRS. KEENEY *appears in the doorway in rear and looks on with startled eyes. None of the men notice her.*)

JOE (*with bravado*)—Then we're a-goin' to mutiny and take the old hooker home ourselves. Ain't we boys? (*As he turns his head to look at the others* KEENEY'*s fist shoots out to the side of his jaw.* JOE *goes down in a heap and lies there.* MRS. KEENEY *gives a shriek and hides her face in her hands. The men pull out their sheath knives and start a rush, but stop when they find themselves confronted by the revolvers of* KEENEY *and* THE MATE.)

KEENEY (*his eyes and voice snapping*)—Hold still! (*The men stand huddled together in a sullen silence.* KEENEY'*s voice is full of mockery.*) You's found out it ain't safe to mutiny on this ship, ain't you? And now git for'ard where ye belong, and—(*he gives* JOE'*s body a contemptuous kick*)—drag him with you. And remember, the first man of ye I see shirkin' I'll shoot dead as sure as there's a sea under us, and you can tell the rest the same. Git for'ard now! Quick! (*The men leave in cowed silence, carrying* JOE *with them.* KEENEY *turns to* THE MATE *with a short laugh and puts his revolver back in his pocket.*) Best get up on deck, Mr. Slocum, and see to it they don't try none of their skulkin' tricks. We'll have to keep an eye peeled from now on. I know 'em.

MATE—Yes, sir. (*He goes out, right.* KEENEY *hears his wife's hysterical weeping and turns around in surprise—then walks slowly to her side.*)

KEENEY (*putting an arm around her shoulder—with gruff tenderness*)—There, there, Annie. Don't be feared. It's all past and gone.

MRS. KEENEY (*shrinking away from him*)—Oh, I can't bear it! I can't bear it any longer!

KEENEY (*gently*)—Can't bear what, Annie?

MRS. KEENEY (*hysterically*)—All this horrible brutality, and these brutes of men, and this terrible ship and this prison cell of a room, and the ice all around and the silence. (*After this outburst she calms down and wipes her eyes with her handkerchief.*)

KEENEY (*after a pause, during which he looks down at her with a puzzled frown*)—Remember, I warn't hankerin' to have you come on this voyage, Annie.

MRS. KEENEY—I wanted to be with you, David, don't you see? I didn't want to wait back there in the house all alone as I've been doing these last six years since we were married—waiting, and watching, and fearing—with nothing to keep my mind occupied—not able to go back teaching school on account of being Dave Keeney's wife. I used to dream of sailing on the great, wide, glorious ocean. I wanted to be by your side in the danger and vigorous life of it all. I wanted to see you the hero they make you out to be in Homeport. And instead

99

(*her voice grows tremulous*) all I find is ice and cold—and brutality! (*Her voice breaks.*)

KEENEY—I warned you what it'd be, Annie. "Whalin' ain't no ladies' tea party," I says to you, "and you better stay to home where you've got all your woman's comforts." (*Shaking his head*) But you was so set on it.

MRS. KEENEY (*wearily*)—Oh, I know it isn't your fault, David. You see, I didn't believe you. I guess I was dreaming about the old Vikings in the story books, and I thought you were one of them.

KEENEY (*protestingly*)—I done my best to make it as cozy and comfortable as could be. (MRS. KEENEY *looks around her in wild scorn.*) I even sent to the city for that organ for ye, thinkin' it might be soothin' to ye to be playin' it times when they was calms and things was dull-like.

MRS. KEENEY (*wearily*)—Yes, you were very kind, David. I know that. (*She goes to left and lifts the curtains from the port-hole and looks out—then suddenly bursts forth*) I won't stand it—I can't stand it—pent up by these walls like a prisoner. (*She runs over to him and throws her arms around him, weeping. He puts his arm protectingly over her shoulders.*) Take me away from here, David! If I don't get away from here, out of this terrible ship, I'll go mad! Take me home, David! I can't think any more. I feel as if the cold and the silence were crushing down on my brain. I'm afraid. Take me home!

KEENEY (*holds her at arm's length and looks at her face anxiously*)—Best go to bed, Annie. You ain't yourself. You got fever. Your eyes look so strange-like. I ain't never seen you look this way before.

MRS. KEENEY (*laughing hysterically*)—It's the ice and the cold and the silence—they'd make anyone look strange.

KEENEY (*soothingly*)—In a month or two, with good luck, three at the most, I'll have her filled with ile, and then we'll give her everything she'll stand and p'int for home.

MRS. KEENEY—But we can't wait for that—I can't wait. I want to get home. And the men won't wait. They want to get home. It's cruel, it's brutal for you to keep them. You must sail back. You've got no excuse. There's clear water to the south now. If you've a heart at all you've got to turn back.

KEENEY (*harshly*)—I can't, Annie.

MRS. KEENEY—Why can't you?

KEENEY—A woman couldn't rightly understand my reason.

MRS. KEENEY (*wildly*)—Because it's a stubborn reason. Oh, I heard you talking with the second mate. You're afraid the other captains will sneer at you because you didn't come back with a full ship. You want to live up to your silly reputation even if you have to beat and starve men and drive me mad to do it.

KEENEY (*his jaw set stubbornly*)—It ain't that, Annie. Them skippers would never dare sneer to my face. It ain't so much what anyone'd say—but—(*he hesitates, struggling to express his meaning*) you see—I've always done it—since my first voyage as skipper. I always come back—with a full ship—and—it don't seem right not to—somehow. I been always first whalin' skipper out o' Homeport, and—don't you see my meanin', Annie? (*He glances at her. She is not looking at him, but staring dully in front of her, not hearing a word he is saying.*) Annie! (*She comes to herself with a start.*) Best turn in, Annie, there's a good woman. You ain't well.

MRS. KEENEY (*resisting his attempts to guide her to the door in rear*)—David! Won't you please turn back?

KEENEY (*gently*)—I can't Annie—not yet a while. You don't see my meanin'. I got to git the ile.

MRS. KEENEY—It'd be different if you needed the money, but you don't. You've got more than plenty.

KEENEY (*impatiently*)—It ain't the money I'm thinkin' of. D'you think I'm as mean as that?

MRS. KEENEY (*dully*)—No—I don't know—I can't understand. (*Intensely*) Oh, I want to be home in the old house once more, and see my own kitchen again, and hear a woman's voice talking to me and be able to talk to her. Two years! It seems so long ago—as if I'd been dead and could never go back.

KEENEY (*worried by her strange tone and the faraway look in her eyes*)—Best go to bed, Annie. You ain't well.

MRS. KEENEY (*not appearing to hear him*)—I used to think Homeport was a stupid, monotonous place. Then I used to go down on the beach, especially when it was windy and the breakers were rolling in, and I'd dream of the fine, free life you must be leading. (*She gives a laugh which is half a sob.*) I used to love the sea then. (*She pauses; then continues with slow intensity*) But now—I don't ever want to see the sea again.

KEENEY (*thinking to humor her*)—'Tis no fit place for a woman, that's sure. I was a fool to bring ye.

MRS. KEENEY (*after a pause—passing her hand over her eyes with a gesture of pathetic weariness*)—How long would it take us to reach home—if we started now?

101

KEENEY (*frowning*)—'Bout two months, I reckon, Annie, with fair luck.

MRS. KEENEY (*counts on her fingers—then murmurs with a rapt smile*)— That would be August, the latter part of August, wouldn't it? It was on the twenty-fifth of August we were married, David, wasn't it?

KEENEY (*trying to conceal the fact that her memories have moved him— gruffly*)—Don't *you* remember?

MRS. KEENEY (*vaguely—again passes her hand over her eyes*)—My memory is leaving me—up here in the ice. It was so long ago. (*A pause—then she smiles dreamily.*) It's June now. The lilacs will be all in bloom in the front yard—and the climbing roses on the trellis to the side of the house—they're budding—(*She suddenly covers her face with her hands and commences to sob.*)

KEENEY (*disturbed*)—Go in and rest, Annie. You're all worn out cryin' over what can't be helped.

MRS. KEENEY (*suddenly throwing her arms around his neck and clinging to him*)—You love me, don't you, David?

KEENEY (*in amazed embarrassment at this outburst*)—Love you? Why d'you ask me such a question, Annie?

MRS. KEENEY (*shaking him fiercely*)—But you do, don't you, David? Tell me!

KEENEY—I'm your husband, Annie, and you're my wife. Could there be aught but love between us after all these years?

MRS. KEENEY (*shaking him again—still more fiercely*)—Then you do love me. Say it!

KEENEY (*simply*)—I do, Annie.

MRS. KEENEY (*gives a sigh of relief—her hands drop to her sides.* KEENEY *regards her anxiously. She passes her hand across her eyes and murmurs half to herself*)—I sometimes think if we could only have had a child— (KEENEY *turns away from her, deeply moved. She grabs his arm and turns him around to face her—intensely.*) And I've always been a good wife to you, haven't I, David?

KEENEY (*his voice betraying his emotion*—No man has ever had a better, Annie.

MRS. KEENEY—And I've never asked for much from you, have I, David? Have I?

KEENEY—You know you could have all I got the power to give ye, Annie.

MRS. KEENEY (*wildly*)—Then do this, this once, for my sake, for God's sake—take me home! It's killing me, this life—the brutality and cold and horror of it. I'm going mad. I can feel the threat in the air. I can't bear the silence threatening me—day after gray day and every day the same. I can't bear it. (*Sobbing*) I'll go mad, I know I will. Take me home, David, if you love me as you say. I'm afraid. For the love of God, take me home! (*She throws her arms around him, weeping against his shoulder. His face betrays the tremendous struggle going on within him. He holds her out at arm's length, his expression softening. For a moment his shoulders sag, he becomes old, his iron spirit weakens as he looks at her tearstained face.*)

KEENEY (*dragging out the words with an effort*)—I'll do it, Annie—for your sake—if you say it's needful for ye.

MRS. KEENEY (*wild with joy—kissing him*)—God bless you for that, David! (*He turns away from her silently and walks toward the companionway. Just at that moment there is a clatter of footsteps on the stairs and* THE MATE *enters the cabin.*)

MATE (*excitedly*)—The ice is breakin' up to no'the'ard, sir. There's a clear passage through the floe, and clear water beyond, the lookout says. (KEENEY *straightens himself like a man coming out of a trance.* MRS. KEENEY *looks at* THE MATE *with terrified eyes.*)

KEENEY (*dazedly—trying to collect his thoughts*)—A clear passage? To no'the'ard?

MATE—Yes, sir.

KEENEY (*his voice suddenly grim with determination*)—Then get ready and we'll drive her through.

MATE—Aye, aye, sir.

MRS. KEENEY (*appealingly*)—David! David!

KEENEY (*not heeding her*)—Will the men turn to willin' or must we drag 'em out?

MATE—They'll turn to willin' enough. You put the fear o' God into 'em, sir. They're meek as lambs.

KEENEY—Then drive 'em—both watches. (*With grim determination*) They's whale t'other side o' this floe and we're agoin' to git 'em.

MATE—Aye, aye, sir. (*He goes out hurriedly. A moment later there is the sound of scuffling feet from the deck outside and* THE MATE's *voice shouting orders.*)

KEENEY (*speaking aloud to himself—derisively*)—And I was agoin' home like a yaller dog!

MRS. KEENEY (*imploringly*)—David!

KEENEY (*sternly*)—Woman, you ain't a-doin' right when you meddle in men's business and weaken 'em. You can't know my feelin's. I got to prove a man to be a good husband for ye to take pride in. I got to git the ile, I tell ye.

Mrs. Keeney (*supplicatingly*)—David! Aren't you going home?

Keeney (*ignoring this question—commandingly*)—You ain't well. Go and lay down a mite. (*He starts for the door.*) I got to git on deck. (*He goes out. She cries after him in anguish, "David!" A pause. She passes her hand across her eyes—then commences to laugh hysterically and goes to the organ. She sits down and starts to play wildly an old hymn, "There Is Rest for the Weary." Keeney re-enters from the doorway to the deck and stands looking at her angrily. He comes over and grabs her roughly by the shoulder.*)

Keeney—Woman, what foolish mockin' is this? (*She laughs wildly, and he starts back from her in alarm.*) Annie! What is it? (*She doesn't answer him. Keeney's voice trembles.*) Don't you know me, Annie? (*He puts both hands on her shoulders and turns her around so that he can look into her eyes. She stares up at him with a stupid expression, a vague smile on her lips. He stumbles away from her, and she commences softly to play the organ again.*)

Keeney (*swallowing hard—in a hoarse whisper, as if he had difficulty in speaking*)—You said—you was a-goin' mad—God! (*A long wail is heard from the deck above, "Ah, bl-o-o-o-ow!" A moment later The Mate's face appears through the skylight. He cannot see Mrs. Keeney.*)

Mate (*in great excitement*)—Whales, sir—a whole school of 'em—off the star-b'd quarter, 'bout five miles away—big ones!

Keeney (*galvanized into action*)—Are you lowerin' the boats?

Mate—Yes, sir!

Keeney (*with grim decision*)—I'm a-comin' with ye.

Mate—Aye, aye, sir. (*Jubilantly*) You'll git the ile now right enough, sir. (*His head is withdrawn and he can be heard shouting orders.*)

Keeney (*turning to his wife*)—Annie! Did you hear him? I'll git the ile. (*She doesn't answer or seem to know he is there. He gives a hard laugh which is almost a groan.*) I know you're foolin' me, Annie. You ain't out of your mind—(*anxiously*) be you? I'll git the ile now right enough—jest a little while longer, Annie—then we'll turn home'ard. I can't turn back now, you see that, don't you? I've got to git the ile. (*In sudden terror*) Answer me! You ain't mad, be you? (*She keeps on playing the organ, but makes no reply. The Mate's face appears again through the skylight.*)

Mate—All ready, sir. (*Keeney turns his back on his wife and strides to the *doorway, where he stands for a moment and looks back at her in anguish, fighting to control his feelings.*)

MATE—Comin', sir?

KEENEY (*his face suddenly grows hard with determination*)—Aye. (*He turns abruptly and goes out.* MRS. KEENEY *does not appear to notice his departure. Her whole attention seems centered in the organ. She sits with half-closed eyes, her body swaying a little from side to side to the rhythm of the hymn. Her fingers move faster and faster and she is playing wildly and discordantly as the*

CURTAIN FALLS.)

pearl s. buck

(1892–1973)

Prize awarded 1938 "for her rich and truly epic descriptions of peasant life in China and for her biographical masterpieces." ★ *Born in Hillsboro, West Virginia, Pearl Buck lived in China with her missionary parents until 1934, although she returned to the United States for her college education (Randolph Macon Women's College, bachelor's 1914; Cornell, master's 1925; and Yale, master's 1933). While she wrote in diverse genres, all of her subject matter relates to China. She was moved by what she saw happening to the Chinese people under the onslaught of cultural changes, and her first novel,* East Wind, West Wind *(1930), describes the clash of traditional values with social change. For the deeply moving account of Chinese peasant life in her second book,* The Good Earth *(1931), Buck received fame and a Pulitzer Prize. Her novels* The Mother *(1934) and* A House Divided *(1935), along with the biographies of her parents,* The Exile *(1936) and* The Fighting Angel *(1936), helped win her the Nobel Prize in 1938.*

Buck was a strong and vocal proponent of improved Sino-American relations through a clearer racial understanding, and she was a champion of children, especially those displaced by war and famine. Examples of her literature for children include The Water Buffalo Children *(1943),* The Beech Tree *(1955),* Christmas Miniature *(1957), and* The Christmas Ghost *(1960).* Dragon Seed *(1942) was her best-selling book.*

THE GOOD DEED

MR. PAN WAS WORRIED ABOUT HIS mother. He had been worried about her when she was in China, and now he was worried about her in New York, although he had thought that once he got her out of his ancestral village in the province of Szechuen and safely away from the local bullies, who took over when the distant government fell, his anxieties would be ended. To this end he had risked his own life and paid out large sums of sound American money, and he felt that day when he saw her on the wharf, a tiny, dazed little old woman, in a lavender silk coat and black skirt, that now they would live happily together, he and his wife, their four small children and his beloved mother, in the huge safety of the American city.

It soon became clear, however, that safety was not enough for old Mrs. Pan. She did not even appreciate the fact, which he repeated again and again, that had she remained in the village, she would now have been dead, because she was the widow of the large land-owner who had been his father and therefore deserved death in the eyes of the rowdies in power.

Old Mrs. Pan listened to this without reply, but her eyes, looking very large in her small withered face, were haunted with homesickness.

"There are many things worse than death, especially at my age," she replied at last, when again her son reminded her of her good fortune in being where she was.

He became impassioned when she said this. He struck his breast with clenched fists and he shouted, "Could I have forgiven myself if

107

I had allowed you to die? Would the ghost of my father have given me rest?"

"I doubt his ghost would have traveled over such a wide sea," she replied. "That man was always afraid of the water."

Yet there was nothing that Mr. Pan and his wife did not try to do for his mother in order to make her happy. They prepared the food that she had once enjoyed, but she was now beyond the age of pleasure in food, and she had no appetite. She touched one dish and another with the ends of her ivory chopsticks, which she had brought with her from her home, and she thanked them prettily. "It is all good," she said, "but the water is not the same as our village water; it tastes of metal and not of earth, and so the flavor is not the same. Please allow the children to eat it."

She was afraid of the children. They went to an American school and they spoke English very well and Chinese very badly, and since she could speak no English, it distressed her to hear her own language maltreated by their careless tongues. For a time she tried to coax them to a few lessons, or she told them stories, to which they were too busy to listen. Instead they preferred to look at the moving pictures in the box that stood on a table in the living room. She gave them up finally and merely watched them contemplatively when they were in the same room with her and was glad when they were gone. She liked her son's wife. She did not understand how there could be a Chinese woman who had never been in China, but such her son's wife was. When her son was away, she could not say to her daughter-in-law, "Do you remember how the willows grew over the gate?" For her son's wife had no such memories. She had grown up here in the city and she did not even hear its noise. At the same time, though she was so foreign, she was very kind to the old lady, and she spoke to her always in a gentle voice, however she might shout at the children, who were often disobedient.

The disobedience of the children was another grief to old Mrs. Pan. She did not understand how it was that four children could all be disobedient, for this meant that they had never been taught to obey their parents and revere their elders, which are the first lessons a child should learn.

"How is it," she once asked her son, "that the children do not know how to obey?"

Mr. Pan had laughed, though uncomfortably. "Here in America the children are not taught as we were in China," he explained.

"But my grandchildren are Chinese nevertheless," old Mrs. Pan said in some astonishment.

"They are always with Americans," Mr. Pan explained. "It is very difficult to teach them."

Old Mrs. Pan did not understand, for Chinese and Americans are different beings, one on the west side of the sea and one on the east, and the sea is always between. Therefore, why should they not continue to live apart even in the same city? She felt in her heart that the children should be kept at home and taught those things which must be learned, but she said nothing. She felt lonely and there was no one who understood the things she felt and she was quite useless. That was the most difficult thing: She was of no use here. She could not even remember which spout the hot water came from and which brought the cold. Sometimes she turned on one and then the other, until her son's wife came in briskly and said, "Let me, Mother."

So she gave up and sat uselessly all day, not by the window, because the machines and the many people frightened her. She sat where she could not see out; she looked at a few books, and day by day she grew thinner and thinner until Mr. Pan was concerned beyond endurance.

One day he said to his wife, "Sophia, we must do something for my mother. There is no use in saving her from death in our village if she dies here in the city. Do you see how thin her hands are?"

"I have seen," his good young wife said. "But what can we do?"

"Is there no woman you know who can speak Chinese with her?" Mr. Pan asked. "She needs to have someone to whom she can talk about the village and all the things she knows. She cannot talk to you because you can only speak English, and I am too busy making our living to sit and listen to her."

Young Mrs. Pan considered. "I have a friend," she said at last, "a schoolmate whose family compelled her to speak Chinese. Now she is a social worker here in the city. She visits families in Chinatown and this is her work. I will call her up and ask her to spend some time here so that our old mother can be happy enough to eat again."

"Do so," Mr. Pan said.

That very morning, when Mr. Pan was gone, young Mrs. Pan made the call and found her friend, Lili Yang, and she explained everything to her.

"We are really in very much trouble," she said finally. "His mother is thinner every day, and she is so afraid she will die here. She has made us promise that we will not bury her in foreign soil but will send her coffin back to the ancestral village. We have promised, but can we keep this promise, Lili? Yet I am so afraid, because I think she will die, and Billy will think he must keep his promise and he will try to take the coffin back and then he will be killed. Please help us, Lili."

Lili Yang promised and within a few days she came to the apartment and young Mrs. Pan led her into the inner room, which was old Mrs. Pan's room and where she always sat, wrapped in her satin coat and holding a magazine at whose pictures she did not care to look. She took up the magazine when her daughter-in-law came in, because she did not want to hurt her feelings, but the pictures frightened her. The women looked bold and evil, their bosoms bare, and sometimes they wore only a little silk stuff over their legs and this shocked her. She wondered that her son's wife would put such a magazine into her hands, but she did not ask questions. There would have been no end to them had she once begun, and the ways of foreigners did not interest her. Most of the time she sat silent and still, her head sunk on her breast, dreaming of the village, the big house there where she and her husband had lived together with his parents and where their children were born. She knew that the village had fallen into the hands of their enemies and that strangers lived in the house, but she hoped even so that the land was tilled. All that she remembered was the way it had been when she was a young woman and before the evil had come to pass.

She heard now her daughter-in-law's voice, "Mother, this is a friend. She is Miss Lili Yang. She has come to see you."

Old Mrs. Pan remembered her manners. She tried to rise but Lili took her hands and begged her to keep seated.

"You must not rise to one so much younger," she exclaimed.

Old Mrs. Pan lifted her head. "You speak such good Chinese!"

"I was taught by my parents," Lili said. She sat down on a chair near the old lady.

Mrs. Pan leaned forward and put her hand on Lili's knee. "Have you been in our own country?" she asked eagerly.

Lili shook her head. "That is my sorrow. I have not and I want to know about it. I have come here to listen to you tell me."

"Excuse me," young Mrs. Pan said, "I must prepare the dinner for the family."

She slipped away so that the two could be alone and old Mrs. Pan looked after her sadly. "She never wishes to hear; she is always busy."

"You must remember in this country we have no servants," Lili reminded her gently.

"Yes," old Mrs. Pan said, "and why not? I have told my son it is not fitting to have my daughter-in-law cooking and washing in the kitchen. We should have at least three servants: one for me, one for the children and one to clean and cook. At home we had many more but here we have only a few rooms."

Lili did not try to explain. "Everything is different here and let us not talk about it," she said. "Let us talk about your home and the village. I want to know how it looks and what goes on there."

Old Mrs. Pan was delighted. She smoothed the gray satin of her coat as it lay on her knees and she began.

"You must know that our village lies in a wide valley from which the mountains rise as sharply as tiger's teeth."

"Is it so?" Lili said, making a voice of wonder.

"It is, and the village is not a small one. On the contrary, the walls encircle more than one thousand souls, all of whom are relatives of our family,"

"A large family," Lili said.

"It is," old Mrs. Pan said, "and my son's father was the head of it. We lived in a house with seventy rooms. It was in the midst of the village. We had gardens in the courtyards. My own garden contained also a pool wherein are aged goldfish, very fat. I fed them millet and they knew me."

"How amusing." Lili saw with pleasure that the old lady's cheeks were faintly pink and that her large beautiful eyes were beginning to shine and glow. "And how many years did you live there, Ancient One?"

"I went there as a bride. I was seventeen." She looked at Lili, questioning, "How old are you?"

Lili smiled, somewhat ashamed. "I am twenty-seven."

Mrs. Pan was shocked. "Twenty-seven? But my son's wife called you Miss."

"I am not married," Lili confessed.

Mrs. Pan was instantly concerned. "How is this?" she asked. "Are your parents dead?"

111

"They are dead," Lili said, "but it is not their fault that I am not married."

Old Mrs. Pan would not agree to this. She shook her head with decision. "It is the duty of the parents to arrange the marriage of the children. When death approached, they should have attended to this for you. Now who is left to perform the task? Have you brothers?

"No," Lili said, "I am an only child. But please don't worry yourself, Madame Pan. I am earning my own living and there are many young women like me in this country."

Old Mrs. Pan was dignified about this. "I cannot be responsible for what other persons do, but I must be responsible for my own kind," she declared. "Allow me to know the names of the suitable persons who can arrange your marriage. I will stand in the place of your mother. We are all in a foreign country now and we must keep together and the old must help the young in these important matters."

Lili was kind and she knew that Mrs. Pan meant kindness. "Dear Madame Pan," she said. "Marriage in America is very different from marriage in China. Here the young people choose their own mates."

"Why do you not choose, then?" Mrs. Pan said with some spirit.

Lili Yang looked abashed. "Perhaps it would be better for me to say that only the young men choose. It is they who must ask the young women."

"What do the young women do?" Mrs. Pan inquired.

"They wait," Lili confessed.

"And if they are not asked?"

"They continue to wait," Lili said gently.

"How long?" Mrs. Pan demanded.

"As long as they live."

Old Mrs. Pan was profoundly shocked. "Do you tell me that there is no person who arranges such matters when it is necessary?"

"Such an arrangement is not thought of here," Lili told her.

"And they allow their women to remain unmarried?" Mrs. Pan exclaimed. "Are there also sons who do not marry?"

"Here men do not marry unless they wish to do so."

Mrs. Pan was even more shocked. "How can this be?" she asked. "Of course, men will not marry unless they are compelled to do so to provide grandchildren for the family. It is necessary to make laws and create customs so that a man who will not marry is denounced as an unfilial son and one who does not fulfill his duty to his ancestors."

"Here the ancestors are forgotten and parents are not important," Lili said unwillingly.

"What a country is this," Mrs. Pan exclaimed. "How can such a country endure?"

Lili did not reply. Old Mrs. Pan had unknowingly touched upon a wound in her heart. No man had ever asked her to marry him. Yet above all else she would like to be married and to have children. She was a good social worker, and the head of the Children's Bureau sometimes told her that he would not know what to do without her and she must never leave them, for then there would be no one to serve the people in Chinatown. She did not wish to leave except to be married, but how could she find a husband? She looked down at her hands, clasped in her lap, and thought that if she had been in her own country, if her father had not come here as a young man and married here, she would have been in China and by now the mother of many children. Instead what would become of her? She would grow older and older, and twenty-seven was already old, and at last hope must die. She knew several American girls quite well; they liked her, and she knew that they faced the same fate. They, too, were waiting. They tried very hard; they went in summer to hotels and in winter to ski lodges, where men gathered and were at leisure enough to think about them, and in confidence they told one another of their efforts. They compared their experiences and they asked anxious questions. "Do you think men like talkative women or quiet ones?" "Do you think men like lipstick or none?" Such questions they asked of one another and who could answer them? If a girl succeeded in winning a proposal from a man, then all the other girls envied her and asked her special questions and immediately she became someone above them all, a successful woman. The job which had once been so valuable then became worthless and it was given away easily and gladly. But how could she explain this to old Mrs. Pan?

Meanwhile Mrs. Pan had been studying Lili's face carefully and with thought. This was not a pretty girl. Her face was too flat, and her mouth was large. She looked like a girl from Canton and not from Hangchow or Soochow. But she had nice skin, and her eyes, though small, were kind. She was the sort of girl, Mrs. Pan could

113

see, who would make an excellent wife and a good mother, but certainly she was one for whom a marriage must be arranged. She was a decent, plain, good girl and, left to herself, Mrs. Pan could predict, nothing at all would happen. She would wither away like a dying flower.

Old Mrs. Pan forgot herself and for the first time since she had been hurried away from the village without even being allowed to stop and see that the salted cabbage, drying on ropes across the big courtyard, was brought in for the winter. She had been compelled to leave it there and she had often thought of it with regret. She could have brought some with her had she known it was not to be had here. But there it was, and it was only one thing among others that she had left undone. Many people depended upon her and she had left them, because her son compelled her, and she was not used to this idleness that was killing her day by day.

Now as she looked at Lili's kind, ugly face it occurred to her that here there was something she could do. She could find a husband for this good girl, and it would be counted for merit when she went to heaven. A good deed is a good deed, whether one is in China or in America, for the same heaven stretches above all.

She patted Lili's clasped hands. "Do not grieve anymore," she said tenderly. "I will arrange everything."

"I am not grieving," Lili said.

"Of course you are," Mrs. Pan retorted. "I see you are a true woman, and women grieve when they are not wed so that they can have children. You are grieving for your children."

Lili could not deny it. She would have been ashamed to confess to any other person except this old Chinese lady who might have been her grandmother. She bent her head and bit her lip; she let a tear or two fall upon her hands. Then she nodded. Yes, she grieved in the secret places of her heart, in the darkness of the lonely nights, when she thought of the empty future of her life.

"Do not grieve," old Mrs. Pan was saying, "I will arrange it; I will do it."

It was so comforting a murmur that Lili could not bear it. She said, "I came to comfort you, but it is you who comfort me." Then she got up and went out of the room quickly because she did not want to sob aloud. She was unseen, for young Mrs. Pan had gone to market and the children were at school, and Lili went away telling herself that it was all absurd, that an old woman from the middle of

114

China who could not speak a word of English would not be able to change this American world, even for her.

Old Mrs. Pan could scarcely wait for her son to come home at noon. She declined to join the family at the table, saying that she must speak to her son first.

When he came in, he saw at once that she was changed. She held up her head and she spoke to him sharply when he came into the room, as though it was her house and not his in which they now were.

"Let the children eat first," she commanded, "I shall need time to talk with you and I am not hungry."

He repressed his inclination to tell her that he was hungry and that he must get back to the office. Something in her look made it impossible for him to be disobedient to her. He went away and gave the children direction and then returned.

"Yes, my mother," he said, seating himself on a small and uncomfortable chair.

Then she related to him with much detail and repetition what had happened that morning; she declared with indignation that she had never before heard of a country where no marriages were arranged for the young, leaving to them the most important event of their lives and that at a time when their judgment was still unripe, and a mistake could bring disaster upon the whole family.

"Your own marriage," she reminded him, "was arranged by your father with great care, our two families knowing each other well. Even though you and my daughter-in-law were distant in this country, yet we met her parents through a suitable go-between, and her uncle here stood in her father's place, and your father's friend in place of your father, and so it was all done according to custom though so far away."

Mr. Pan did not have the heart to tell his mother that he and his wife Sophia had fallen in love first, and then, out of kindness to their elders, had allowed the marriage to be arranged for them as though they were not in love, and as though, indeed, they did not know each other. They were both young people of heart, and although it would have been much easier to be married in the American fashion, they considered their elders.

"What has all this to do with us now, my mother?" he asked.

"This is what is to do," she replied with spirit. "A nice, ugly girl of our own people came here today to see me. She is twenty-seven years old and she is not married. What will become of her?"

"Do you mean Lili Yang?" her son asked.

"I do," she replied. "When I heard that she has no way of being married because, according to the custom of this country, she must wait for a man to ask her—"

Old Mrs. Pan broke off and gazed at her son with horrified eyes. "What now?" he asked.

"Suppose the only man who asks is one who is not at all suitable?"

"It is quite possible that it often happens thus," her son said, trying not to laugh.

"Then she has no choice," old Mrs. Pan said indignantly. "She can only remain unmarried or accept one who is unsuitable."

"Here she has no choice," Mr. Pan agreed, "unless she is very pretty, my mother, when several men may ask and then she has a choice." It was on the tip of his tongue to tell how at least six young men had proposed to his Sophia, thereby distressing him continually until he was finally chosen, but he thought better of it. Would it not be very hard to explain so much to his old mother, and could she understand? He doubted it. Nevertheless, he felt it necessary at least to make one point.

"Something must be said for the man also, my mother. Sometimes he asks a girl who will not have him, because she chooses another, and then his sufferings are intense. Unless he wishes to remain unmarried he must ask a second girl, who is not the first one. Here also is some injustice."

Old Mrs. Pan listened to this attentively and then declared, "It is all barbarous. Certainly it is very embarrassing to be compelled to speak of these matters, man and woman, face to face. They should be spared; others should speak for them."

She considered for a few seconds and then she said with fresh indignation, "And what woman can change the appearance her ancestors have given her? Because she is not pretty is she less a woman? Are not her feelings like any woman's; is it not right to have husband and home and children? It is well-known that men have no wisdom in such matters; they believe that a woman's face is all she has, forgetting that everything else is the same. They gather about the pretty woman, who is surfeited with them, and leave alone the good woman. And I do not know why heaven has created ugly women always good but so it is, whether here or in our own

116

country, but what man is wise enough to know that? Therefore his wife should be chosen for him, so that the family is not burdened with his follies."

Mr. Pan allowed all this to be said and then he inquired, "What is on your mind, my mother?"

Old Mrs. Pan leaned toward him and lifted her forefinger. "This is what I command you to do for me, my son. I myself will find a husband for this good girl of our people. She is helpless and alone. But I know no one; I am a stranger, and I must depend upon you. In your business there must be young men. Inquire of them and see who stands for them, so that we can arrange a meeting between them and me; I will stand for the girl's mother. I promised it."

Now Mr. Pan laughed heartily. "Oh, my mother!" he cried. "You are too kind, but it cannot be done. They would laugh at me, and do you believe that Lili Yang herself would like such an arrangement? I think she would not. She has been in America too long."

Old Mrs. Pan would not yield, however, and in the end he was compelled to promise that he would see what he could do. Upon this promise she consented to eat her meal, and he led her out, her right hand resting upon his left wrist. The children were gone and they had a quiet meal together, and after it she said she felt that she would sleep. This was good news, for she had not slept well since she came, and young Mrs. Pan led her into the bedroom and helped her to lie down and placed a thin quilt over her.

When young Mrs. Pan went back to the small dining room where her husband waited to tell her what his mother had said, she listened thoughtfully.

"It is absurd," her husband said, "but what shall we do to satisfy my mother? She sees it as a good deed if she can find a husband for Lili Yang."

Here his wife surprised him. "I can see some good in it myself," she declared. "I have often felt for Lili. It is a problem, and our mother is right to see it as such. It is not only Lili—it is a problem here for all young women, especially if they are not pretty." She looked quizzically at her husband for a moment and then said, "I too used to worry when I was very young, lest I should not find a husband for myself. It is a great burden for a young woman. It would be nice to have someone else arrange the matter."

"Remember," he told her, "how often in the old country the wrong men are arranged for and how often the young men leave

117

home because they do not like the wives their parents choose for them."

"Well, so do they here," she said pertly. "Divorce, divorce, divorce!"

"Come, come," he told her. "It is not so bad."

"It is very bad for women," she insisted. "When there is divorce here, then she is thrown out of the family. The ties are broken. But in the old country, it is the man who leaves home and the woman stays on, for she is still the daughter-in-law and her children will belong to the family, and however far away the man wants to go, she has her place and she is safe."

Mr. Pan looked at his watch. "It is late and I must go to the office."

"Oh, your office," young Mrs. Pan said in an uppish voice, "what would you do without it?"

They did not know it but their voices roused old Mrs. Pan in the bedroom, and she opened her eyes. She could not understand what they said for they spoke in English, but she understood that there was an argument. She sat up on the bed to listen, then she heard the door slam and she knew her son was gone. She was about to lie down again when it occurred to her that it would be interesting to look out of the window to the street and see what young men there were coming to and fro. One did not choose men from the street, of course, but still she could see what their looks were.

She got up and tidied her hair and tottered on her small feet over to the window and opening the curtains a little she gazed into the street really for the first time since she came. She was pleased to see many Chinese men, some of them young. It was still not late, and they loitered in the sunshine before going back to work, talking and laughing and looking happy. It was interesting to her to watch them, keeping in mind Lili Yang and thinking to herself that it might be this one or that one, although still one did not choose men from the street. She stood so long that at last she became tired and she pulled the small chair to the window and kept looking through the parted curtain.

Here her daughter-in-law saw her a little later, when she opened the door to see if her mother-in-law was awake, but she did not speak. She looked at the little satin-clad figure, and went away again, wondering why it was that the old lady found it pleasant today to look out of the window when every other day she had refused the same pleasure.

It became a pastime for old Mrs. Pan to look out of the window every day from then on. Gradually she came to know some of the young men, not by name but by their faces and by the way they walked by her window, never, of course looking up at her, until one day a certain young man did look up and smile. It was a warm day, and she had asked that the window be opened, which until now she had not allowed, for fear she might be assailed by the foreign winds and made ill. Today, however, was near to summer, she felt the room airless and she longed for freshness.

After this the young man habitually smiled when he passed or nodded his head. She was too old to have it mean anything but courtesy and so bit by bit she allowed herself to make a gesture of her hand in return. It was evident that he belonged in a china shop across the narrow street. She watched him go in and come out; she watched him stand at the door in his shirt sleeves on a fine day and talk and laugh, showing, as she observed, strong white teeth set off by two gold ones. Evidently he made money. She did not believe he was married, for she saw an old man who must be his father, who smoked a water pipe, and now and then an elderly woman, perhaps his mother, and a younger brother, but there was no young woman.

She began after some weeks of watching to fix upon this young man as a husband for Lili. But who could be the go-between except her own son?

She confided her plans one night to him, and, as always, he listened to her with courtesy and concealed amusement. "But the young man, my mother, is the son of Mr. Lim, who is the richest man on our street."

"That is nothing against him," she declared.

"No, but he will not submit to an arrangement, my mother. He is a college graduate. He is only spending the summer at home in the shop to help his father."

"Lili Yang has also been to school."

"I know, my mother, but, you see, the young man will want to choose his own wife, and it will not be someone who looks like Lili Yang. It will be someone who—"

He broke off and made a gesture which suggested curled hair, a fine figure and an air. Mrs. Pan watched him with disgust. "You are

119

like all these other men, though you are my son," she said, and dismissed him sternly.

Nevertheless, she thought over what he had said when she went back to the window. The young man was standing on the street picking his fine teeth and laughing at friends who passed, the sun shining on his glistening black hair. It was true he did not look at all obedient; it was perhaps true that he was no more wise than other men and so saw only what a girl's face was. She wished that she could speak to him, but that, of course, was impossible. Unless—

She drew in a long breath. Unless she went downstairs and out into that street and crossed it and entered the shop, pretending that she came to buy something! If she did this, she could speak to him. But what would she say, and who would help her cross the street? She did not want to tell her son or her son's wife, for they would suspect her and laugh. They teased her often even now about her purpose, and Lili was so embarrassed by their laughter that she did not want to come anymore.

Old Mrs. Pan reflected on the difficulty of her position as a lady in a barbarous and strange country. Then she thought of her eldest grandson, Johnnie. On Saturday, when her son was at his office and her son's wife was at the market, she would coax Johnnie to lead her across the street to the china shop; she would pay him some money, and in the shop she would say she was looking for two bowls to match some that had been broken. It would be an expedition, but she might speak to the young man and tell him—what should she tell him? That must first be planned.

This was only Thursday and she had only two days to prepare. She was very restless during those two days, and she could not eat. Mr. Pan spoke of a doctor, whom she indignantly refused to see, because he was a man and also because she was not ill. But Saturday came at last and everything came about as she planned. Her son went away, and then her son's wife, and she crept downstairs with much effort to the sidewalk where her grandson was playing marbles and beckoned him to her. The child was terrified to see her there and came at once, and she pressed a coin into his palm and pointed across the street with her cane.

"Lead me there," she commanded, and, shutting her eyes tightly, she put her hand on his shoulder and allowed him to lead her to the shop. Then to her dismay he left her and ran back to play and she stood wavering on the threshold, feeling dizzy, and the young man

saw her and came hurrying toward her. To her joy he spoke good
Chinese, and the words fell sweetly upon her old ears.

"Ancient One, Ancient One," he chided her kindly. "Come in
and sit down. It is too much for you."

He led her inside the cool, dark shop and she sat down on a
bamboo chair.

"I came to look for two bowls," she said faintly.

"Tell me the pattern and I will get them for you," he said. "Are
they blue willow pattern or the thousand flowers?"

"Thousand flowers," she said in the same faint voice, "but I do
not wish to disturb you."

"I am here to be disturbed," he replied with the utmost courtesy.

He brought out some bowls and set them on a small table before
her and she fell to talking with him. He was very pleasant; his rather
large face was shining with kindness and he laughed easily. Now
that she saw him close, she was glad to notice that he was not too
handsome; his nose and mouth were big, and he had big hands and
feet.

"You look like a countryman," she said. "Where is your ancestral
home?"

"It is in the province of Shantung," he replied, "and there are not
many of us here."

"That explains why you are so tall," she said. "These people from
Canton are small. We of Szechuen are also big and our language is
yours. I cannot understand the people of Canton."

From this they fell to talking of their own country, which he had
never seen, and she told him about the village and how her son's
father had left it many years ago to do business here in this foreign
country and how he had sent for their son and then how she had
been compelled to flee because the country was in fragments and
torn between many leaders. When she had told him this much, she
found herself telling him how difficult it was to live here and how
strange the city was to her and how she would never have looked
out of the window had it not been for the sake of Lili Yang.

"Who is Lili Yang?" he asked.

Old Mrs. Pan did not answer him directly. That would not have
been suitable. One does not speak of a reputable young woman to
any man, not even one as good as this one. Instead she began a long
speech about the virtues of young women who were not pretty, and
how beauty in a woman made virtue unlikely, and how a woman not

beautiful was always grateful to her husband and did not consider that she had done him a favor by the marriage, but rather that it was he who conferred the favor, so that she served him far better than she could have done were she beautiful.

To all this the young man listened, his small eyes twinkling with laughter.

"I take it that this Lili Yang is not beautiful," he said.

Old Mrs. Pan looked astonished. "I did not say so," she replied with spirit. "I will not say she is beautiful and I will not say she is ugly. What is beautiful to one is not so to another. Suppose you see her sometime for yourself, and then we will discuss it."

"Discuss what?" he demanded.

"Whether she is beautiful."

Suddenly she felt that she had come to a point and that she had better go home. It was enough for the first visit. She chose two bowls and paid for them and while he wrapped them up she waited in silence, for to say too much is worse than to say too little.

When the bowls were wrapped, the young man said courteously, "Let me lead you across the street, Ancient One."

So, putting her right hand on his left wrist, she let him lead her across and this time she did not shut her eyes, and she came home again feeling that she had been a long way and had accomplished much. When her daughter-in-law came home she said quite easily, "I went across the street and bought these two bowls."

Young Mrs. Pan opened her eyes wide. "My mother, how could you go alone?"

"I did not go alone," old Mrs. Pan said tranquilly. "My grandson led me across and young Mr. Lim brought me back."

Each had spoken in her own language with helpful gestures.

Young Mrs. Pan was astonished and she said no more until her husband came home, when she told him. He laughed a great deal and said, "Do not interfere with our old one. She is enjoying herself. It is good for her."

But all the time he knew what his mother was doing and he joined in it without her knowledge. That is to say, he telephoned the same afternoon from his office to Miss Lili Yang, and when she answered, he said, "Please come and see my old mother again. She asks for you every day. Your visit did her much good."

Lili Yang promised, not for today but for a week hence, and when Mr. Pan went home he told his mother carelessly, as though it were nothing, that Lili Yang had called him up to say she was coming again next week.

Old Mrs. Pan heard this with secret excitement. She had not gone out again, but every day young Mr. Lim nodded to her and smiled, and once he sent her a small gift of fresh ginger root. She made up her mind slowly but she made it up well. When Lili Yang came again, she would ask her to take her to the china shop, pretending that she wanted to buy something, and she would introduce the two to each other; that much she would do. It was too much, but, after all, these were modern times, and this was a barbarous country, where it did not matter greatly whether the old customs were kept or not. The important thing was to find a husband for Lili, who was already twenty-seven years old.

So it all came about, and when Lili walked into her room the next week, while the fine weather still held, old Mrs. Pan greeted her with smiles. She seized Lili's small hand and noticed that the hand was very soft and pretty, as the hands of most plain-faced girls are, the gods being kind to such women and giving them pretty bodies when they see that ancestors have not bestowed pretty faces.

"Do not take off your foreign hat," she told Lili. "I wish to go across the street to that shop and buy some dishes as a gift for my son's wife. She is very kind to me."

Lili Yang was pleased to see the old lady so changed and cheerful and in all innocence she agreed and they went across the street and into the shop. Today there were customers, and old Mr. Lim was there too, as well as his son. He was a tall, withered man, and he wore a small beard under his chin. When he saw old Mrs. Pan he stopped what he was doing and brought her a chair to sit upon while she waited. As soon as his customer was gone, he introduced himself, saying that he knew her son.

"My son has told me of your honored visit last week," he said. "Please come inside and have some tea. I will have my son bring the dishes, and you can look at them in quiet. It is too noisy here."

She accepted his courtesy, and in a few minutes young Mr. Lim came back to the inner room with the dishes while a servant brought tea.

Old Mrs. Pan did not introduce Lili Yang, for it was not well to embarrass a woman, but young Mr. Lim boldly introduced himself, in English.

"Are you Miss Lili Yang?" he asked. "I am James Lim."

"How did you know my name?" Lili asked, astonished.

"I have met you before, not face to face, but through Mrs. Pan," he said, his small eyes twinkling. "She has told me more about you than she knows."

Lili blushed. "Mrs. Pan is so old-fashioned," she murmured. "You must not believe her."

"I shall only believe what I see for myself," he said gallantly. He looked at her frankly and Lili kept blushing. Old Mrs. Pan had not done her justice, he thought. The young woman had a nice, round face, the sort of face he liked. She was shy, and he liked that also. It was something new.

Meanwhile old Mrs. Pan watched all this with amazement. So this was the way it was: The young man began speaking immediately, and the young woman blushed. She wished that she knew what they were saying but perhaps it was better that she did not know.

She turned to old Mr. Lim, who was sitting across the square table sipping tea. At least here she could do her duty. "I hear your son is not married," she said in a tentative way.

"Not yet," Mr. Lim said. "He wants first to finish learning how to be a Western doctor."

"How old is he?" Mrs. Pan inquired.

"He is twenty-eight. It is very old but he did not make up his mind for some years, and the learning is long."

"Miss Lili Yang is twenty-seven," Mrs. Pan said in the same tentative voice.

The young people were still talking in English and not listening to them. Lili was telling James Lim about her work and about old Mrs. Pan. She was not blushing anymore; she had forgotten, it seemed, that he was a young man and she a young woman. Suddenly she stopped and blushed again. A woman was supposed to let a man talk about himself, not about her.

"Tell me about your work," she said. "I wanted to be a doctor, too, but it cost too much."

"I can't tell you here," he said. "There are customers waiting in the shop and it will take a long time. Let me come to see you, may I? I could come on Sunday when the shop is closed. Or we could take a ride on one of the riverboats. Will you? The weather is so fine."

"I have never been on a riverboat," she said. "It would be delightful."

She forgot her work and remembered that he was a young man and that she was a young woman. She liked his big face and the way his black hair fell back from his forehead and she knew that a day on the river could be a day in heaven.

The customers were getting impatient. They began to call out and he got up. "Next Sunday," he said in a low voice. "Let's start early. I'll be at the wharf at nine o'clock."

"We do not know each other," she said, reluctant and yet eager. Would he think she was too eager?

He laughed. "You see my respectable father, and I know old Mrs. Pan very well. Let them guarantee us."

He hurried away, and old Mrs. Pan said immediately to Lili, "I have chosen these four dishes. Please take them and have them wrapped. Then we will go home."

Lili obeyed, and when she was gone, old Mrs. Pan leaned toward old Mr. Lim.

"I wanted to get her out of the way," she said in a low and important voice. "Now, while she is gone, what do you say? Shall we arrange a match? We do not need a go-between. I stand as her mother, let us say, and you are his father. We must have their horoscopes read, of course, but just between us, it looks as though it is suitable, does it not?"

Mr. Lim wagged his head. "If you recommend her, Honorable Old Lady, why not?"

Why not, indeed? After all, things were not so different here, after all.

"What day is convenient for you?" she asked.

"Shall we say Sunday?" old Mr. Lim suggested.

"Why not?" she replied. "All days are good, when one performs a good deed, and what is better than to arrange a marriage?"

"Nothing is better," old Mr. Lim agreed. "Of all good deeds under heaven, it is the best."

They fell silent, both pleased with themselves, while they waited.

Gabriela Mistral

(1889–1957)

Prize awarded 1945 "for her lyric poetry, which, inspired by powerful emotions,

has made her name a symbol of the idealistic aspirations of the entire Latin

American world." ★ *Gabriela Mistral, whose real name was Lucila Godoy de*

Alcayaga, was Latin America's first Nobel laureate. The sincerity of her poetry,

written in an unembellished, succinct, yet lyrical style, brought her international

critical recognition.

    Her early poems, incorporated in Sonnets on Death *(1914), are poignant*

reflections on the death of her lover. Desolations *(1922) and* Tenderness

(1924) explore nature, motherhood, childhood, and mortality, all depicted against

the backdrop of continuing personal suffering. The prevalent mood of her fourth

book, Felling *(1938), is lighter; the poems embody vignettes of Latin American*

life, lullabies, and even an emerging reconciliation with mortality. This theme

remains central to Mistral's later work and is coupled with a heightened sense of

faith and acceptance in Wine Press *(1954), her last book.*

126

    Mistral was a highly regarded educator in her native country and in Mexico,

where she worked to improve the national school system. She later represented

Chile in the League of Nations and the United Nations.

Drops of Gall

Don't sing: A song always
Remains, fixed to your tongue;
The song that must be surrendered

Don't kiss; The kiss always
Remains, by some strange curse,
The kiss unreached by the soul

Pray, pray that it is sweet;
But know you can't hope to say
    with avid tongue
The only paternoster that could save,

And don't call on death for mercy
For in the vast white flesh
A shred remains alive that feels
The choking stone
And the ravenous worm that unbraids your hair.

Rodin's Thinker

With chin fallen in rough hand
The thinker reconciles himself with
    grave—bound flesh
Mortal flesh, naked in the face of destiny
Flesh which abhors death and trembles with delicacy

And trembled with love, all his springtime ardor,
And now in Autumn, overflows with truth and sadness.
That "We must die" passes through his mind
With all the high pitched bells of sundown.
And in anguish, his suffering muscles split
The furrows of his flesh filled with horror,
Split like Autumn leaves, this strong man

That is said to be of bronze, and no sun-twisted tree
Of the plains, no loin-injured lion
Is convoluted like this man who thinks on death.

(Translations by the Editors)

......

Hermann Hesse

(1877–1962)

Prize awarded 1946 "for his inspired writings, which, while growing in bold-ness and penetration, exemplify the classical humanitarian ideals and high quality of style." ★ *The son of missionaries in India, Hesse lived, after 1919, in Switzerland and eventually became a Swiss citizen. His two major influences were Eastern mysticism and the psychological theories of Carl Jung. The former is illustrated in* Journey to the East *(1932) and the lyrical and gentle* Siddartha *(1922), his most famous work.*

*His pleasant lyrical poetry and shorter works in the nineteenth-century tra-dition of German literature (*Diesseits, *1907;* Nachbarn, *1908; and* Umwege, *1912) depict rural settings and personalities. The artist as outsider was explored in* Peter Camenzind *(1904),* Gertrude *(1910), and* Rosshalde *(1914). Later books begin to show greater psychological depth, symbolism, and sociolog-ical complexity:* Klein und Wagner *(1919) views domesticity as a confinement from which to escape, as does the still much-read* Steppenwolf *(1927), in which the experimental narrative devices first introduced in* Demian *(1919) are more fully developed. In the long futuristic novel* Magister Ludi *(1949), Hesse blends Oriental contemplation with romantic activism. His political essays were collected in* Freig und Frieden *(1946), and he has left behind a body of illuminating correspondence with many of the leading minds of Europe.*

128

INSIDE AND OUTSIDE

HERE WAS A MAN BY THE NAME OF Friedrich who occupied himself with intellectual matters and possessed a good deal of knowledge. But to his mind not every kind of knowledge was equal, and not every thought was as the other; he loved a certain kind of thinking and despised and scorned the others. What he loved and honored was logic, that superior method, and everything that he called "science."

"Two times two is four," he used to say. "In that I believe, and on that truth man must base his thinking."

It was not unknown to him that there were other kinds of thought and knowledge, but they were not "science," and he held them in low esteem. Though a freethinker, he was not intolerant toward religion. This was because of a tacit agreement among scientists. For some centuries their science concerned itself with almost everything worth knowing on earth, with one exception: the human soul. In the course of time it had become customary to leave this matter to religion and to tolerate its speculations about the soul, though without taking them seriously. Despite his tolerance toward religion, Friedrich abhorred everything that he viewed as superstition. Such beliefs were all very well for foreign, uneducated, and backward peoples, and no one would deny the existence of mystical or magical thinking in remote antiquity—but now that science and logic existed there was no more point in such outmoded and dubious tools.

So he said and so he thought, and when he noticed traces of superstition he became annoyed as if something hostile had touched him.

What angered him most, however, was to find such traces of superstition among men of his own kind, educated men acquainted with the principles of scientific thought. And nothing was more painful and unbearable to him than that blasphemous idea, which he had recently had to hear expounded and discussed even among highly educated men, that absurd idea that scientific thought might not be supreme, timeless, eternal, predestined, and unshakable, but only one of many modes of thought, limited in time and not immune to change and decline. This disrespectful, destructive, poisonous idea was all around, that even Friedrich could not deny; a result of the suffering that war, revolution, and hunger had brought into the world, it had sprung up here and there like an admonition, a ghostly saying written by a white hand on a white wall.

The more Friedrich suffered from the existence of this idea and from its ability to cause him such anxiety, the more passionately he hated it and all those whom he suspected of believing in it. Up until now only a very few of those who were truly educated professed this new teaching, which, if it were to spread and gain power, seemed destined to destroy the intellectual culture on earth and usher in chaos. But things had not yet come so far, and the individual adherents of the idea were still so few that one could dismiss them as cranks and eccentrics. But yet, a drop of poison, a radiation of the idea, was here and there noticeable. Among the common people and the half-educated, all sorts of new teachings, occults, sects, and discipleships had sprung up. The world was full of them; everywhere one could discern superstition, mysticism, spiritism, and other dark powers. These ought to have been fought, of course, but for the present, science, as though from a sense of secret weakness, tolerated them in silence.

One day Friedrich came to the house of a friend with whom he had engaged in various studies. As it happened, he had not seen this friend for some time. While he was climbing the stairs, he tried to remember when and where he had last seen him. But as much as he usually prided himself on his memory, he could not remember. This annoyed him and put him in a bad mood, and it called for some effort to pull himself together as he reached his friend's door.

As soon as he greeted Erwin, his friend, he was struck by the indulgent smile on his friend's friendly face. He had never noticed this smile before. Despite his friendliness he felt something mocking or hostile, and that very moment, the memory for which he had been searching in vain came to him, the memory of his last meeting with Erwin. He recalled that they had parted without a quarrel, but yet with a sense of inner disharmony because Erwin, so it seemed to him, had not supported his attacks on superstition.

It was strange! How could he have forgotten that! And now he also knew that the reason he had not called on his friend for such a long time was only because of the resentment he had felt at the time, and it also came to him that he had known this all along, though he had recounted to himself a number of other reasons for the continual postponement of his visit.

Now they faced each other, and it seemed to Friedrich that the gap between them had grown. He felt intuitively that in that moment something was lacking between him and Erwin, something that had always been present, a sense of immediate understanding, of affection itself. Instead there was a void, an abyss, an estrangement. They greeted each other, spoke of the season, of acquaintances, of their health—and, heaven knows how, at every word Friedrich had the scary feeling that he did not fully understand his friend, that his friend did not really know him, that his words did not reach him, and that no common ground for a genuine conversation could be found. And Erwin wore that friendly, unwavering smile on his face, which Friedrich almost began to hate.

During a pause in their awkward conversation, Friedrich looked around the familiar study and saw a sheet of paper pinned loosely to the wall. The sight affected him strangely and awakened old memories, for he recalled that in the past, during the student years, it had been a habit of Erwin's to remind himself in this way of a saying by a thinker or a verse by a poet. He rose and went up to the wall to read what was written on the sheet.

There was written in Erwin's handsome handwriting: "Nothing is outside, nothing is inside, for that which is outside is inside."

Turning pale, Friedrich stood there a moment. There it was! Here he stood confronting what he dreaded! During any other time he would have let the sheet of paper be, would have tolerated it. He would have passed it off indulgently as a mood, as a harmless and permissible amusement, perhaps as a small sentimentality, to be protected. But now it was different. He felt that these words were not written in the spirit of a passing poetic mood, that after so many

131

years, not a mere whim had brought Erwin back to a habit of his youth.

What was written here was an avowal of his friend's current preoccupation, namely mysticism! Erwin was a traitor.

Slowly he turned toward him and saw a bright smile on his face.

"Explain this to me!" he demanded.

All friendliness, Erwin nodded.

"Have you never read this saying?"

"Yes, of course," cried Friedrich. "I know it. It is mysticism, it is gnosticism. Maybe poetic, but— Now please, explain it to me, and tell me why it is hanging on your wall."

"Gladly," said Erwin. "This saying is a first introduction to a theory of knowledge in which I am interested in at present and to which I owe a great deal of happiness."

Friedrich controlled his annoyance. He asked: "A new theory of knowledge? Is there such a thing? What is it called?"

"Oh," said Erwin, "it's new only to me. It's old and venerable. It's called magic."

The word had been spoken. Filled with consternation by so open an avowal, Friedrich felt that he was confronted with his archenemy in the person of his friend. He was silent. He did not know whether he was closer to anger or tears; he had a sense of irretrievable loss. He remained silent for a long time.

Then, in a tone of affected mockery, he said:

"So now you want to become a magician?"

"Yes," Erwin said without hesitating.

"A kind of sorcerer's apprentice, right?"

"Certainly."

Again Friedrich was silent. It was so still that the ticking of the clock could be heard from the next room.

Then he said: "You realize that you are breaking your ties with serious science and consequently with me?"

"I hope not," Erwin answered. "But if that's how it has to be— what else can I do?"

Friedrich, losing his control, cried: "What else can you do? Give up this nonsense, this dismal, degrading hocus-pocus once and for all. That's what you must do if you want to keep my respect."

Erwin smiled a little, although his good humor had left him.

"You speak as if"—he said this so softly that Friedrich's angry

132

voice still seemed to echo through the room—"you speak as if it were a matter of will, as if I had a choice. That is not so. I have no choice. I did not choose magic. Magic chose me."

Friedrich heaved a deep sigh. "Then good-bye," he said with difficulty, and stood up without offering his hand in good-bye.

"Not like this!" Erwin called out. "No, you must not leave me like this. Suppose one of us were dying—and that is how it is!—and we had to take leave from one another."

"But which one of us, Erwin, is the one dying?"

"Today, my friend, it is undoubtedly myself. The man in search of rebirth must be prepared to die."

Again Friedrich stepped before the sheet of paper and read the saying about inside and outside.

"Very well," he said finally. "You are right. It won't do us any good to part in anger. I'll do as you say and assume that one of us is dying. It could be me. Before I go, I want to ask you a last favor."

"I am glad of that," said Erwin. "Tell me, what can I do for you in parting?"

"I will repeat my first question, that is my favor: explain these words to me as well as you can."

Erwin thought for a short while, then he spoke:

"Nothing is outside, nothing is inside. The religious meaning is well known: God is everywhere. He is in the mind and He is also in nature. All things are divine, because God is the All. We used to call that pantheism. Then the philosophical meaning: the division between inside and outside is habitual to our thinking, but not necessary. There is the possibility for our mind to pass beyond the dividing line we have drawn for it. Beyond the pairs of opposites of which the world consists for us, other, new insights begin. But dear friend, I must admit to you: since my thinking has changed, no word and saying has a single meaning for me, but every word has ten, a hundred meanings. Here, then, begins what you fear so much: magic."

Friedrich frowned and wanted to interrupt him, but Erwin looked at him reassuringly and continued in a louder voice: "Permit me to give you an example to take with you. Take something of mine along, an object, and observe it a little from time to time, and soon the saying of inside and outside will reveal one of its many meanings to you."

133

He looked around him and reached for a small clay figure with a glazed surface and gave it to Friedrich.

"Take this as my parting gift. When this object I am putting into your hands ceases to be outside of you and is inside you, come back to me. But if it remains forever outside you as it is now, then let our parting also be forever."

Friedrich wanted to say a good deal more, but Erwin pressed his hand and said good-bye with a look that did not allow another word.

Friedrich left and went down the stairs (how unbelievably long it had been since he had climbed up these stairs!); he passed through the streets and went home with the little clay figure in his hand, feeling confused and intensely unhappy. Outside his house he stopped, shook his fist angrily, and felt very much like smashing the ridiculous little object to the ground. He did not do so but bit his lips and went inside. Never had he been so agitated, so tortured by conflicting emotions.

He searched for a place for his friend's gift and chose the upper shelf of a bookcase. There he left it for the time being.

Sometimes, during the course of the day, he looked at it and wondered about its origin and what meaning this absurd object was supposed to have for him. It was a small figure of a man, god, or idol with two faces like the Roman god Janus, rather clumsily modeled of clay and covered with a fired glaze that was cracked in several places. The little thing looked crude and insubstantial; it was surely not the work of a Greek or Roman, more likely from some backward African or South Sea Islands people. On both faces, which were identical, there was a glum, lazy, almost grinning smile—it was positively ugly, like a small goblin that continually squanders its silly smile.

Friedrich could not yet get used to the figure. It repulsed and annoyed him, and was in his way—in short, it disturbed him. The very next day he took it down and set it on the stove, and a few days later he set it on top of a closet. Time and time again it caught his eye as if insinuating itself, and smiled at him coldly and stupidly, made itself important, demanded attention. Two or three weeks later he moved it out to the vestibule, between photographs of Italy and the small, playful souvenirs that stood around there and that no one ever looked at. Now at least he only saw the idol on his way in and out; he passed quickly, never stopping to look at it more closely. But even here, though he would not admit it, the thing disturbed him. With this lump of clay, this two-faced monster, trouble and torment had come into his life.

One day, months later, he returned home from a short trip; he had taken to going off on such trips now and then, as if something were making him restless. He stepped into his house, passed through the vestibule, was greeted by the maid, and read some letters that had been waiting for him. But he was restless and distracted, as if he had forgotten something important; none of his books attracted him, he found no ease in any of the chairs. He began to examine himself, trying to remember what had caused this sudden change in his mood. Had he missed something important? Had something irritated him? Had he eaten something that disagreed with him? He guessed and searched, and he realized that this uneasy feeling had come over him as soon as he had entered the apartment, in the vestibule. He walked out into the vestibule, and his eyes searched, quite involuntarily, for the clay figure.

A peculiar shudder passed through him when he failed to see the idol. It had disappeared. It was not there. Had it walked away on its tiny clay legs? Flown away? Had a magic spell summoned it back from whence it came?

Friedrich pulled himself together, smiled, shook his head, and began to search the entire room. When he could not find anything, he called the maid. She came, she was embarrassed and admitted at once that she had dropped the thing as she was dusting it.

"Where is it?"

It no longer existed. It had seemed so solid, she had often held it in her hand , but yet it had broken into tiny bits and pieces and could not be mended; she had brought the shards to the glazier, who had laughed at her. Then she had thrown them away.

Friedrich dismissed the maid. He smiled. He did not mind. God knows, the idol was no loss. Now the monster was gone, and he would have peace. If he had only smashed the thing to bits the very first day! How he had suffered all this time! How the goblin had smiled at him, sly, evil, demonically. Now that the idol was gone he could admit to himself: he had feared it, he had honestly and truly been scared of that clay god! Was it not a sign and a symbol of everything that was loathsome and intolerable to Friedrich, everything he had always re-

135

garded as harmful, hostile, and to be fought, all superstition, all darkness, all that restrained conscience and mind? Did it not represent that feared subterranean power whose rumblings he sometimes heard, that distant earthquake that would destroy civilization and usher in chaos? Had this repulsive figure not robbed him of his best friend—no, not only robbed—but made him into an enemy! Well, now the thing was gone. Away. Smashed. Done with. It was good like this, it was far better than if he had destroyed it himself.

Thus he thought, or he said, and went after his business in the usual way.

But it was like a curse. Just now, now that he had gotten used to the absurd figure, now that the sight of it in its accustomed place in the vestibule had become increasingly familiar and almost a matter of indifference to him, now its absence began to torment him. Yes, he missed it. Whenever he went through the room he saw nothing but the empty place where it had stood, and from this place emanated an emptiness that filled the entire room with foreignness and rigidity.

Bad days and even worse nights began for Friedrich. He could not pass through the vestibule without thinking of the two-faced idol, without missing it, without feeling his thoughts tied to it. These feelings became a tormenting compulsion. And it was not only during the times when he passed through the vestibule that this compulsion seized him. Just as an emptiness and barrenness radiated from the empty table, so this compulsion radiated from deep within him, gradually displacing everything else, corroding all other thoughts and filling everything with emptiness and strangeness.

Time and again he recalled the figure in detail, if only to convince himself how absurd it was to grieve over its loss. He visualized it in all its stupid barbaric ugliness, with its empty or deceitful smile and its two faces. At times he even caught himself curling his lips as if propelled by an extrinsic force, in an attempt to imitate that hateful smile. A question pursued him: had the two faces really been identical? Did not some slight roughness or a crack in the glaze give one of them a slightly different expression? A questioning look? Something sphinxlike? And how uncanny, or at least peculiar, the color of the glaze had been! There had been green and blue and gray in it, but also red; a glaze that he now found in other objects, too, in the shine of the windowpane in the sun, in the reflection of a wet pavement.

He brooded a lot about this glaze, even during the night. G-l-a-s-u-r, what a peculiar, strange, unpleasant, and unfamiliar, almost malicious, word this was. He dissected the word, he hatefully split it apart, and once he even reversed it. Then it became R-u-s-a-l-g. Only the devil knew from where this word took its sound. He knew the word "Rusalg," he was certain, he knew it, and it was a hostile, unpleasant word, a word with ugly, disruptive overtones. For a long time he tortured himself, and finally it came to him that Rusalg reminded him of a book he had purchased and read on a trip. The book had dismayed and tormented him but had also secretly fascinated him. Its title had been *Countess Rusalga*. It was as if a curse were connected to the figurine; everything that was related to the figure, with its glaze, the blue, the green, and the smile, signified hostility, stung, tormented, contained poison! And how very strangely he smiled, Erwin, his former friend, as he put the idol into his hands! How very strange, how significant, how hostile!

Friedrich fought bravely and on some days even successfully against the thoughts that forced themselves upon him. He felt the danger keenly—he did not want to go mad! No, rather dead. Reason was a necessity. Life was not. And it occurred to him that perhaps precisely this was magic, that perhaps Erwin had cast a spell on him with the help of this figurine and that he, the victim, a defender of reason and science, must fall. But, if this was so, if he could even conceive of it as a possibility . . . then magic did exist. No, rather be dead!

A doctor recommended hikes and baths; during the evening he also sought distraction in a tavern. But this did little good. He cursed Erwin, he cursed himself.

One night he woke up frightened as he often did at that time without finding himself able to fall asleep again. He felt thoroughly anguished and ill at ease. He tried to think, he tried to find consolation. He looked for words to say to himself, comforting, reassuring words, filled with soothing peace and clarity, such as "Two times two is four." Nothing came to him, yet he stammered, half-crazed in his condition, sounds and syllables. Little by little, words formed on his lips, and several times, without grasping the meaning, he repeated a short sentence that had somehow taken form within him. He mumbled it over and over as though to deaden his mind, as

137

though to grope his way back to his lost sleep, on a narrow path bordering on the abyss.

But suddenly his voice grew somewhat louder, and the mumbled words entered his consciousness. He knew them. They were: "Yes, now you are in me!" And all at once he knew. He knew what they meant, he knew that they referred to the clay idol and that now, in this gray hour of the night, he had fulfilled, exactly and on time, the prediction that Erwin had made on that strange day: now the figure, which he had then held contemptuously in his hands, was no longer outside him but within him! "For that which is outside is inside."

Leaping out of bed, he felt ice and fire running through his body. The world turned round and round, the planets stared madly at him. He gathered his clothes, turned on the light, left bed and house, and walked in the middle of the night to Erwin's house. There he saw light behind the familiar window of the study; the door unlocked, everything seemed to await him. He staggered up the stairs. He trembled as he stepped into Erwin's study and propped his shaking hands on the table. Erwin sat in the soft lamplight, smiling thoughtfully.

His friend rose to welcome him: "You came. That is good."

"Did you expect me?" Friedrich whispered.

"I expected you, as you know yourself, ever since the hour that you left and took my small gift with you. Has that happened of which I spoke back then?"

Friedrich said in a low voice: "It has happened. The idol is now inside me. I can't bear it any longer."

"Can I help you?" Erwin asked.

"I don't know. Do as you will. Tell me more about your magic! Tell me how to get the idol out of myself."

Erwin put his hand on his friend's shoulder. He led him to an easy chair and made him sit down.

Then he smiled and said in a warm, almost motherly tone:

"The idol will come out. Trust me. Trust yourself. You have learned to believe in him. Now learn to love him! He is inside you, but he is still dead, he is still a ghost to you. Wake him, speak to him, ask him! For he is yourself! Stop hating him, don't fear him, don't torture him—how you have tortured the poor idol, who was only yourself! How you have tortured yourself!"

"Is this the way to magic?" Friedrich asked. He sat slumped in his chair, as though aged; his voice was gentle.

Erwin said: "This is the way, and the most difficult step you have perhaps already taken. You experienced: outside can become inside. You have been beyond the pairs of opposites. It seemed like hell to you: learn, friend, that this hell is heaven! Because it is heaven that confronts you. See, this is magic: to exchange inside and outside, not out of compulsion, not suffering as you have done, but willingly. Summon the past, summon the future: they are both within you! Today you have been the slave of what is inside you. Learn to become its master. That is magic."

André Gide

(1869–1951)

Prize awarded 1947 "for his comprehensive and artistically significant writings in which human problems and conditions have been presented with a fearless love of truth and keen psychological insight." ★ *Throughout his long and active life, André Gide was a figure of controversy: he espoused communism, then disavowed it; he defended homosexuality; his books* Travels in the Congo *(1927) and* Retour du Tchad *(1928) influenced the reform of France's colonial policies. He was a founder in 1909 of the prestigious literary magazine* Nouvelle Revue Francais. *He translated Tagore, Shakespeare, and Blake into French.*

Gide's works are flooded with highly personal, introspective questions. He challenged the modernist view of moral ambiguities and attempted to reconcile spirit and flesh, science and art. He was an exceptional stylist, influenced by people like Paul Valéry and Stéphane Mallarmé, and later incorporated ideas of Nietzsche and Dostoyevsky.

Gide considered The Counterfeiters *(1927) to be his only novel, dismissing the rest as "mere narratives." Written long after* The Immoralist *(1902) and his first popular success,* Strait Is the Gate *(1909),* The Counterfeiters *is notable for its examination of writing within the narrative itself, with many levels of self-criticism. All of Gide's works advocate the assertion of man's individuality, encouraging his readers to free themselves from conformist modes of thought.*

140

The Return of
the Prodigal Son

I HAVE PAINTED HERE, FOR MY OWN DELECTA-
tion, as they used to do in the old triptychs, the parable told us by
our Lord Jesus Christ. Leaving scattered and confused, as it were,
the twofold inspiration which has moved me, I have not tried to
show the victory of any god over me—nor my victory over any god.
Perhaps, however, if the reader should seek some expression of
piety from me, he would not look in vain for it in my picture, where
like the donor of a triptych, I kneel in one corner—a companion-
figure to the Prodigal Son, my face, like his, smiling and at the same
time wet with tears.

THE PRODIGAL

When the Prodigal, after his long absence, has grown tired of his
waywardness and has almost fallen out of love with himself, he
dreams, in the very depths of his misery of his father's face; of the
room that is not so very small, where every night his mother used to
lean over his bed; of the garden refreshed by a running brook—yet
closed in so that he always yearned to escape; and he dreams of that
thrifty elder brother, whom he never loved, who is keeping back the
portion of his substance that in his prodigality he has been unable
to squander. He confesses to himself that he has not found happiness, and cannot even feel any longer the mad rapture which he
sought instead of happiness. Perhaps, he thinks, if my father, who
was at first angry with me, has believed me dead, he would, in spite
of my sin, rejoice to see me returning to him in great humility, my
head bowed and covered with ashes, kneeling before him and say-

141

ing: "Father, I have sinned against Heaven and against you." What should I do, if he should raise me up and say to me, "Come into the house, my son!" And already filled with reverent love, the Prodigal sets out on his journey.

When, through an interval of the hills, he finally sees the smoke rising from the roof of the house, it is dusk; but he waits until the gathering darkness shrouds his wretchedness. He hears in the distance his father's voice; his knees shake; he falls down and hides his face in his hands, ashamed of his shame, for he knows that he is, nevertheless, the true son of his father. He is hungry; he has nothing left in his tattered cloak but a handful of sweet acorns—which have been his food as well as the food of the swine he has been tending. He sees supper being prepared. He can just make out his mother coming down the steps before the house. He can contain himself no longer; so he runs down the hill and into the courtyard, his dog, which does not recognize him, barking at him. He tries to speak to the servants, but they draw back suspiciously and hasten to warn their master, who at once comes out.

He was undoubtedly expecting the Prodigal Son, for he recognizes him immediately. He holds out his arms; then the young man kneels before him, covering his brow with one arm and raising his right hand to entreat forgiveness.

"Father, Father," he cries, "I have sinned grievously against Heaven and against you. I am no longer worthy to be called your son; but at least let me live, even as the humblest of your hired servants; in some corner of our house—let me live—"

The father lifts him up and embraces him. "My son, blessed be the day of your return"—and his joy overflows his heart in tears. Kissing his son's brow, he raises his head and turns to the servants: "Bring the best robe, put shoes on his feet and a precious ring on his finger, choose the fattest calf in our stables; kill it; make ready a joyous feast, for the son whom I thought dead lives."

And as the news is already spreading, he hurries on; he does not want to let anyone else say: "Mother, the son we have been mourning for has come back to us."

The joy of all, rising like a chant, fills the elder brother with anxiety. If he consents to sit at the common table, it is because the father, by his urgent plea, has constrained him. Alone among all the guests—for even the least of the servants has been invited to the feast—he sits with a frown on his face. Why give more honor to a repentant sinner than to him who has never sinned? He puts order above love. If he consents to appear at the feast it is because, making allowance for his brother, he can indulge him in his joy for one evening; it is also because his mother and father have promised to reprove the Prodigal Son on the morrow, and he himself is preparing to admonish him severely.

The smoke of the torches mounts to heaven. The feast is done; the tables are cleared. Now it is night, and not a breath stirs as the tired household, one soul after another, goes to rest. But in the room next to the Prodigal Son, there is a boy, his younger brother, who all through the night, even to the coming of dawn, tries in vain to sleep.

THE REPROOF OF THE FATHER

"My son, why did you leave me?"

"Did I really leave you? Father, are you not everywhere? I have never ceased to love you."

"Let us not quibble. I had a house to keep you in. It was built for you. Generations labored to build it so that your spirit might find shelter, might live in luxury worthy of it with comfort and employment. You were the son, the heir—why did you run away from it?"

"Because the house shut me in. The house is not mine father."

"I was the one who built it, and for you."

"Those are not your words but my brother's. You rule all the earth, and the house, and all that is not the house. The house was built by others, not you; in your name, I know, but by others."

"Man needs a roof under which to lay his head. Do you in your pride think that you can sleep in the open? Were you happy far away from me?"

"I did not feel far away from you."

"What was it, then, that made you come back? Tell me."

"I don't know. Idleness perhaps."

"Idleness, son! Then it was not love?"

"Father, I have told you I never loved you more than when I was in the desert. But I was worn out every morning trying to find the means of subsistence. At home, at least, there was plenty to eat."

"Yes, the servants take care of that. So it was hunger that called you back?"

"Perhaps it was cowardice, too, sickness. In the end, that hazardous existence weakened me, for I was living on wild fruits, locusts,

143

and honey. Less and less was I able to endure the discomfort that in the beginning fanned my enthusiasm. At night when I was cold, I dreamed of my bed in my father's house, so nicely tucked in. Famished, I dreamed that in my father's house there was always abundance of food, and to spare, for my hunger. I weakened. I no longer felt brave enough, strong enough—and yet—"

"So the fatted calf yesterday seemed good to you?"

The Prodigal Son, sobbing, throws himself down.

"Father, Father, in spite of everything, the wild taste of the sweet acorns is still in my mouth. Nothing can ever take that taste away."

"Poor child," the father begins again, raising him up, "Perhaps I have spoken too harshly to you. Your brother asked me to; his word is law here. It was he who bade me say to you 'Out of the house, there is no hope for you.' But then it was I who made you; what is in you I know, I know what drove you away on your wanderings. I was waiting for you at the end. If you had called me, I would have been there."

"Then I could have found you without coming back, Father?"

"If you had begun to grow weak, you did well to come back. Go now. Return to the room I have made ready for you. Enough for today. Rest. Tomorrow you can talk with your brother."

THE REPROOF OF THE ELDER BROTHER

At first, the Prodigal Son tries to carry it off with a high hand. "My big brother," he begins, "we resemble each other very little. We are not alike, brother."

"That is your fault," the elder brother answers.

"Why my fault?"

"Because I do everything in order. Everything that may be distinguished from order is the fruit or the seed of pride."

"Is there nothing, then, to distinguish me but my faults?"

"Call virtue only what brings you back to order, and, as for all the rest, subdue it."

"That would mean mutilation—it is this that I dread. The very thing you would suppress in me comes from the father."

"I did not say suppress it—subdue it."

"I understand you perfectly. All the same, that is how I have subdued my virtues."

"And that is why I now find them in you again. You should exalt them. Understand me well: it is not a lowering of yourself but rather an exaltation that I am proposing whereby the most conflicting and insubordinate element of your flesh and spirit must be made to move together in harmony, whereby the worst in you must sustain the best, and the best must yield—"

"It was, also, an exaltation that I was seeking, and that I found in the desert—perhaps not very different from what you are thinking of."

"To say the truth, what I should like to do is to impose it upon you."

"Our father did not speak so harshly."

"I know what Father said to you. It was vague. He no longer explains himself clearly; so one can make him say whatever one wishes. But I understand his thoughts. I alone can interpret them to the servants, and whoever would understand the father must listen to me."

"I used to understand him very easily without your help."

"So it seemed to you, but you understood him wrongly. There is not more than one way of understanding Father, there is not more than one way of listening to him, not more than one way of loving him, if we are to be united in that love."

"In his own house."

"That love leads you back to it; you see that, don't you, since you have returned."

"I know, I know, I returned; I admit it."

"What can you seek elsewhere that you do not find in abundance here? Nay, it is only here that you can find what is yours."

"I know that you have kept riches for me."

"All of your possessions that you have not squandered—that is to say, the part that we hold in common—the estate."

"Do I no longer own anything in my own right?"

"Yes, the personal part of our gift that our father may perhaps consent to allow you."

"That is what I want to keep. I agree that I am to receive nothing else."

"My proud brother, you are not going to be consulted. Between ourselves, that part is uncertain: I rather advise you to renounce it. It was your personal part of the gift that was your ruin, that you squandered as soon as you received it."

"The rest I could not take with me."

"And you will find it just as you left it. That is enough for today. Enter into the peace of the house."

145

"That will be good, for I am tired."

"Blessed by your fatigue, then. Go to sleep now. Tomorrow your mother will speak to you."

THE MOTHER

Prodigal Son, though your mind still rebels against your brother's words, speak out from your heart. How sweet you find it, as your mother sits here, to lie at her knees with your head buried in her lap, and to feel her caressing hand bend your stubborn neck!

"Why did you leave me so long?"

Your tears are your only answer.

"Why do you weep now, my son? You have come back to me. While I was waiting for you, I wept my tears dry."

"Were you still waiting for me?"

"I never ceased hoping. Every night before I fell asleep, I thought, If he returns tonight, will he remember how to open the door? and I was a long time going to sleep. Every morning before I was quite awake, I thought, Will he come back today? Then I would pray. I prayed so hard that you were bound to come back."

"Your prayers made me return."

"What are you going to do now?"

"I told you before: try to be like my elder brother, manage our estate, like him, take a wife."

"That means that you have someone in mind?"

"Oh, it does not matter who she may be, so long as you choose her. Do for me as you did for my brother."

"I should like to choose her according to your heart's desire."

"What does it matter if my heart had chosen? I yield up the pride that took me far away from you. Guide my choice. I submit, I tell you. I will see that my children also submit, and thus my attempt to escape will no longer seem so futile to me."

"Listen; there is a child you might take care of even now."

"What do you mean? Who is it?"

"Your younger brother, who was barely ten years old when you went away, whom you hardly recognized, and yet—"

"Go on, Mother, tell me what troubles you."

"He is a boy in whom you should have been able to recognize yourself, for he is now just like you as you were when you left."

"Like me?"

"Like what you were, I say, not, alas, like what you have become."

"But he will become like that."

"We must make him. Talk to him. I am sure he will listen to you, the Prodigal. Make him realize what disappointment you met on the way; spare him—"

"But what alarms you so about my brother? Perhaps it is just that we look alike—"

"No, no. The resemblance between you is deeper. What disturbs me about him is the very thing that I did not at first let disturb me enough about you. He reads too much, and does not always choose good books."

"Is that all?"

"Often he climbs to the highest spot in the garden—you know, up on the walls—from which you can see the whole countryside."

"I remember. Is that all?"

"He is less with us than off on the farm."

"What does he do there?"

"Nothing bad. But it is not the farmer he seeks out, it is the ne'er-do-wells farthest away, those that are not from this part of the country. There is one especially who comes from a long distance, who tells him all sorts of stories."

"The swineherd."

"Yes, you know him? To listen to him, your brother follows him every evening into the pigsty. He does not come home until dinner, and then it is with no appetite and with vile-smelling clothes. Remonstrating with him makes no difference. He becomes rigid under restraint. Some mornings at dawn, before any of us are up, he runs to go with the swineherd as far as the gate when he drives his herd out to pasture."

"Does he know he ought not to go?"

"You knew it, too. Someday he will slip away from me, I am sure. Someday he will leave."

"No, I will speak to him, Mother. Don't worry."

"To you I know he will listen. Did you see how he looked at you that first evening? What glamour your rags had for him—and then the purple robe which your father put on you! I was afraid that in his mind he confused one with the other; that it might have been the rags that attracted him first. But now that fear seems foolish to me, for if you, my child, could have foreseen so much misery, you would not have left us, would you?"

147

"I do not understand now how I could leave you—you, my mother."

"Well, then, tell him all that."

"Yes, I will tell him tomorrow night. Kiss me now on my brow just as you used to when I was a little child and you watched me fall asleep. I am sleepy now."

"Go to sleep. I am going to pray for you all."

DIALOGUE WITH THE YOUNGER BROTHER

Next to the Prodigal's there is a room, not so very small, a room with bare walls. The Prodigal, lamp in hand, comes close to the bed where his younger brother lies, his face turned to the wall. He begins in a low voice, so as not to disturb the boy should he be asleep.

"I want to speak to you, brother."

"What prevents you?"

"I thought you might be asleep."

"One doesn't have to sleep in order to dream."

"You were dreaming? Of what?"

"What is that to you? If I myself do not understand my dreams, I don't suppose you can explain them to me."

"Are they then so subtle? If you will tell them to me, I will try."

"Can you choose your own dreams? Mine are what they want to be; they are freer than I. What did you come here for? Why do you disturb my sleep?"

"But you are not asleep, and I have come to speak to you quietly."

"What have you to say to me?"

"Nothing, if you take that tone."

"Then good-bye."

The Prodigal Son moves toward the door but puts the lamp down on the floor, where it lights the room only feebly; then, going back, he sits down on the edge of the bed in the uncertain shadow and, for a long time, strokes the boy's brow, which is turned away from him.

148

"You answer me more rudely than I ever did our brother, although I too was against him."

The restive boy raises himself up abruptly.

"Tell me, did our brother send you to me?"

"No, child, it was not he but your mother."

"Then you would not have come of your own accord?"

"But I come as a friend."

Half sitting up in his bed, the boy stares at the Prodigal.

"How can one of my own people be my friend?"

"You are mistaken about our brother."

"Don't speak to me of him. I hate him—I am utterly out of patience with him. It is because of him that I answered you so rudely."

"How is that?"

"You would not understand."

"Anyhow, tell me."

The Prodigal draws his brother into his arms, and the boy drops his restraint.

"The evening you returned I could not sleep. All through the night I kept musing—I had another brother and I did not know him. It was this that made my heart beat so loud when I saw you coming in the courtyard covered with glory."

"Oh, but then I was covered with rags."

"Yes, I saw you, but even so you were glorious, and I saw what our father did: he put a ring on your finger—our brother has no such ring. I did not like to ask anyone about you. I only knew that you came from very far away, and I watched your expression at table—"

"Were you at the feast?"

"Oh, I know very well that you did not see me. All through the meal you were looking far away without seeing anything; and the second evening you talked with Father. That was all right, but the third—"

"Go on."

"If you had only said one loving word to me—just one word!"

"You were counting on me, then?"

"So much! Do you think I would have hated our brother so bitterly if you had not talked with him such a long time that evening? What did you have to say to each other? You know very well that if you are like me you can have nothing in common with him."

"I had wronged him gravely."

"Was that possible?"

"At least, wronged Father and Mother. You know that I ran away from home?"

"Yes, I know. A long time ago, wasn't it?"

"When I was just about your age."

149

"Oh, is that what you call doing wrong?"

"Yes, that was my offense, my sin."

"When you went away did you realize that you were doing wrong?"

"No, I felt as if something inside me were compelling me to go."

"What has happened since to change the thing that was the truth to you then into an error?"

"I have suffered."

"And that is what makes you say, 'I did wrong'?"

"No, not exactly: it has made me think."

"Before that, then, you didn't think?"

"Yes, but my weak reason let itself be imposed upon by my desires."

"As later by your sufferings. So that today you return—beaten."

"No, not beaten, exactly—resigned."

"At any rate, you have given up being what you wanted to be."

"What my pride persuaded me to be."

The boy remained silent a moment, then, bursting into sobs, cried:

"My brother, I am now as you were when you went away. Tell me, did you meet on the way with nothing but disillusionment? All those far-off things of which I have had glimpses—which are so different from things here—are they only a mirage? All this new life that I feel in me, is it only madness? Tell me, what did you find on your way that disheartened you so? Oh, what made you come back?"

"The freedom I was seeking, I lost; I was a captive, I had to serve."

"I am a captive here."

"Yes, but serving evil masters is another thing; here you serve your parents."

"If one must serve, has not one at least the freedom to choose one's servitude?"

"I had hoped so. As far as my feet would carry me I kept following after my desire, like Saul after his asses but a kingdom was waiting for him, while it was misery that I found—and still—"

"Did you not take the wrong road?"

"I went straight ahead."

"Are you sure of that? But there must be still other kingdoms, and lands without a king, to discover."

"Who told you so?"

"I know it; I feel it. It seems to me that already I rule there."

"Proud boy!"

"Oh, that is what our brother said to you. Why do you repeat it to me now? Had you only kept that pride, you would not have come back."

"Then I never should have known you."

"Yes, out there I should have joined you. You would have known I was your brother. Indeed it seems to me it is to find you that I am going away."

"That you are going away?"

"Haven't you understood? Are you yourself not encouraging me to go?"

"I should like to spare you the return—by sparing you the start."

"No, no, don't say that! That is not what you mean. Did you not, also, go away as a conqueror?"

"Yes, and that was just what made servitude seem hard."

"Then why did you submit? Did you tire so soon?"

"No, not till toward the end, but I began to doubt."

"What do you mean?"

"To doubt about everything, about myself. I wanted too, to settle down somewhere. The comfort which the master promised me tempted me. Yes, I realize it now; I have failed."

The Prodigal bows his head, shielding his eyes with his hands.

"But how was it at first?"

"I traveled for a long time across the great unconquered earth."

"The desert?"

"It was not always the desert."

"What were you looking for?"

"I no longer know myself."

"Get up. Look on the table at my bedside—there near that torn book."

"I see an opened pomegranate."

"The swineherd brought it to me the other night after he had been away for three days."

151

"Yes, it is a wild pomegranate."

"I know. It is almost unbearably bitter; yet I feel that if I were thirsty enough, I would bite into it."

"Then I may tell you now. It was a thirst like that that I was seeking in the desert."

"A thirst that only this fruit without sweetness can quench?"

"Oh, but it makes one love that thirst."

"Do you know where to gather it?"

"In a little neglected orchard you reach just before nightfall. No wall now separates it from the desert. A brook flows through it. Some half-ripe fruit hangs from the branches."

"What fruit?"

"Like that in our garden, only wild. It had been very hot all that day."

"Listen, do you know why I was waiting for you this evening? I shall leave before the night ends. This very night, as soon as the sky grows pale. I have girded my loins. Tonight I have kept on my sandals."

"What, are you going to do all that I could not do?"

"You have opened the way for me, and the thought of you will sustain me."

"I can only admire you, but you must forget me. What are you taking with you?"

"You know very well that I, the youngest brother, have no part in the heritage. I leave empty-handed."

"It is better so."

"What are you looking at out of the window?"

"The garden where our forefathers lie buried."

"My brother!" The boy, who has risen from the bed, gently puts his arm around the neck of the Prodigal Son, and his embrace becomes as loving as his voice. "Come with me!"

"Leave me, leave me. I stay to comfort our mother. Without me you will be braver. Now it is time to start. The sky is growing pale. Don't make any noise. Kiss me, little brother. You take all my hopes with you. Be strong; forget us; forget me. And may you never come back. Go down the stairs softly. I'll bring the lamp for you."

"Let me keep hold of your hand as far as the door."

"Mind the steps outside."

T. S. Eliot

(1888–1965)

Prize awarded 1948 "for his outstanding pioneer contribution to present-day poetry." ★ Thomas Stearns Eliot is among the most influential poets (and critics) of the twentieth century. "The Love Song of J. Alfred Prufrock" (1917), "The Waste Land" (1922), and his drama Murder in the Cathedral *(1935) are some of the best known and finest examples of twentieth-century literature.*

Descended from a distinguished New England family, Eliot was born in St. Louis, Missouri, the grandson of William Greenleaf Eliot, who founded Washington University in St. Louis. Eliot went to Harvard in 1904, majoring in philosophy and contributing poetry to the Harvard Advocate. *He received a master's degree from Harvard, then attended the Sorbonne and Oxford, after which he made his home in England. He began to earn his living as a writer in 1917 after a stint as a bank clerk and was the assistant editor of the* Egoist, *a British literary magazine, from 1917 to 1919. In 1922 he founded the* Criterion, *a quarterly review that flourished until 1939. During that time Eliot also worked for Faber & Faber, the British publishing house that would become his own publisher.*

Eliot was deeply concerned with the individual's loss of identity and sense of isolation from the world, and with the barrenness of contemporary society. He developed these themes with increasing richness and complexity through the years. His eventual conversion to Catholicism in the twenties, however, coincided with an increasing optimism in his writings, especially Ash Wednesday *(1930) and* Four Quartets *(1943).*

Eliot could be cynical and lyrical, and both come through his often mystical, consciously literary themes, religious as well as secular. These selections, drawn from some of his earliest writing, hint at the major contributions yet to come. Drafted while Eliot was still a student at Harvard, they have been lost to the general public for decades.

153

SONG

When we came home across the hill
  No leaves were fallen from the trees;
  The gentle fingers of the breeze
Had torn no quivering cobweb down.

The hedgerow bloomed with flowers still,
  No withered petals lay beneath;
  But the wild roses in your wreath
Were faded, and the leaves were brown.

ON A PORTRAIT

Among a crowd of tenuous dreams, unknown
To us of restless brain and weary feet,
Forever hurrying, up and down the street,
She stands at evening in the room alone.

Not like a tranquil goddess carved of stone
But evanescent, as if one should meet
A pensive lamia in some wood-retreat,
An immaterial fancy of one's own.

No meditations glad or ominous
Disturb her lips, or move the slender hands;
Her dark eyes keep their secrets hid from us,
Beyond the circle of our thought she stands.

The parrot on his bar, a silent spy,
Regards her with a patient curious eye.

At Graduation 1905

I

Standing upon the shore of all we know
We linger for a moment doubtfully,
Then with a song upon our lips, sail we
Across the harbor bar—no chart to show,
No light to warn of rocks which lie below,
But let us yet put forth courageously.

II

As colonists embarking from the strand
To seek their fortunes on some foreign shore
Well know they lose what time shall not restore,
And when they leave they fully understand
That though again they see their fatherland
They there shall be as citizens no more.

Spleen

Sunday: this satisfied procession
Of definite Sunday faces;
Bonnets, silk hats, and conscious graces
In repetition that displaces
Your mental self-possession
By this unwarranted digression.

Evening, lights, and tea!
Children and cats in the alley;
Dejection unable to rally
Against this dull conspiracy.

And Life, a little bald and gray,
Languid, fastidious, and bland,
Waits, hat and gloves in hand,
Punctilious of tie and suit
(Somewhat impatient of delay)
   On the doorstep of the Absolute.

155

william Faulkner

(1897–1962)

Prize awarded 1949 "for his powerful and artistically unique contribution to the modern American novel." ★ *Faulkner gained an enormous reputation abroad ("to the young people of France he is a god," said Sartre) before achieving recognition in the United States; he was awarded the Nobel Prize in 1949 and the French Legion of Honor in 1951 but didn't win the Pulitzer Prize until 1955. American indifference to Faulkner resulted, in part, from a lack of interest in the rural southern setting of his major works (fictionalized as Yoknapatawpha County, Mississippi). In addition, Faulkner's style—dense, poetic, and often stream-of-consciousness—was extremely experimental for his time, with a subjective narrative (first emerging in* The Sound and the Fury, *1929), which, while absorbing, was difficult for the average reader.*

Critics derided his choice of locale and subject matter, but Faulkner was encouraged by his friend Sherwood Anderson (who successfully transcended parochialism with his own masterpiece, Winesburg, Ohio*).* Absalom, Absalom! *(1936),* The Unvanquished *(1938),* Go Down, Moses *(1942), and* The Reivers *(1962)—just a part of the Yoknapatawpha series—reflect Faulkner's continuing fascination with the deep South: the passions of rich and poor, black and white, and the moral consequences of slavery, the Civil War, and Reconstruction.*

Financial concerns in the 1930s and 1940s drove Faulkner to accept work as a "film doctor" in Hollywood. In 1932 alone he rewrote nine scripts, including Today We Live *(based on his own short story* Turn About*) and* The Story of Temple Drake *(based on* Sanctuary*). Still, he never stopped writing stories and novels, and by the time of his death in 1962 his fame in the United States equaled his reputation abroad. Today he is considered one of the finest American writers of all time.*

THRIFT

I

I

N MESSES THEY TOLD OF MACWYRGLINCHBEATH
how, a first-class air mechanic of a disbanded Nieuport squadron, he went three weeks A.W.O.L. He had been given a week's leave for England while the squadron was being reequipped with British-made machines, and he was last seen in Boulogne, where the lorry set him and his mates down. That night he disappeared. Three weeks later the hitherto unchallenged presence of an unidentifiable first-class air mechanic was discovered in the personnel of a bombing squadron near Boulogne. At the ensuing investigation the bomber gunnery sergeant told how the man had appeared among the crew one morning on the beach, where the flight had landed after a raid. Replacements had come up the day before, and the sergeant said he took the man to be one of the new mechanics. He told how the man showed at once a conscientious aptitude, revealing an actual affection for the aeroplane of whose crew he made one, speaking in a slow, infrequent Scottish voice of the amount of money it represented and of the sinfulness of sending so much money into the air in a single lump.

"He even asked to be put on flying," the sergeant testified. "He downright courted me till I did it, volunteering for all manner of off-duty jobs for me, until I put him on once or twice. I'd keep him with me, on the toggles, though."

They did not discover that anything was wrong until pay day. His name was not on the pay officer's list; the man's insistence—his was either sublime courage or sublime effrontery—brought his presence to the attention of the squadron commander. But when they looked for him, he was gone.

The next day, in Boulogne, an air mechanic with a void seven-day pass, issued three weeks ago by a now disbanded scout squadron, was arrested while trying to collect three weeks' pay, which he said was owing to him from the office of the acting provost marshal himself. His name, he said, was MacWyrglinchbeath.

Thus it was discovered that MacWyrglinchbeath was a simultaneous deserter from two military units. He repeated his tale—for the fifth time in three days fetched from his cell by a corporal and four men with bayoneted rifles—standing bareheaded to attention before the table where a general now say, and the operations officer of the bomber squadron and the gunnery sergeant:

"A had gone doon tae thae beach tae sleep, beca' A kenned they wud want money for-r thae beds in the town. A was ther-re when the bombers cam' doon. Sae A went wi' thae boombers."

"But why didn't you go home on your leave?" the general asked.

"A wou'na be spendin' sic useless money, sir'r."

The general looked at him. The general had little pig's eyes, and his face looked as though it had been blown up with a bicycle pump.

"Do you mean to tell me that you spent seven days' leave and a fortnight more without leave, as the member of the personnel of another squadron?"

"Well, sir-r," MacWyrglinchbeath said, "naught wud do they but A sud tak' thae week's fur-rlough. I didna want it. And wi' the big machines A cud get flying pay."

The general looked at him. Rigid, motionless, he could see the general's red face swell and swell.

"Get that man out of here!" the general said at last.

" 'Bout face," the corporal said.

"Get me that squadron commander," the general said. "At once! I'll cashier him! Gad's teeth, I'll put him in jail for the rest of his life!"

" 'Bout face!" the corporal said, a little louder. MacWyrglinchbeath had not moved.

"Sir-r," he said. The general, in midvoice, looked at him, his mouth still open a little. Behind his mustache he looked like a boar in a covert. "Sir-r," MacWyrglinchbeath said, "wull A get ma pay for thae thr-r-ree weeks and thae seven hour-rs and for-rty minutes in the air'r?"

It was Ffollansbye, who was to first recommend him for a commission, who knew most about him.

"I give you," he said, "a face like a ruddy walnut, maybe sixteen, maybe fifty-six; squat, with arms not quite as long as an ape's, lugging petrol tins across the aerodrome. So long his arms were that he would have to hunch his shoulders and bow his elbows a little so the bottoms of the tins wouldn't scrape the ground. He walked with a limp—he told me about that. It was just after they came down from Stirling in 'fourteen. He had enlisted for infantry; they had not told him that there were other ways of going in.

"So he began to make inquiries. Can't you see him, listening to all the muck they told recruits then, about privates not lasting two days after reaching Dover—they told him, he said, that the enemy killed only the English and Irish and Lowlanders; the Highlands having not yet declared war—and such. Anyway, he took it all in, and then he would go to bed at night and sift it out. Finally he decided to go for the Flying Corps; decided with pencil and paper that he would last longer there and so have more money saved. You see, neither courage nor cowardice had ever functioned in him at all; I don't believe he had either. He was just like a man who, lost for a time in a forest, picks up a fagot here and there against the possibility that he might some day emerge.

"He applied for transfer, but they threw it out. He must have been rather earnest about it, for they finally explained that he must have a better reason than personal preference for desiring to transfer, and that a valid reason would be mechanical knowledge or a disability leaving him unfit for infantry service.

"So he thought that out. And the next day he waited until the barracks was empty, prodded the stove to a red heat, removed his boot and putty, and laid the sole of his foot to the stove.

"That was where the limp came from. When his transfer went through and he came out with his third-class air mechanic's rating, they thought that he had been out before.

"I can see him stiff at attention in the squadron office, his b.o. on the table, Whiteley and the sergeant trying to pronounce his name.

159

" 'What't the name, sergeant?' Whiteley says.

"Sergeant looks at b.o., rubs hands on thighs. 'Mac——' he says, and bogs down again. Whiteley leans to look-see himself.

" 'Mac——' bogs himself; then: 'Beath. Call him MacBeath.'

" 'A'm ca'd MacWyrglinchbeath,' newcomer says.

" 'Sir,' sergeant prompts.

" 'Sir-r,' newcomer says.

" 'Oh,' Whiteley says, 'Magillinbeath. Put it down, sergeant.' Sergeant takes up pen, writes M-a-c with flourish, then stops, handmaking concentric circles with pen above page while owner tries for a peep at b.o. in Whiteley's hands. 'Rating, three ack emma,' Whiteley says. 'Put that down, sergeant.'

" 'Very good, sir,' sergeant says. Flourishes grow richer, like sustained cavalry threat; leans yet nearer Whiteley's shoulder, beginning to sweat.

"Whiteley looks up, says, 'Eh?' sharply. 'What's matter?' he says.

" 'The nyme, sir,' sergeant says. 'I can't get—'

"Whiteley lays b.o. on table; they look at it. 'People at Wing never could write,' Whiteley says in fretted voice.

" ' 'Tain't that, sir,' sergeant says. 'Is people just 'aven't learned to spell. Wot's yer nyme agyne, my man?'

" 'A'm ca'd MacWyrglinchbeath,' newcomer says.

" 'Ah, the devil,' Whiteley says. 'Put him down MacBeath and give him to C. Carry on.'

"But newcomer holds ground, polite but firm. 'A'm ca'd MacWyrglinchbeath,' he says without heat.

"Whiteley stares at him. Sergeant stares at him. Whiteley takes pen from sergeant, draws record sheet to him. 'Spell it.' Newcomer does so as Whiteley writes it down. 'Pronounce it again, will you?' Whiteley says. Newcomer does so. 'Magillinbeath,' Whiteley says. 'Try it, sergeant.'

"Sergeant stares at written word. Rubs ear. 'Mac-wigglinbeech,' he says. Then, in hushed tone: 'Blimey.'

"Whiteley sits back. 'Right,' he says. 'We've it correctly. Carry on.'

" 'Ye ha' it MacWyrglinchbeath, sir-r?' newcomer says. 'A'd no ha' ma pay gang wrong.'

"That was before he soloed. Before he deserted, of course. Lugging his petrol tins back and forth, a little slower than anyone else, but always at it if you could suit your time to his. And sending his money, less what he smoked—I have seen his face as he watched the men drinking beer in the canteen—back home to the neighbor who was keeping his horse and cow for him.

"He told me about that arrangement too. When he and the neighbor agreed, it was in emergency; they both believed it would be over and he would be home in three months. That was a year ago. ' 'Twull be a sore sum A'll be owin' him for foragin' thae twa beasties,' he told me. Then he quit shaking his head. He became quite still for a while; you could almost watch his mind ticking over. 'Aweel,' he says at last, 'A doot not thae beasts wull ha' increased in value, too, wi' thae har-rd times.'

"In those days, you know, the Hun came over your aerodrome and shot at you while you ran and got into holes they had already dug for that purpose, while the Hun sat overhead and dared you to come out.

"So we could see fighting from the mess windows; we were carting off the refuse ourselves then. One day it crashed not two hundred yards away. When we got there, they were just dragging the pilot clear—all but his legs. He was lying on his back, looking up at the sky with that expression they have, until someone closed his eyes.

"But Mac—they were still calling him MacBeath—was looking at the crash. He was walking around it, clicking his tongue. 'Tzut, tzut,' he says. ' 'Tis a sinfu' waste. Sinfu'. Tzut. Tzut. Tzut.'

"That was while he was still a three ack emma. He was a two soon, sending a little more money back to the neighbor. He was keeping books now, with a cheap notebook and a pencil, and a candle stub for nights. The first page was his bank book; the others were like a barograph of this war, tighter than a history.

"Then he was a one A.M. He began then to work over his ledger late into the night. I supposed it was because he had more money to worry him now, drawing, as he probably did, more a month than he ever had in his life, until he came to me for an N.C.O. rating sheet. I gave it to him. A week later he had to buy a new candle. I met him.

" 'Well, Mac,' I said, 'have you decided to go for a sergeant yet?'

"He looked at me, without haste, without surprise. 'Ay, sir-r,' he says. He hadn't heard about flying pay then, you see."

161

* * *

Ffollansbye told about his solo:

"His new squadron were pups. I suppose as soon as he saw they were single seaters, he realized that there would be no flying pay here. He applied for transfer to bombers. It was denied. It must have been about this time that he had the letter from his neighbor, telling that the cow had calved. I can see him now, reading the letter through to the last word, keeping all judgment and speculation and concern in abeyance until he had done, then sitting there—his pencil and paper useless in this case—weighing that delicate and unanticipated situation and its unpredictable ramifications of ownership, then deciding that circumstances would take care of it in good time.

"One day he waked up; the impulse, the need to, may have come like a germ in that letter. Not that he had ever soldiered, but now he began to show interest in the machines and in the operation of the controls, talking with the pilots, asking questions about flight, sifting and cataloguing the answers in his bunk at night. He became so— well, ubiquitous, tireless, made such an up-and-doing appearance when brass hats were about, that they made him a corporal. I suppose if I'd been there then I'd have believed that was his aim all along.

"But this time he had hitched to a star, in more than allegorical sense, it proved. It was in the middle of lunch one day when the alarm goes off. They rush out, officer and man, clutching napkins, in time to see a pup go down the aerodrome, the wings at forty-five-degree angle, the tip practically dragging. It righted itself by putting the other wing down, and with a crash car waiting behind, it nosed up and shot perpendicularly for perhaps two hundred feet, hung for ten thousand years on the prop, flipped its tail up, and vanished from view, still at that forty-five-degree angle.

" 'What—' the major says.

" 'It's a mine!' a subaltern shouts. 'It's my machine!'

" 'Who—' the major says. The crash car comes wailing back, and at about a hundred m.p.h. the pup comes into view again, upside down now. The pilot wears neither goggles nor helmet; in the fleeting glimpse they have of him, his face wears an expression of wary and stubborn concern. He goes on, half rolls into a skid that swaps him end for end. He is now headed straight for the crash car; driver jumps out and flees for nearest hangar, the pup in vicious pursuit. Just as the driver, clutching head in both arms, hurls himself into the hangar, the pup shoots skyward again, hangs again on the prop, then ducks from sight, disappearance followed immediately by dull crash.

"They removed Mac from its intricate remains, intact but unconscious. When he waked he was again under arrest."

II

"And so," Ffollansbye said, "for the second time Mac had caused near apoplexy in high places. But this time he was not present. He was in detention camp, where he was calculating the amount of deficit which bade fair to be the first entry on the flying-pay page of his ledger. Meanwhile, at B.H.Q. and in London they considered his case, with its accumulated documents. At last they decided, as a matter of self-protection and to forestall him before he invented any more crimes for which K. R. & O. had no precedent, to let him have his way.

"They came and told him that he was for England and the school of aeronautics.

" 'If A gang, wull they be char-rgin' thae leetle unfor-rtunate machine against me?'

" 'No,' they said.

" 'Verra weel,' he said. 'A'm ready noo.'

"He returned to England, setting foot on his native side of the Channel for the first time in more than two years, refusing to leave to go home, as usual. Perhaps it was that matter of the calf's economic legitimacy; perhaps he had figured the most minimated minimum of unavoidable outlay for the trip, knowing, too, that whatever he discovered, he could not remain long enough to solidify against what he might find when he got there. But perhaps not. Perhaps it was just MacWyrglinchbeath."

Seven months later, a sergeant pilot, he was trundling an obsolete and unwieldly Reconnaissance Experimental back and forth above the Somme while his officer observer spotted artillery fire from the blunt, bathtubish nose of it. Big, broad-winged, the heavy four-cylinder Beardmore engine thundering sedately behind and above

163

MacWyrglinchbeath's head a temptation and potential victim to anything with a gun on it that could move seventy miles an hour. But all the same, flying hours accumulated slowly in MacWyrglinch-beath's log book.

He and his officer carried on a long, intermittent conversation as they pottered about the ancient thing between flights. The officer was an artilleryman by instinct and a wireless enthusiast by inclination; between him and aviation was an antipathy which never flagged. MacWyrglinchbeath's passion for accumulating flying time was an enigma to him until, by patient probing, he learned of the neighbor and the mounting hoard of shillings.

"So you came to the war to make money?" he said.

"Aweel," MacWyrglinchbeath said. "A wou'na be wastin' ma time."

The officer repeated MacWyrglinchbeath's history to the mess. A day or two later another pilot—an officer—entered the hangar and found MacWyrglinchbeath head down in the nacelle of his machine.

"I say, sergeant," the officer said to the seat of MacWyrglinch-beath's breeks. MacWyrglinchbeath backed slowly into complete sight and turned over his shoulder a streaked face.

"Ay, sir-r."

"Come down a moment, will you?" MacWyrglinchbeath climbed down, carrying a wrench and a bit of foul waste. "Robinson tells me you're a sort of financier," the officer said.

MacWyrglinchbeath laid the wrench down and wiped his hands on the waste. "Aweel, A wou'na say just that."

"Now, sergeant, don't deny it. Mr. Robinson has told on you. . . . Have a cigarette?"

"A'll no' mind." MacWyrglinchbeath wiped his hands on his thighs and took the cigarette. "A smawk a pipe masel'." He accepted a light.

"I've a bit of business in your line," the officer said. "This day, each month, you're to give me one pound, and for every day I get back, I give you a shilling. What do you say?"

MacWyrglinchbeath smoked slowly, holding the cigarette as though it were a dynamite cap. "And thae days when ye'll no fly?"

"Just the same. I owe you a shilling."

MacWyrglinchbeath smoked slowly for a while. "Wull ye gang wi' me as ma obsair-rver-r?"

"Who'll take up my bus? No, no; if I flew with you, I'd not need underwriting. . . . What do you say?"

MacWyrglinchbeath mused, the cigarette in his soiled hand. " 'Twill tak' thinkin'," he said at last. "A'll tell ye the mor-rn."

"Right. Take the night and think it out." The officer returned to the mess.

"I've got him! I've got him hooked."

"What's your idea?" the C.O. said. "Are you spending all this ingenuity for a pound which you can only win by losing?"

"I just want to watch the old Shylock lose flesh. I should give his money back, even if I won it."

"How?" the C.O. said.

"Look here," Robinson said, "why don't you let Mac be? You don't know those people, those Highlanders. It takes forti- tude just to live as they do, let alone coming away without protest to fight for a king whom they probably still consider a Ger- man peasant, and for a cause that, however it ends, he'll only lose. And the man who can spend three years in this mess and still look forward to a future with any sanity, strength to his arm, say I."

"Hear, hear!" someone cried.

"Oh, have a drink," the other said. "I shan't hurt your Scot."

The next morning MacWyrglinchbeath paid down the pound, slowly and carefully, but without reluctance. The officer accepted it as soberly.

"We'll start wi' today," MacWyrglinchbeath said.

"Righto," the officer said. "We'll start in a half hour."

Three days later, after a short conversation with Robinson, the C.O. called MacWyrglinchbeath's client aside.

"Look here. You must call that silly wager off. You're disrupting my whole squadron. Robinson says that if you're anywhere in sight, he can't even keep MacBeath in their sector long enough after the battery fires to see the bursts."

"It's not my fault, sir. I wasn't buying a watchdog. At least, I thought not. I was just pulling Mac's leg."

"Well, you look him out tomorrow and ask him to release you. We'll have Brigade about our ears at this rate."

The next morning the client talked to MacWyrglinchbeath. That afternoon Robinson talked to MacWyrglinchbeath. That evening

165

after dinner, the C.O. sent for him. But MacWyrglinchbeath was firm, polite, and without heat, and like granite.

The C.O. drummed on the table for a while. "Very well, sergeant," he said at last. "But I order you to keep to your tour of duty. If you are reported off your patrol once more, I'll ground you. Carry on."

MacWyrglinchbeath saluted. "Verra gude, sir-r."

After that he kept to his tour. Back and forth, back and forth above the puny shell puffs, the gouts of slow smoke. From time to time, he scanned the sky above and behind him, but always his eyes returned northward, where the other R.E. was a monotonous speck in the distance.

This was day after day, while Mr. Robinson, with his binoculars, hung over the leading edge of the nacelle like a man in a bath who has dropped the soap overside. But every day the client returned, daily the shillings grew, until that day came when the shilling was profit, followed by another and another. Then the month was complete, and MacWyrglinchbeath paid down another pound. The profit was gone now, and his gaze was a little more soberly intent as he stared northward at brief intervals.

Mr. Robinson was leaning down, peering over the nacelle when the heavy engine behind him burst into thunderous crescendo and the earth pivoted one hundred and eighty degrees in a single swoop. He jerked himelf up and looked behind, swinging his gun about. The sky was clear, yet they were moving at the R.E.'s sedate top speed. MacWyrglinchbeath was staring straight ahead and Robinson turned and saw, indicated by A-A bursts, the other R.E. plunging and darting like an ancient stiff-kneed horse. Shrapnel unfolded and bloomed above it, and at last he made out the Fokker clinging to the R.E.'s blind spot. He swung his gun forward and cleared the mechanism with a short burst.

The two R.E.'s approached at a quartering angle, the first zigzagging just above the clinging German, all three losing altitude. The first and last intimation the German had of the presence of the second R.E. was a burst from Robinson's gun. The German shot straight up, stalled, and burst into flames. Then MacWyrglinchbeath, yawing violently to dodge the zooming German, saw Robinson

fall forward over the edge of the nacelle, and at the same time a
rake of tracer smoke along the fuselage beside him. He swerved;
without pausing, the second German shot past and plumped full
upon the tail of the first R.E., and again bullets ripped about
MacWyrglinchbeath, coming from beneath now, where British infantry were firing at the German.

The three of them were not a hundred feet high when they
flashed above the secondary lines and the tilted pink faces of the
A-A battery. The German utterly disregarded MacWyrglinchbeath.
He hung upon the tail of the first R.E., which was still zigzagging
in wild and sluggish yaws, and putting his nose down a little more
and unfastening his belt, MacWyrglinchbeath brought his machine
directly above the German and a little behind him. Still the German seemed utterly unaware of his presence, and MacWyrglinchbeath put one leg over the nacelle and got from directly beneath
the engine and pushed the stick forward. The German disappeared completely beneath the nacelle and Robinson's dead body
sprawled there; immediately afterward, MacWyrglinchbeath felt
the prolonged shock. He cut the switch and climbed free of
the nacelle, onto the bottom wing, where the engine wouldn't fall
on him. "Sax shillin'," he said as the sudden earth swooped and
tilted.

III

He climbed stiffly down from his Bristol and limped across the
tarmac, toward his hut. His limp was pronounced now, a terrific
crablike gait, for in the wet, chill October days his broken hips
stiffened, even after fourteen months.

The flight was all in, the windows of the officers' mess glowed
cheerily across the dusk; he limped on, thinking of tea, a drink, a
cozy evening in his hut behind the locked door. That was against
the young devils from the mess. Children they took now. The old
pilots, mature men, were all dead or promoted to remote Wing
offices, their places filled by infants not done with public school,
without responsibility or any gift for silence. He went on and opened
the door to his hut.

He stopped, the open door in his hand, then he closed it and
entered the cubby-hole of a room. His batman had built the fire up
in the miniature stove; the room was quite warm. He laid his helmet

and goggles aside and slowly unfastened and removed his flying boots. Only then did he approach the cot and stand there, looking quietly at the object which had caught his eye when he entered. It was his walking-out tunic. It had been pressed, but that was not all. The Royal Flying Corps tabs and the chevrons had been ripped from the shoulder and sleeve, and on each shoulder strap a subaltern's pip was fixed, and upon the breast, above the D.S.M. ribbon, were wings. Beside it his scarred belt lay, polished, with a new and shining shoulder strap buckled on. He was still looking soberly at them when the door burst open upon a thunderous inrush.

"Now, old glum-face!" a young voice cried. "He'll have to buy a drink now. Hey, fellows?"

They watched him from the mess windows as he crossed the aerodrome in the dusk.

"Wait, now," they told one another. "Wait till he's had time to dress."

Another voice rose: "Gad, wouldn't you like to see the old blighter's face when he opens the door?"

"Old blighter?" a flight commander sitting with a newspaper beneath the lamp said. "He's not old. I doubt if he's thirty."

"Good fad! Thirty! Gad, I'll not live to see thirty by ten years."

"Who cares? Who wants to live forever?"

"Stow it. Stow it."

"*Ave, Caesar! Morituri—*"

"Stow it, stow it! Don't be a mawkish fool!"

"Gad, yes! What ghastly taste!"

"Thirty! Good gad!"

"He looks about a hundred, with that jolly walnut face of his."

"Let him. He's a decent sort. Shame it wasn't done sooner for him."

"Yes. Been a D.S.O. and an M.C. twice over by now."

"Got quite a decent clink record too. Deserted once, you know."

"Go on."

"'Struth. And first time he was ever off the ground he nipped off alone on a pup. No instruction; ack emma then. Sort of private solo."

"I say, do you know that yarn they tell about him about hoarding his pay against peace? Sends it all home. Done it for years."

"Well, why not?" the flight commander said. "If some of you young puppies would just—" They shouted him down. "Clear off, the lot of you!" the flight commander said above the din. "Why don't you go and fetch him up here?"

They charged from the room; the noise faded in the outer dusk. The three flight commanders sat down again, talking quietly among themselves.

"I'm glad too. Trouble is, they should have done it years ago. Ffollansbye recommended him once. Dare say some ass hipped on precedent quashed it."

"Too bad Ffollansbye couldn't have lived to see it done."

"What a putrid shame."

"Yes. But you'd not know it from Mac. Ffollansbye told him when he put him up. Old Mac never said anything at all; just went on about his business. And then, when Ffollansbye had to tell him it was no go, he just sort of grunted and thanked him and carried on as though it had never come up."

"What a ruddy shame."

"Yes. Sort of makes you glad you belong to the same squadron with a chap like that. Does his bit and be damned to you." They sat in the cozy warmth, talking quietly of MacWyrglinchbeath. Feet rushed again beyond the door; it opened and two of the deputation stood in it with their young, baffled faces.

"Well?" someone said. "Where's the victim?"

But they were beckoning the senior flight commander, in whose flight MacWyrglinchbeath was.

"Come here, skipper," they said. The senior looked at them. He did not rise.

"What's row?"

But they were merely urgent and mysterious; not until the three of them were outside did they explain. "The old fool won't take it," they said in hushed tones. "Can you believe it? Can you?"

"We'll see," the flight commander said. Beyond MacWyrglinch-beath's door the sound of voices indistinguishable and expostulant came.

The flight commander entered and thrust among them as they stood about the cot. The tunic and belt lay untouched upon it; beside it MacWyrglinchbeath sat in the lone chair.

"Clear off, now," the flight commander said, herding them to-

169

ward the door. "Off with you, the whole lot." He pushed the last one out and shut the door and returned and straddled his legs before the stove.

"What's all the hurrah, Mac?"

"Weel, skipper," MacWyrglinchbeath said slowly, "thae bairns mean weel, A doot not—" He looked up. "Ye ha' disfeegur-red ma walkin-oot tunic, and thae bairns think A sud just dress up in a' thae leather-r and brass, and gang wi' they tae thae awf-ficer-rs' mess." He mused again upon the tunic.

"Right," the flight commander said. "Shame it wasn't done a year ago. Hop into it now, and come along. Dinner's about ready."

But MacWyrglinchbeath did not stir. He put his hand out slowly and musingly, and touched the gallant sweep of the embroidered wings above the silken candy stripe.

"Thae bairns mean weel. A mak' nae doot," he said.

"Silly young pups. But we're all damned glad. You should have seen the major when it came through this morning. Like a chile on Christmas Eve. The lads could hardly wait until they could sneak your tunic out."

"Ay." MacWyrglinchbeath said. "They mean well. A mak' nae doot. But 'twill tak' thinkin'." He sat, slowly and gently touching the wings with blunt hand, pitted and grained with four years of grease. The flight commander watched quietly and with what he thought was comprehension. He moved.

"Right you are. Take the night and think it out. Better show up at breakfast, though, or those devils will be after you again."

"Ay," MacWyrglinchbeath said. " 'Twill tak' thinkin'."

Dark was fully come. The flight commander strode savagely back to the mess, swearing. He opened the door, and, still cursing, he entered. The others faced him quickly.

"Is he coming?"

The flight commander cursed steadily—Wing, Brigade, Staff, the war, Parliament.

"Do you think he will? Would any of you yourselves, after they'd let you rot for four ruddy years, and then gave you a second lieutenancy as though it were a garter? The man has pride and he's damned well right."

After his dinner, MacWyrglinchbeath went to the sergeant of the officers' mess and talked with him. Then he went to the squadron commander's orderly and talked with him. Then he returned and sat on his cot—he had yet the stub of candle, for light was furnished him now; but he was well into his second pencil—and calculated. He roughly computed the cost of a new uniform and accessories, with an allowance for laundry. Then he calculated a monthly average battle bill, added the amounts, and subtracted the total from a subaltern's pay. He compared the result with his present monthly net, sitting above the dead yet irrevocable assertion of the figures for a long time. Then he tied the ledger up in its bit of greasy cord and went to bed.

The next morning he sought the flight commander. "Thae bairns mean well, A mak' nae doot," he said, with just a trace of apology. "And the major-r. A'm gritfu' tae ya a'. But 'twina do, skipper. Ye ken that."

"Yes," the flight commander said. "I see. Yes." Again and aloud he cursed the whole fabric of the war. "Stupid fools, with their ruddy tabs and brass. No wonder they can't win a war in four years. You're right, Mac; 'course it's no go at this late day. And I'm sorry, old fellow." He wrung MacWyrglinchbeath's limp, callused hand hard.

"A'm gritfu'," MacWyrglinchbeath said. "A'm obleeged."

That was in October 1918.

By two o'clock there was not a mechanic on the place. On the tarmac the squadron commander's machine stood, the engine idling; in the cockpit the major sat. He was snoring. Up and down the aerodrome the senior flight commander and a wing commander and an artillery officer raced in the squadron's car, while a fourth man in an S.E.5 played tag with them. He appeared to be trying to set his landing gear down in the tonneau of the car; at each failure the occupants of the car howled, the artillery officer waving a bottle; each time the flight commander foiled him by maneuvering, they howled again and passed the bottle from mouth to mouth.

The mess was littered with overturned chairs and with bottles and other objects small enough to throw. Beneath the table lay two men to whom three hours of peace had been harder than that many years of fighting; above and upon and across them the unabated tumult raged. At last one climbed upon the table and stood swaying and shouting until he made himself heard:

171

"Look here! Where's old Mac?"

"Mac!" they howled. "Where's old Mac? Can't have a binge without old Mac!"

They rushed from the room. In his cockpit the major snored; the squadron car performed another last-minute skid as the S.E.'s propeller flicked the cap from the artillery officer's head. They rushed on to MacWyrglinchbeath's hut and crashed the door open. MacWyrglinchbeath was sitting on his cot, his ledger upon his knees and his pencil poised above it. He was taking stock.

With the hammer which he had concealed beneath the well coping four years ago he carefully drew the nails in the door and window frames and put them into his pocket and opened his house again. He put the hammer and the nails away in their box, and from another box he took his kilts and shook them out. The ancient folds were stiff, reluctant, and moths had been among them, and he clicked his tongue soberly.

Then he removed his tunic and breeks and putties, and donned the kilts. With the fagots he had stored there four years ago he kindled a meager fire on the hearth and cooked and ate his supper. Then he smoked his pipe, put the dottle carefully away, smothered the fire, and went to bed.

The next morning he walked three miles down the glen to the neighbor's. The neighbor, from his tilted doorway, greeted him with sparse unsurprise:

"Weel, Wully. A thocht ye'd be comin' hame. A heer-rd thae war-r was done wi'."

"Ay," MacWyrglinchbeath said, and together they stood beside the angling fence of brush and rocks and looked at the shaggy, small horse and the two cows balanced, seemingly without effort, on the forty-five-degree slope of the barn lot.

"Ye'll be takin' away thae twa beasties," the neighbor said.

"Thae three beasties, ye mean," MacWyrglinchbeath said. They did not look at each other. They looked at the animals in the lot.

"Ye'll mind ye left but twa wi' me."

They looked at the three animals. "Ay," MacWyrglinchbeath said. Presently they turned away. They entered the cottage. The neighbor lifted a hearthstone and counted down MacWyrglinchbeath's remittances to the last ha'penny. The total agreed exactly with the ledger.

"A'm gritfu'," MacWyrglinchbeath said.

"Ye'll ha' ither spol frae thae war-r, A doot not?" the neighbor said.

"Naw. 'Twas no that kind o' a war-r," MacWyrglinchbeath said.

"Ay,'" the neighbor said. "No Hieland Scots ha' ever won aught in English war-rs."

MacWyrglinchbeath returned home. The next day he walked to the market town, twelve miles away. Here he learned the current value of two-year-old cattle; he consulted a lawyer also. He was closeted with the lawyer for an hour. Then he returned home, and with pencil and paper and the inch-long butt of the candle he calculated slowly, proved his figures, and sat musing above the result. Then he snuffed the candle and went to bed.

The next morning he walked down the glen. The neighbor, in his tilted doorway, greeted him with sparse unsurprise.

"Weel, Wully. Ye ha' cam' for thae twa beasties?"

"Ay," MacWyrglinchbeath said.

Bertrand Russell

(1872–1970)

Prize awarded in 1950 "in recognition of his varied and significant writings in which he champions humanitarian ideals and freedom of thought." ★ *Russell was the personification of the British intellectual eccentric and a figure of monumental importance not only to mathematical philosophy, but to the cause of peace. Stimulated by his early exposure to Euclid, mathematics and logic remained Russell's chief preoccupations at Cambridge. His close association there with Alfred North Whitehead resulted in the publication of the seminal work* Principia Mathematica *in 1903, in which all math was demonstrated to be an internally consistent, self-contained branch of logic.*

A member of the Cambridge intellectual circle that included G. E. Moore, John Maynard Keynes, Lytton Strachey, and, later, Ludwig Wittgenstein, Russell authored works on metaphysical philosophy that were firmly in the mainstream of British empirical thought. But he later became a renegade, continuing his maverick ways well into his nineties, in his social philosophies (as in Marriage and Morals, *1929), his pacifist politics, and his educational theories (*Education, Especially in Early Childhood, *1932).*

A man of regal bearing, Russell was willingly arrested for civil disobedience when he acted as flagbearer for the Committee on Nuclear Disarmament. He was even imprisoned for six months in 1918 for his alleged libel against the U.S. Army and British government. In 1940 he was dismissed by the City College of New York for recommending "temporary marriages" for college students, a sentiment he also expressed in Marriage and Morals *(1929), which was alleged to be sexually immoral. Bertrand Russell is remembered for the rigorous logic with which he tried to bring his world into greater harmony and order.*

HAS RELIGION MADE USEFUL CONTRIBUTIONS TO CIVILIZATION?

Y OWN VIEW ON RELIGION IS that of Lucretius. I regard it as a disease born of fear and as a source of untold misery to the human race. I cannot, however, deny that it has made some contributions to civilization. It helped in early days to fix the calendar, and it caused Egyptian priests to chronicle eclipses with such care that in time they became able to predict them. These two services I am prepared to acknowledge, but I do not know of any others.

The word *religion* is used nowadays in a very loose sense. Some people, under the influence of extreme Protestantism, employ the word to denote any serious personal convictions as to morals or the nature of the universe. This use of the word is quite unhistorical. Religion is primarily a social phenomenon. Churches may owe their origin to teachers with strong individual convictions, but these teachers have seldom had much influence upon the churches that they founded, whereas churches have had enormous influence upon the communities in which they flourished. To take the case that is of most interest to members of Western civilization: the teaching of Christ, as it appears in the Gospels, has had extraordinarily little to do with the ethics of Christians. The most important thing about Christianity, from a social and historical point of view, is not Christ but the church, and if we are to judge of Christianity as a social force we must not go to the Gospels for our material. Christ taught that you should give your goods to the poor, that you should not fight, that you should not go to church, and that you should not punish adultery. Neither Catholics nor Protestants have shown any

175

strong desire to follow His teaching in any of these respects. Some of the Franciscans, it is true, attempted to teach the doctrine of apostolic poverty, but the Pope condemned them, and their doctrine was declared heretical. Or, again, consider such a text as "Judge not, that ye be not judged," and ask yourself what influence such a text has had upon the Inquisition and the Ku Klux Klan.

What is true of Christianity is equally true of Buddhism. The Buddha was amiable and enlightened; on his deathbed he laughed at his disciples for supposing that he was immortal. But the Buddhist priesthood—as it exists, for example, in Tibet—has been obscurantist, tyrannous, and cruel in the highest degree.

There is nothing accidental about this difference between a church and its founder. As soon as absolute truth is supposed to be contained in the sayings of a certain man, there is a body of experts to interpret his sayings, and these experts infallibly acquire power, since they hold the key to truth. Like any other privileged caste, they use their power for their own advantage. They are, however, in one respect worse than any other privileged caste, since it is their business to expound an unchanging truth, revealed once for all in utter perfection, so that they become necessarily opponents of all intellectual and moral progress. The church opposed Galileo and Darwin; in our own day it opposes Freud. In the days of its greatest power it went further in its opposition to the intellectual life. Pope Gregory the Great wrote to a certain bishop a letter beginning: "A report has reached us which we cannot mention without a blush, that thou expoundest grammar to certain friends." The bishop was compelled by pontifical authority to desist from this wicked labor, and Latinity did not recover until the Renaissance. It is not only intellectually but also morally that religion is pernicious. I mean by this that it teaches ethical codes which are not conducive to human happiness. When, a few years ago, a plebiscite was taken in Germany as to whether the deposed royal houses should still be allowed to enjoy their private property, the churches in Germany officially stated that it would be contrary to the teaching of Christianity to deprive them of it. The churches, as everyone knows, opposed the abolition of slavery as long as they dared, and with a few well-advertised exceptions they oppose at the present day every movement toward economic justice. The Pope has officially condemned Socialism.

CHRISTIANITY AND SEX

The worst feature of the Christian religion, however, is its attitude toward sex—an attitude so morbid and so unnatural that it can be understood only when taken in relation to the sickness of the civilized world at the time the Roman Empire was decaying. We sometimes hear talk to the effect that Christianity improved the status of women. This is one of the grossest perversions of history that it is possible to make. Women cannot enjoy a tolerable position in society where it is considered of the utmost importance that they should not infringe a very rigid moral code. Monks have always regarded Woman primarily as the temptress; they have thought of her mainly as the inspirer of impure lusts. The teaching of the church has been, and still is, that virginity is best, but that for those who find this impossible marriage is permissible. "It is better to marry than to burn," as St. Paul brutally puts it. By making marriage indissoluble, and by stamping out all knowledge of the *ars amandi,* the church did what it could to secure that the only form of sex which it permitted should involve very little pleasure and a great deal of pain. The opposition to birth control has, in fact, the same motive: if a woman has a child a year until she dies worn out, it is not to be supposed that she will derive much pleasure from her married life; therefore birth control must be discouraged.

The conception of Sin which is bound up with Christian ethics is one that does an extraordinary amount of harm, since it affords people an outlet for their sadism which they believe to be legitimate, and even noble. Take, for example, the question of the prevention of syphilis. It is known that, by precautions taken in advance, the danger of contracting this disease can be made negligible. Christians, however, object to the dissemination of knowledge of this fact, since they hold it good that sinners should be punished. They hold this so good that they are even willing that punishment should extend to the wives and children of sinners. There are in the world at the present moment many thousands of children suffering from congenital syphilis who would never have been born but for the desire of Christians to see sinners punished. I cannot understand how doctrines leading to this fiendish cruelty can be considered to have any good effects upon morals.

It is not only in regard to sexual behavior but also in regard to knowledge on sex subjects that the attitude of Christians is danger-

177

ous to human welfare. Every person who has taken the trouble to study the question in an unbiased spirit knows that the artificial ignorance on sex subjects which orthodox Christians attempt to enforce upon the young is extremely dangerous to mental and physical health, and causes in those who pick up their knowledge by the way of "improper" talk, as most children do, an attitude that sex is in itself indecent and ridiculous. I do not think there can be any defense for the view that knowledge is ever undesirable. I should not put barriers in the way of the acquisition of knowledge by anybody at any age. But in the particular case of sex knowledge there are much weightier arguments in its favor than in the case of most other knowledge. A person is much less likely to act wisely when he is ignorant than when he is instructed, and it is ridiculous to give young people a sense of sin because they have a natural curiosity about an important matter.

Every boy is interested in trains. Suppose we told him that an interest in trains is wicked; suppose we kept his eyes bandaged whenever he was in a train or on a railway station; suppose we never allowed the word "train" to be mentioned in his presence and preserved an impenetrable mystery as to the means by which he is transported from one place to another. The result would not be that he would cease to be interested in trains; on the contrary, he would become more interested than ever but would have a morbid sense of sin, because this interest had been represented to him as improper. Every boy of active intelligence could by this means be rendered in a greater or less degree neurasthenic. This is precisely what is done in the matter of sex; but, as sex is more interesting than trains, the results are worse. Almost every adult in a Christian community is more or less diseased nervously as a result of the taboo on sex knowledge when he or she was young. And the sense of sin which is thus artificially implanted is one of the causes of cruelty, timidity, and stupidity in later life. There is no rational ground of any sort or kind for keeping a child ignorant of anything that he may wish to know, whether on sex or on any other matter. And we shall never get a sane population until this fact is recognized in early education, which is impossible so long as the churches are able to control educational politics.

Leaving these comparatively detailed objections on one side, it is clear that the fundamental doctrines of Christianity demand a great deal of ethical perversion before they can be accepted. The world,

178

we are told, was created by a God who is both good and omnipotent. Before He created the world He foresaw all the pain and misery that it would contain; He is therefore responsible for all of it. It is useless to argue that the pain in the world is due to sin. In the first place, this is not true; it is not sin that causes rivers to overflow their banks or volcanoes to erupt. But even if it were true, it would make no difference. If I were going to beget a child knowing that the child was going to be a homicidal maniac, I should be responsible for his crimes. If God knew in advance the sins of which man would be guilty, He was clearly responsible for all the consequences of those sins when He decided to create man. The usual Christian argument is that the suffering in the world is a purification for sin and is therefore a good thing. This argument is, of course, only a rationalization of sadism; but in any case it is a very poor argument. I would invite any Christian to accompany me to the children's ward of a hospital, to watch the suffering that is there being endured, and then to persist in the assertion that those children are so morally abandoned as to deserve what they are suffering. In order to bring himself to say this, a man must destroy in himself all feelings of mercy and compassion. He must, in short, make himself as cruel as the God in whom he believes. No man who believes that all is for the best in this suffering world can keep his ethical values unimpaired, since he is always having to find excuses for pain and misery.

THE OBJECTIONS TO RELIGION

The objections to religion are of two sorts—intellectual and moral. The intellectual objection is that there is no reason to suppose any religion true; the moral objection is that religious precepts date from a time when men were more cruel than they are and therefore tend to perpetuate inhumanities which the moral conscience of the age would otherwise outgrow.

To take the intellectual objection first: there is a certain tendency in our practical age to consider that it does not much matter whether religious teaching is true or not, since the important question is whether it is useful. One question cannot, however, well be decided without the other. If we believe the Christian religion, our notions of what is good will be different from what they will be if we do not believe it. Therefore, to Christians, the effects of Christianity may seem good, while to unbelievers they may seem bad. Moreover, the

179

attitude that one ought to believe such and such a proposition, independently of the question whether there is evidence in its favor, is an attitude which produces hostility to evidence and causes us to close our minds to every fact that does not suit our prejudices.

A certain kind of scientific candor is a very important quality, and it is one which can hardly exist in a man who imagines that there are things which it is his duty to believe. We cannot, therefore, really decide whether religion does good without investigating the question whether religion is true. To Christians, Mohammedans, and Jews the most fundamental question involved in the truth of religion is the existence of God. In the days when religion was still triumphant the word "God" had a perfectly definite meaning; but as a result of the onslaughts of Rationalists the word has become paler and paler, until it is difficult to see what people mean when they assert that they believe in God. Let us take, for purposes of argument, Matthew Arnold's definition: "A power not ourselves that makes for righteousness." Perhaps we might make this even more vague and ask ourselves whether we have any evidence of purpose in the universe apart from the purposes of living beings on the surface of this planet.

The usual argument of religious people on this subject is roughly as follows: "I and my friends are persons of amazing intelligence and virtue. It is hardly conceivable that so much intelligence and virtue could have come about by chance. There must, therefore, be someone at least as intelligent and virtuous as we are who set the cosmic machinery in motion with a view to producing Us." I am sorry to say that I do not find this argument so impressive as it is found by those who use it. The universe is large; yet, if we are to believe Eddington, there are probably nowhere else in the universe beings as intelligent as men. If you consider the total amount of matter in the world and compare it with the amount forming the bodies of intelligent beings, you will see that the latter bears an almost infinitesimal proportion to the former. Consequently, even if it is enormously improbable that the laws of chance will produce an organism capable of intelligence out of a casual selection of atoms, it is nevertheless probable that there will be in the universe that very small number of such organisms that we do in fact find.

Then again, considered as the climax to such a vast process, we do not really seem to me sufficiently marvelous. Of course, I am aware that many divines are far more marvelous than I am, and that

180

I cannot wholly appreciate merits so far transcending my own. Nevertheless, even after making allowances under this head, I cannot but think that Omnipotence operating through all eternity might have produced something better. And then we have to reflect that even this result is only a flash in the pan. The earth will not always remain habitable; the human race will die out, and if the cosmic process is to justify itself hereafter it will have to do so elsewhere than on the surface of our planet. And even if this should occur, it must stop sooner or later. The second law of thermodynamics makes it scarcely possible to doubt that the universe is running down, and that ultimately nothing of the slightest interest will be possible anywhere. Of course, it is open to us to say that when that time comes God will wind up the machinery again; but if we do say this, we can base our assertion only upon faith, not upon one shred of scientific evidence. So far as scientific evidence goes, the universe has crawled by slow stages to a somewhat pitiful result on this earth and is going to crawl by still more pitiful stages to a condition of universal death. If this is to be taken as evidence of purpose, I can only say that the purpose is one that does not appeal to me. I see no reason, therefore, to believe in any sort of God, however vague and however attenuated. I leave on one side the old metaphysical arguments, since religious apologists themselves have thrown them over.

THE SOUL AND IMMORTALITY

The Christian emphasis on the individual soul has had a profound influence upon the ethics of Christian communities. It is a doctrine fundamentally akin to that of the Stoics, arising as theirs did in communities that could no longer cherish political hopes. The natural impulse of the vigorous person of decent character is to attempt to do good, but if he is deprived of all political power and of all opportunity to influence events, he will be deflected from his natural course and will decide that the important thing is to be good. This is what happened to the early Christians; it led to a conception of personal holiness as something quite independent of beneficent action, since holiness had to be something that could be 181 achieved by people who were impotent in action. Social virtue came therefore to be excluded from Christian ethics. To this day conventional Christians think an adulterer more wicked than a politician who takes bribes, although the latter probably does a thousand times as much harm. The medieval conception of virtue, as one sees in their pictures, was of something wishy-washy, feeble, and sentimental. The most virtuous man was the man who retired from the world; the only men of action who were regarded as saints were those who wasted the lives and substance of their subjects in fighting the Turks, like St. Louis. The church would never regard a man as a saint because he reformed the finances, or the criminal law, or the judiciary. Such mere contributions to human welfare would be regarded as of no importance. I do not believe there is a single saint in the whole calendar whose saintship is due to work of public utility. With this separation between the social and the moral person there went an increasing separation between soul and body, which has survived in Christian metaphysics and in the systems derived from Descartes. One may say, broadly speaking, that the body represents the social and public part of a man, whereas the soul represents the private part. In emphasizing the soul, Christian ethics has made itself completely individualistic. I think it is clear that the net result of all the centuries of Christianity has been to make men more egotistic, more shut up in themselves, than nature made them; for the impulses that naturally take a man outside the walls of his ego are those of sex, parenthood, and patriotism or herd instinct. Sex the church did everything it could to decry and degrade; family affection was decried by Christ himself and by the bulk of his followers; and patriotism could find no place among the subject populations of the Roman Empire. The polemic against the family in the Gospels is a matter that has not received the attention it deserves. The church treats the Mother of Christ with reverence, but He Himself showed little of this attitude. "Woman, what have I to do with thee?" (John ii, 4) is His way of speaking to her. He says also that He has come to set a man at variance against his father, the daughter against her mother, and the daughter-in-law against her mother-in-law, and that he that loveth father and mother more than Him is not worthy of Him (Matt. x, 35–37). All this means the breakup of the biological family tie for the sake of creed—an attitude which had a great deal to do with the intolerance that came into the world with the spread of Christianity.

182

This individualism culminated in the doctrine of the immortality of the individual soul, which was to enjoy hereafter endless bliss or endless woe according to circumstances. The circumstances upon which this momentous difference depended were somewhat curious. For example, if you died immediately after a priest had sprinkled water upon you while pronouncing certain words, you inherited eternal bliss; whereas, if after a long and virtuous life you happened to be struck by lightning at a moment when you were using bad language because you had broken a bootlace, you would inherit eternal torment. I do not say that the modern Protestant Christian believes this, nor even perhaps the modern Catholic Christian who has not been adequately instructed in theology; but I do say that this is the orthodox doctrine and was firmly believed until recent times. The Spaniards in Mexico and Peru used to baptize Indian infants and then immediately dash their brains out: by this means they secured that these infants went to Heaven. No orthodox Christian can find any logical reason for condemning their action, although all nowadays do so. In countless ways the doctrine of personal immortality in its Christian form has had disastrous effects upon morals, and the metaphysical separation of soul and body has had disastrous effects upon philosophy.

SOURCES OF INTOLERANCE

The intolerance that spread over the world with the advent of Christianity is one of its most curious features, due, I think, to the Jewish belief in righteousness and in the exclusive reality of the Jewish God. Why the Jews should have had these peculiarities I do not know. They seem to have developed during the captivity as a reaction against the attempt to absorb the Jews into alien populations. However that may be, the Jews, and more especially the prophets, invented emphasis upon personal righteousness and the idea that it is wicked to tolerate any religion except one. These two ideas have had an extraordinarily disastrous effect upon Occidental history. The church has made much of the persecution of Christians by the Roman State before the time of Constantine. This persecution, however, was slight and intermittent and wholly political. At all times, from the age of Constantine to the end of the seventeenth century, Christians were far more fiercely persecuted by other Christians than they ever were by the Roman emperors. Before the rise of Christianity this persecuting atittude was unknown to the ancient world except among the Jews. If you read, for example, Herodotus, you find a bland and tolerant account of the habits of the foreign nations he visited. Sometimes, it is true, a peculiarly barbarous custom may shock him, but in general he is hospitable to foreign gods and foreign customs. He is not anxious to

183

prove that people who call Zeus by some other name will suffer eternal perdition and ought to be put to death in order that their punishment may begin as soon as possible. This attitude has been reserved for Christians. It is true that the modern Christian is less robust, but that is not thanks to Christianity; it is thanks to the generations of freethinkers, who, from the Renaissance to the present day, have made Christians ashamed of many of their traditional beliefs. It is amusing to hear the modern Christian telling you how mild and rationalistic Christianity really is and ignoring the fact that all its mildness and rationalism is due to the teaching of men who in their own day were persecuted by all orthodox Christians. Nobody nowadays believes that the world was created in 4004 B.C.; but not so very long ago skepticism on this point was thought an abominable crime. My great-great-grandfather, after observing the depth of the lava on the slopes of Etna, came to the conclusion that the world must be older than the orthodox supposed and published this opinion in a book. For this offense he was cut by the county and ostracized from society. Had he been a man in humbler circumstances, his punishment would doubtless have been more severe. It is no credit to the orthodox that they do not now believe all the absurdities that were believed 150 years ago. The gradual emasculation of the Christian doctrine has been effected in spite of the most vigorous resistance, and solely as the result of the onslaughts of freethinkers.

THE DOCTRINE OF FREE WILL

The attitude of the Christians on the subject of natural law has been curiously vacillating and uncertain. There was, on the one hand, the doctrine of free will, in which the great majority of Christians believed; and this doctrine required that the acts of human beings at least should not be subject to natural law. There was, on the other hand, especially in the eighteenth and nineteenth centuries, a belief in God as the Lawgiver and in natural law as one of the main evidences of the existence of a Creator. In recent times the objection to the reign of law in the interests of free will has begun to be felt more strongly than the belief in natural law as affording evidence for a Lawgiver. Materialists used the laws of physics to show, or attempt to show, that the movements of human bodies are mechanically determined, and that consequently everything that we say and every change of position that we effect fall outside the sphere of any possible free will. If this be so, whatever may be left for our unfettered volitions is of little value. If, when a man writes a poem or commits a murder, the bodily movements involved in his act result solely from physical causes, it would seem absurd to put up a statue to him in the one case and to hang him in the other. There might in certain metaphysical systems remain a region of pure thought in which the will would be free; but, since that can be communicated to others only by means of bodily movement, the realm of freedom would be one that could never be the subject of communication and could never have any social importance.

Then, again, evolution has had a considerable influence upon those Christians who have accepted it. They have seen that it will not do to make claims on behalf of man which are totally different from those which are made on behalf of other forms of life. Therefore, in order to safeguard free will in man, they have objected to every attempt at explaining the behavior of living matter in terms of physical and chemical laws. The position of Descartes, to the effect that all lower animals are automata, no longer finds favor with liberal theologians. The doctrine of continuity makes them inclined to go a step further still and maintain that even what is called dead matter is not rigidly governed in its behavior by unalterable laws. They seem to have overlooked the fact that, if you abolish the reign of law, you also abolish the possibility of miracles, since miracles are acts of God which contravene the laws governing ordinary phenomena. I can, however, imagine the modern liberal theologian maintaining with an air of profundity that all creation is miraculous, so that he no longer needs to fasten upon certain occurrences as special evidence of Divine intervention.

Under the influence of this reaction against natural law, some Christian apologists have seized upon the latest doctrines of the atom, which tend to show that the physical laws in which we have hitherto believed have only an approximate and average truth as applied to large numbers of atoms, while the individual electron behaves pretty much as it likes. My own belief is that this is a temporary phase, and that the physicists will in time discover laws governing minute phenomena, although these laws may differ very considerably from those of traditional physics. However that may be, it is worth while to observe that the modern doctrines as to minute phenomena have no bearing upon anything that is of practical importance. Visible motions, and indeed all motions that make

185

any difference to anybody, involve such large numbers of atoms that they come well within the scope of the old laws. To write a poem or commit a murder (reverting to our previous illustration), it is necessary to move an appreciable mass of ink or lead. The electrons composing the ink may be dancing freely around their little ballroom, but the ballroom as a whole is moving according to the old laws of physics, and this alone is what concerns the poet and his publisher. The modern doctrines, therefore, have no appreciable bearing upon any of those problems of human interest with which the theologian is concerned.

The free-will question consequently remains just where it was. Whatever may be thought about it as a matter of ultimate metaphysics, it is quite clear that nobody believes in it in practice. Everyone has always believed that it is possible to train character; everyone has always known that alcohol or opium will have a certain effect on behavior. The apostle of free will maintains that a man can by will power avoid getting drunk, but he does not maintain that when drunk a man can say "British Constitution" as clearly as if he were sober. And everybody who has ever had to do with children knows that a suitable diet does more to make them virtuous than the most eloquent preaching in the world. The one effect that the free-will doctrine has in practice is to prevent people from following out such common-sense knowledge to its rational conclusion. When a man acts in ways that annoy us we wish to think him wicked, and we refuse to face the fact that his annoying behavior is the result of antecedent causes which, if you follow them long enough, will take you beyond the moment of his birth and therefore to events for which he cannot be held responsible by any stretch of imagination.

No man treats a motorcar as foolishly as he treats another human being. When the car will not go, he does not attribute its annoying behavior to sin; he does not say, "You are a wicked motorcar, and I shall not give you any more petrol until you go." He attempts to find out what is wrong and to set it right. An analogous way of treating human beings is, however, considered to be contrary to the truths of our holy religion. And this applies even in the treatment of little children. Many children have bad habits which are perpetuated by punishment but will probably pass away of themselves if left unnoticed. Nevertheless, nurses, with very few exceptions, consider it right to inflict punishment, although by so doing they run the risk of causing insanity. When insanity has been caused it is cited in courts of law as proof of the harmfulness of the habit, not of the punishment. (I am alluding to a recent prosecution for obscenity in the state of New York.)

Reforms in education have come very largely through the study of the insane and feeble-minded, because they have not been held morally responsible for their failures and have therefore been treated more scientifically than normal children. Until very recently it was held that, if a boy could not learn his lessons, the proper cure was caning or flogging. This view is nearly extinct in the treatment of children, but it survives in the criminal law. It is evident that a man with a propensity to crime must be stopped, but so must a man who has hydrophobia and wants to bite people, although nobody considers him morally responsible. A man who is suffering from plague has to be imprisoned until he is cured, although nobody thinks him wicked. The same thing should be done with a man who suffers from a propensity to commit forgery; but there should be no more idea of guilt in the one case than in the other. And this is only common sense, though it is a form of common sense to which Christian ethics and metaphysics are opposed.

To judge of the moral influence of any institution upon a community, we have to consider the kind of impulse which is embodied in the institution and the degree to which the institution increases the efficacy of the impulse in that community. Sometimes the impulse concerned is quite obvious, sometimes it is more hidden. An Alpine club, for example, obviously embodies the impulse to adventure, and a learned society embodies the impulse toward knowledge. The family as an institution embodies jealousy and parental feeling; a football club or a political party embodies the impulse toward competitive play; but the two greatest social institutions—namely, the church and the state—are more complex in their psychological motivation. The primary purpose of the state is clearly security against both internal criminals and external enemies. It is rooted in the tendency of children to huddle together when they are frightened and to look for a grown-up person who will give them a sense of security. The church has more complex origins. Undoubtedly the most important source of religion is fear; this can be seen in the present day, since anything that causes alarm is apt to turn people's thoughts to God. Battle, pestilence, and shipwreck all tend to make people religious. Religion has, however, other appeals besides that of terror; it appeals especially to our human self-esteem.

187

If Christianity is true, mankind are not such pitiful worms as they seem to be; they are of interest to the Creator of the universe, who takes the trouble to be pleased with them when they behave well and displeased when they behave badly. This is a great compliment. We should not think of studying an ants' nest to find out which of the ants performed their formicular duty, and we should certainly not think of picking out those individual ants who were remiss and putting them into a bonfire. If God does this for us, it is a compliment to our importance; and it is even a pleasanter compliment if he awards to the good among us everlasting happiness in heaven. Then there is the comparatively modern idea that cosmic evolution is all designed to bring about the sort of results which we call good— that is to say, the sort of results that give us pleasure. Here again it is flattering to suppose that the universe is controlled by a Being who shares our tastes and prejudices.

THE IDEA OF RIGHTEOUSNESS

The third psychological impulse which is embodied in religion is that which has led to the conception of righteousness. I am aware that many freethinkers treat this conception with great respect and hold that it should be preserved in spite of the decay of dogmatic religion. I cannot agree with them on this point. The psychological analysis of the idea of righteousness seems to me to show that it is rooted in undesirable passions and ought not to be strengthened by the *imprimatur* of reason. Righteousness and unrighteousness must be taken together; it is impossible to stress the one without stressing the other also. Now, what is "unrighteousness" in practice? It is in practice behavior of a kind disliked by the herd. By calling it unrighteousness, and by arranging an elaborate system of ethics around this conception, the herd justifies itself in wreaking punishment upon the objects of its own dislike, while at the same time, since the herd is righteous by definition, it enhances its own self-esteem at the very moment when it lets loose its impulse to cruelty. This is the psychology of lynching, and of the other ways in which criminals are punished. The essence of the conception of righteousness, therefore, is to afford an outlet for sadism by cloaking cruelty as justice.

But, it will be said, the account you have been giving of righteousness is wholly inapplicable to the Hebrew prophets, who, after all, on your own showing, invented the idea. There is truth in this:

righteousness in the mouths of the Hebrew prophets meant what was approved by them and Yahweh. One finds the same attitude expressed in the Acts of the Apostles, where the Apostles began a pronouncement with the words "For it seemed good to the Holy Ghost, and to us" (Acts xv, 28). This kind of individual certainty as to God's tastes and opinions cannot, however, be made the basis of any institution. That has always been the difficulty with which Protestantism has had to contend: a new prophet could maintain that his revelation was more authentic than those of his predecessors, and there was nothing in the general outlook of Protestantism to show that this claim was invalid. Consequently Protestantism split into innumerable sects, which weakened one another; and there is reason to suppose that a hundred years hence Catholicism will be the only effective representative of the Christian faith. In the Catholic Church inspiration such as the prophets enjoyed has its place; but it is recognized that phenomena which look rather like genuine divine inspiration may be inspired by the Devil, and it is the business of the church to discriminate, just as it is the business of an art connoisseur to know a genuine Leonardo from a forgery. In this way revelation becomes institutionalized at the same time. Righteousness is what the church approves, and unrighteousness is what it disapproves. Thus the effective part of the conception of righteousness is a justification of herd antipathy.

It would seem, therefore, that the three human impulses embodied in religion are fear, conceit, and hatred. The purpose of religion, one may say, is to give an air of respectability to these passions, provided they run in certain channels. It is because these passions make, on the whole, for human misery that religion is a force for evil, since it permits men to indulge these passions without restraint, where but for its sanction they might, at least to a certain degree, control them.

I can imagine at this point an objection, not likely to be urged perhaps by most orthodox believers but nevertheless worthy to be examined. Hatred and fear, it may be said, are essential human characteristics; mankind always has felt them and always will. The best that you can do with them, I may be told, is to direct them into certain channels in which they are less harmful than they would be in certain other channels. A Christian theologian might say that their treatment by the church is analogous to its treatment of the sex impulse, which it deplores. It attempts to render concupiscence

189

innocuous by confining it within the bounds of matrimony. So, it may be said, if mankind must inevitably feel hatred, it is better to direct this hatred against those who are really harmful, and this is precisely what the church does by its conception of righteousness.

To this contention there are two replies—one comparatively superficial; the other going to the root of the matter. The superficial reply is that the church's conception of righteousness is not the best possible; the fundamental reply is that hatred and fear can, with our present psychological knowlege and our present industrial technique, be eliminated altogether from human life.

To take the first point first. The church's conception of righteousness is socially undesirable in various ways—first and foremost in its depreciation of intelligence and science. This defect is inherited from the Gospels. Christ tells us to become as little children, but little children cannot understand the differential calculus, or the principles of currency, or the modern methods of combating disease. To acquire such knowledge is no part of our duty, according to the church. The church no longer contends that knowledge is in itself sinful, though it did so in its palmy days; but the acquisition of knowledge, even though not sinful, is dangerous, since it may lead to pride of intellect, and hence to a questioning of the Christian dogma. Take, for example, two men, one of whom has stamped out yellow fever throughout some large region in the tropics but has in the course of his labors had occasional relations with women to whom he was not married; while the other has been lazy and shiftless, begetting a child a year until his wife died of exhaustion and taking so little care of his children that half of them died from preventable causes, but never indulging in illicit sexual intercourse. Every good Christian must maintain that the second of these men is more virtuous than the first. Such an attitude is, of course, superstitious and totally contrary to reason. Yet something of this absurdity is inevitable so long as avoidance of sin is thought more important than positive merit, and so long as the importance of knowledge as a help to a useful life is not recognized.

190

The second and more fundamental objection to the utilization of fear and hatred in the way practiced by the church is that these emotions can now be almost wholly eliminated from human nature by educational, economic, and political reforms. The educational reforms must be the basis, since men who feel hate and fear will also admire these emotions and wish to perpetuate them, although this admiration and wish will probably be unconscious, as it is in the ordinary Christian. An education designed to eliminate fear is by no means difficult to create. It is only necessary to treat a child with kindness, to put him in an environment where initiative is possible without disastrous results, and to save him from contact with adults who have irrational terrors, whether of the dark, of mice, or of social revolution. A child must also not be subject to severe punishment, or to threats, or to grave and excessive reproof. To save a child from hatred is a somewhat more elaborate business. Situations arousing jealousy must be very carefully avoided by means of scrupulous and exact justice as between different children. A child must feel himself the object of warm affection on the part of some at least of the adults with whom he has to do, and he must not be thwarted in his natural activities and curiosities except when danger to life or health is concerned. In particular, there must be no taboo on sex knowledge, or on conversation about matters which conventional people consider improper. If these simple precepts are observed from the start, the child will be fearless and friendly.

On entering adult life, however, a young person so educated will find himself or herself plunged into a world full of injustice, full of cruelty, full of preventable misery. The injustice, the cruelty, and the misery that exist in the modern world are an inheritance from the past, and their ultimate source is economic, since life-and-death competition for the means of subsistence was in former days inevitable. It is not inevitable in our age. With our present industrial technique we can, if we choose, provide a tolerable subsistence for everybody. We could also secure that the world's population should be stationary if we were not prevented by the political influence of churches which prefer war, pestilence, and famine to contraception. The knowledge exists by which universal happiness can be secured; the chief obstacle to its utilization for that purpose is the teaching of religion. Religion prevents our children from having a rational education; religion prevents us from removing the fundamental causes of war; religion prevents us from teaching the ethic of scientific cooperation in place of the old fierce doctrines of sin and punishment. It is possible that mankind is on the threshold of a golden age; but, if so, it will be necessary first to slay the dragon that guards the door, and this dragon is religion.

191

Pär Lagerkvist

(1891–1974)

Prize awarded 1951 "for the artistic vigor and true independence of mind with which he endeavors . . . to find answers to the eternal questions confronting mankind." ★ *Pär Lagerkvist, poet, playwright, essayist, and novelist, was preoccupied with the existential problems of faith and the meaning of life in an indifferent cosmos. His forceful and original narratives brought a renown to this Swedish writer rivaled only by Strindberg, with whom he is often compared.*

In his early poems (Anguish, *1916*), *plays, and short stories* (Chaos, *1919*), *Lagerkvist struggled with modern dilemmas of good and evil. By 1925, however, when he wrote his personal novel of childhood,* Guest of Reality, *he turned to expressionist, surrealist forms appropriate to his theme: the emptiness of the universe. Like Camus, Lagerkvist found (in* The Triumph Over Life, *1927) salvation in bringing order out of chaos. His political position crystallized in opposition to the totalitarianism of the thirties, as reflected in the plays* The Hangman *(1933) and* Man Without a Soul *(1936). The Clenched Fist (1934), a manifesto, introduced a humanist theme that Lagerkvist carried into his wartime and postwar writings (such as* The Dwarf, *1944). Spirituality was increasingly emphasized in his later works* (Barabbas, *1951;* The Sibyl, *1956;* The Death of Ahasuerus, *1960;* Pilgrim at Sea, *1964;* Marianne, *1967), and the attendant optimism enabled Lagerkvist's vividly drawn characters to transcend indifference and despair.*

THE MYTH OF MANKIND

ONCE UPON A TIME THERE WAS A WORLD. Two people came to it one morning, but not to stay there for long, only for a short visit. They had many other worlds as well; this one seemed to them more insignificant and poorer than the others. It was beautiful here with the trees and the large drifting clouds, it was beautiful with the mountains, with the woods and glades, and with the wind which came, invisible, as it began to grow dark and touched everything so mysteriously; but it was nothing compared with the worlds they owned far away. That is why they wanted to stay only for a little while. But they did want to be there for a time, for they loved one another, and it was as if their love had nowhere been so wondrous as here. It seemed as though love was not something to be taken for granted in this world, something which completely filled everything, but that it was received as a guest of whom was expected the greatest things that could possibly happen here. It was, in fact, as if all that was clearest and brightest in their being became as secret here, as obscure, veiled, as if it were being kept hidden from them. They were strangers here, alone, left to the mercy of unknown powers. And the love that united them was a miracle, something that could be annihilated, that could wither away and die. That is why they wanted to stay only for a little while.

In this world it was not always day. After the light, dusk fell over everything; it was obliterated, was no longer there. They lay in the darkness, listening. They heard the wind soughing heavily in the trees. They crept together beneath them. "Why do we live here?"

The man made a house for them, only of moss and stones because they were soon to move on again. The woman spread fragrant grass on the trodden-down floor and waited for him when evening came. They loved one another more deeply than they ever seemed to have done before and carried out the tasks of life here laid upon them.

One day as the man was roaming about in the woods he got such a longing for her whom he held dear above all else that he knelt down and kissed the earth because she had rested on it. But the woman began to love the clouds and the great trees, because the man returned home beneath them, and she loved the hour of twilight because it was then that he came. It was an unfamiliar world; it was not like those they owned far away.

And the woman bore a son. The holly trees outside the house sang for him; he looked wonderingly about him and then fell asleep to the sound, unafraid. But the man came home each evening with bleeding animals; he was tired and lay down heavily. They talked to each other happily in the darkness, they would soon be making a move now.

How strange it was, this world; after the summer came autumn and a cold winter, after the winter the most delightful spring. In this way they could see how time passed, everything here was changeable. The woman again bore a son, and after a few years yet another. The children grew up, they began to do things for themselves, running about and playing and finding something new every day. They just played with the whole strange world, with everything in it. What was meant in all seriousness they turned into something meant only for themselves. The man's hands grew rough from working with the soil and from his labors in the woods. The woman's features began to harden, too, and she walked more slowly, but her voice was gentle and singing as before.

One evening when she had settled down in the twilight, tired after a long day, with the children gathered around her, she said to them; "Now we shall soon be leaving here, now we shall soon be going away to the other worlds where we have our home."

194   The children looked at her in wonder. "What do you mean, Mother? Are there other worlds than this?"

Then she and the man looked at each other, a stab went through them, a smarting pain.

She answered in a lower voice, "Of course there are other worlds than this." And she began to tell them, tell them about these worlds that were so different from the one they lived in now; where everything was so much bigger and more wonderful than here, so light and happy, where there was not this darkness, where no trees soughed as they did here, where no struggle weighed down as this one did. The children closed around her, listening, now and then looking wonderingly over at the father as if to ask whether it was true. He nodded his head, lost in thought. The smallest sat right against the mother's feet; he was pale, his eyes gleamed with a strange light. But the eldest son, who was twelve years old, sat farther away, looking down at the ground; at last he got up and went out into the darkness.

The mother went on, they listened and listened; it was as if she were looking away into the distance, her gaze was far off; sometimes she fell silent, just as if she could not see, could not remember anything more, as if she had forgotten; then she spoke again, in a voice even more remote than before. The fire flickered on the sooty hearth, lighting up their faces, casting its glow around the heated room; the father held his hand before his face, the children listened with shining eyes. They sat like this, motionless, until it was almost midnight. Then the door opened, letting in the cold air from outside, and the eldest son came in. He looked around him. In his hand he had a large black bird with a gray belly. Blood ran from its breast; it was the first he had brought down himself. He threw it down on the ground beside the fire. The warm blood steamed. Without a word he went farthest into the semidarkness and lay down to sleep.

There was not a sound. The mother stopped speaking. They looked wonderingly at the bleeding bird, which was staining the ground red around its breast. They got up in silence and all went to rest.

After that evening they didn't speak together very much for a time, each going his own way. It was summer, the bumblebees hummed, the grass round about was lush, the glades were green after the spring rain that had fallen, the air was so clear. One day the smallest boy went up to the mother as she sat outside the house at noonday. He was pale and quiet, and asked her to tell him about another world. The mother looked up in surprise. "I can't talk to you about this now, dear. The sun is high in the heavens; why aren't you playing with all that is yours?" He left her without a word and cried, unknown to anyone.

He never asked again. He just grew paler and paler, his eyes burned with a strange luster, one morning he had to lie where he was, couldn't raise himself up. He lay motionless day after day, hardly speaking, just looking into the far distance with his dilated eyes. They asked him if he was in pain. They said that he would soon be able to go out into the sun again, there were other flowers now, bigger than before; he didn't answer, seemed not to see them. The mother watched over him and cried; she asked if he would like her to tell him all the wonderful things she knew, but he smiled and just lay still as before.

And one evening he closed his eyes and was dead. They all gathered around him. The mother laid his small hands across his breast. Later, when the twilight came, they sat together in the darkened room, speaking about him in whispers. Now he had left this world. Now he was no longer here. Now he had gone to another world, better and happier than this one. But they said it despondently, sighing heavily. Shyly they went to rest on the far side from the dead boy; he lay lonely and cold.

In the morning they buried him in the earth; he was to lie there. The country smelled sweet, the sun shone everywhere, soft and warm. The mother said, "He is not here." By the grave was a rose tree that was now in bloom.

And the years passed. The mother often sat out by the grave of an evening, staring away over the mountains that shut everything in. The father stood there for a while if he was passing. But the children kept away, for it was not like elsewhere on earth.

The two sons were growing up now. Soon they were fullgrown and tall and had a new and more spirited air about them than before; but the man and the woman faded away. They became gray and bent; something venerable and tranquil came over them. The father still tried to go hunting with his sons; when the quarry was dangerous it was no longer he but they who fought with it. But the aged mother sat outside the house, she groped with her hand when they came toward her in the evening, her eyes were so tired that she could only see at noonday when the sun was at its height; otherwise it was too dark. She would ask them, "Why is it so dark here?" One autumn she withdrew into the house, lay listening to the wind as to memories from long, long ago. The man sat and held her hand in his, they talked between themselves, it was as though they were again alone here. She wasted away, but her face seemed to become transfigured by light. And one evening she said to them all in her quavering voice, "Now I want to leave this world where I have lived, now I shall go home." And she went away. They buried her in the earth; she was to lie there.

Winter and cold came again, the old man stayed by the hearth, was too feeble to go out. The sons came home with animals, which they would cut up together. With shaking hand he turned the spit, watching how the fire grew redder as the meat roasted in it. But when the spring came he went into the meadows, gazing at the trees and the grass that were growing green all around him. He stopped by the trees he recognized, he stopped everywhere, recognizing everything. He stopped by the flowers he had picked for her whom he loved the first morning they came here. He stopped by his hunting implements, which were bloodstained because one of the sons had used them. Then he went into the house and lay down, and he said to the sons standing by his deathbed, "Now I must leave this world where I have lived my life, now I must go away. Our home is not here." And he clasped them by the hand until he was dead. They buried him in the earth, as he had bidden them; he wanted to lie there.

Now the old ones were dead. The young ones felt such a strange relief, liberation, as if something had been severed. It was as if life had been freed from something that did not belong to it. They rose early on the morning of the following day. What a scent from the trees that had just come into leaf and from the rain that had fallen in the night! Together they went out, side by side, both tall and newly young; it was joy for the earth to bear them. Now human life was beginning, they went out to take possession of this world.

....

Ernest Hemingway

(1899–1961)

Prize awarded 1954 "for his mastery of the art of narrative . . . and for the influence he exerted on contemporary style." ★ *Hemingway's early training in journalism left its mark in his highly stylized narration, which is marked by lucid, uninterrupted development, clear depictions of action, and staccato rhythms. Preoccupied with "grace under pressure," Hemingway was himself no stranger to adventure or adversity. His writings often reflect personal experiences in World War I and the Spanish Civil War, and with bullfighting and wild-game hunting. His novels typically call for the protagonist to demonstrate extreme determination and fortitude in response to conflict.*

He drew the material for his earlier collections, especially the Nick Adams stories, from his childhood and post–World War I residence in the American Midwest. His rich feeling for locale is remarkable given his verbal leanness and the absence of lyrical, descriptive passages. While a foreign correspondent in Paris from 1920 to 1926, Hemingway chronicled the "lost" generation in his first novel, The Sun Also Rises, *which uses tight narrative evolution to render a vivid historical and geographical flavor. We see the "Hemingway style" not only in his short-story collections* (Three Short Stories and Ten Poems, *1923;* In Our Time, *1924;* Men Without Women, *1927; and* Winner Take Nothing, *1933), but also in his novels* A Farewell to Arms *(1929) and* For Whom the Bell Tolls *(1940). His experimental nonfiction panegyric on the bullfight* (Death in the Afternoon, *1932) brings the peacetime energies of Spain to life. The masculine theme of man meeting challenges and struggling alone continues into his late work,* The Old Man and the Sea, *(1952). In his time, Hemingway's tautly controlled and forceful storytelling style was enormously influential in freeing contemporary writers from the verbose conventions of Edwardian prose.*

INDIAN CAMP

AT THE LAKE SHORE THERE WAS AN-other rowboat drawn up. The two Indians stood waiting.

Nick and his father got in the stern of the boat and the Indians shoved it off and one of them got in to row. Uncle George sat in the stern of the camp rowboat. The young Indian shoved the camp boat off and got in to row Uncle George.

The two boats started off in the dark. Nick heard the oarlocks of the other boat quite a way ahead of them in the mist. The Indians rowed with quick choppy strokes. Nick lay back with his father's arm around him. It was cold on the water. The Indian who was rowing them was working very hard, but the other boat moved farther ahead in the mist all the time.

"Where are we going, Dad?" Nicked asked.

"Over to the Indian camp. There is an Indian lady very sick."

"Oh," said Nick.

Across the bay they found the other boat beached. Uncle George was smoking a cigar in the dark. The young Indian pulled the boat way up the beach. Uncle George gave both the Indians cigars.

They walked up from the beach through a meadow that was soaking wet with dew, following the young Indian who carried a lantern. Then they went into the woods and followed a trail that led to the logging road that ran back into the hills. It was much lighter on the logging road as the timber was cut away on both sides. The young Indian stopped and blew out his lantern and they all walked on along the road.

They came around a bend and a dog came out barking. Ahead

were the lights of the shanties where the Indian barkpeelers lived. More dogs rushed out at them. The two Indians sent them back to the shanties. In the shanty nearest the road there was a light in the window. An old woman stood in the doorway holding a lamp.

Inside on a wooden bunk lay a young Indian woman. She had been trying to have her baby for two days. All the old women in the camp had been helping her. The men had moved off up the road to sit in the dark and smoke out of range of the noise she made. She screamed just as Nick and the two Indians followed his father and Uncle George into the shanty. She lay in the lower bunk, very big under a quilt. Her head was turned to one side. In the upper bunk was her husband. He had cut his foot very badly with an ax three days before. He was smoking a pipe. The room smelled very bad.

Nick's father ordered some water to be put on the stove, and while it was heating he spoke to Nick.

"This lady is going to have a baby, Nick," he said.

"I know," said Nick.

"You don't know," said his father. "Listen to me. What she is going through is called being in labor. The baby wants to be born and she wants it to be born. All her muscles are trying to get the baby born. That is what is happening when she screams."

"I see," Nick said.

Just then the woman cried out.

"Oh, Daddy, can't you give her something to make her stop screaming?" asked Nick.

"No. I haven't any anesthetic," his father said. "But her screams are not important. I don't hear them because they are not important."

The husband in the upper bunk rolled over against the wall.

The woman in the kitchen motioned to the doctor that the water was hot. Nick's father went into the kitchen and poured about half of the water out of the big kettle into a basin. Into the water left in the kettle he put several things he unwrapped from a handkerchief.

"Those must boil," he said, and began to scrub his hands in the basin of hot water with a cake of soap he had brought from the camp. Nick watched his father's hands scrubbing each other with the soap. While his father washed his hands very carefully and thoroughly, he talked.

"You see, Nick, babies are supposed to be born head first but sometimes they're not. When they're not they make a lot of trouble for everybody. Maybe I'll have to operate on this lady. We'll know in a little while."

When he was satisfied with his hands he went in and went to work.

"Pull back that quilt, will you, George?" he said. "I'd rather not touch it."

Later when he started to operate, Uncle George and three Indian men held the woman still. She bit Uncle George on the arm and Uncle George said, "Damn squaw bitch!" and the young Indian who had rowed Uncle George over laughed at him. Nick held the basin for his father. It all took a long time.

His father picked the baby up and slapped it to make it breathe and handed it to the old woman.

"See, it's a boy, Nick," he said. "How do you like being an intern?"

Nick said, "All right." He was looking away so as not to see what his father was doing.

"There. That gets it," said his father, and put something into the basin.

Nick didn't look at it.

"Now," his father said, "there's some stitches to put in. You can watch this or not, Nick, just as you like. I'm going to sew up the incision I made."

Nick did not watch. His curiosity had been gone for a long time.

His father finished and stood up. Uncle George and the three Indian men stood up. Nick put the basin out in the kitchen.

Uncle George looked at his arm. The young Indian smiled reminiscently.

"I'll put some peroxide on that, George," the doctor said.

He bent over the Indian woman. She was quiet now and her eyes were closed. She looked very pale. She did not know what had become of the baby or anything.

"I'll be back in the morning," the doctor said, standing up. "The nurse should be here from St. Ignace by noon and she'll bring everything we need."

He was feeling exalted and talkative as football players are in the dressing room after a game.

"That's one for the medical journal, George," he said. "Doing a

201

Caesarian with a jackknife and sewing it up with nine-foot, tapered gut leaders."

Uncle George was standing against the wall, looking at his arm. "Oh, you're a great man, all right," he said.

"Ought to have a look at the proud father. They're usually the worst sufferers in these little affairs," the doctor said. "I must say he took it all pretty quietly."

He pulled back the blanket from the Indian's head. His hand came away wet. He mounted on the edge of the lower bunk with the lamp in one hand and looked in. The Indian lay with his face toward the wall. His throat had been cut from ear to ear. The blood had flowed down into a pool where his body sagged the bunk. His head rested on his left arm. The open razor lay, edge up, in the blankets.

"Take Nick out of the shanty, George," the doctor said.

There was no need of that. Nick, standing in the door of the kitchen, had a good view of the upper bunk when his father, the lamp in one hand, tipped the Indian's head back.

It was just beginning to be daylight when they walked along the logging road back toward the lake.

"I'm terribly sorry I brought you along, Nickie," said his father, all his postoperative exhilaration gone. "It was an awful mess to put you through."

"Do ladies always have such a hard time having babies?" Nick asked.

"No, that was very, very exceptional."

"Why did he kill himself, Daddy?"

"I don't know, Nick. He couldn't stand things, I guess."

"Do many men kill themselves, Daddy?"

"Not very many, Nick."

"Do many women?"

"Hardly ever."

"Don't they ever?"

"Oh, yes. They do sometimes."

"Daddy?"

"Yes."

"Where did Uncle George go?"

"He'll turn up all right."

"Is dying hard, Daddy?"

"No, I think it's pretty easy, Nick. It all depends."

They were seated in the boat, Nick in the stern, his father rowing. The sun was coming up over the hills. A bass jumped, making a circle in the water. Nick trailed his hand in the water. It felt warm in the sharp chill of the morning.

In the early morning on the lake sitting in the stern of the boat with his father rowing, he felt quite sure that he would never die.

......

Albert Camus

(1913–1960)

Prize awarded in 1957 "for his important literary production, which with clear-sighted earnestness illuminates the problems of the human conscience in our times." ★ *Born and educated in Algiers, Camus went to Paris as a journalist in 1939. He was a brilliant student of philosophy but eschewed the academic life-style; instead, he advocated boldness, decisiveness, and the necessity of personal revolt.*

Throughout his career, Camus was more interested in philosophical issues than in lyricism or psychological analysis. His first novel, The Stranger *(1942), is written in a deliberately unembellished manner that accentuates the absurdity of existence. Camus left occupied France for Algeria to write* Myth of Sysiphus *(1942), which demonstrated the futility of suicide. He later returned to France to fight with the Resistance and edit* Combat, *the underground newspaper. During the war, he wrote his first two plays,* Cross Purpose *(1944) and* Caligula *(1944), which featured a hero who, like the Stranger, is struck by the arbitrariness of existence. Between his next two plays (*State of Siege, 1948, *and* The Just Assassins, 1950) *came a second novel,* The Plague *(1948), which represents the German occupation and expounds the moral obligation to oppose evil and alleviate suffering. In a long essay entitled* The Rebel *(1951), Camus distinguished revolt from rebellion and found meaning in resisting absurdity in itself, a position that offended goal-oriented Marxists like Sartre (with whom Camus had a running conflict). His last major book,* The Fall *(1956), was written in the form of a monologue four years before his untimely death in a car accident.*

THE RENEGADE

WHAT A JUMBLE! WHAT A JUMBLE! I must tidy up my mind. Since they cut out my tongue, another tongue, it seems, has been constantly wagging somewhere in my skull, something has been talking, or someone, that suddenly falls silent, and then it all begins again—oh, I hear too many things I never utter, what a jumble, and if I open my mouth, it's like pebbles rattling together. Order and method, the tongue says, and then goes on talking of other matters simultaneously—yes, I always longed for order. At least one thing is certain, I am waiting for the missionary who is to come and take my place. Here I am on the trail, an hour away from Taghâsa, hidden in a pile of rocks, sitting on my old rifle. Day is breaking over the desert, it's still very cold, soon it will be too hot, this country drives men mad, and I've been here I don't know how many years. . . . No, just a little longer. The missionary is to come this morning, or this evening. I've heard he'll come with a guide, perhaps they'll have but one camel between them. I'll wait, I am waiting, it's only the cold making me shiver. Just be patient a little longer, lousy slave!

But I have been patient for so long. When I was home on that high plateau of the Massif Central, my coarse father, my boorish mother, the wine, the pork soup every day, the wine above all, sour and cold, and the long winter, the frigid wind, the snowdrifts, the revolting bracken—oh, I wanted to get away, leave them all at once and begin to live at last, in the sunlight, with fresh water. I believed the priest, he spoke to me of the seminary, he tutored me daily, he had plenty of time in that Protestant region where he used to hug the walls as he crossed the village. He told me of the future and of the sun, Catholicism is the sun, he used to say, and he would get me to read, he beat Latin into my hard head ("The kid's bright but he's pigheaded"). My head was so hard that, despite all my falls, it has never once bled in my life: "Bullheaded," my pig of a father used to say. At the seminary they were proud as punch, a recruit from the Protestant region was a victory, they greeted me like the sun at Austerlitz. The sun was pale and feeble, to be sure, because of the alcohol, they have drunk sour wine and the children's teeth are set on edge, *gra gra,* one really ought to kill one's father, but after all there's no danger that *he*'ll hurl himself into missionary work since he's now long dead, the tart wine eventually cut through his stomach, so there's nothing left but to kill the missionary.

I have something to settle with him and with his teachers, with my teachers who deceived me, with the whole of lousy Europe, everybody deceived me. Missionary work, that's all they could say, go out to the savages and tell them: "Here is my Lord, just look at him, he never strikes or kills, he issues his orders in a low voice, he turns the other cheek, he's the greatest of masters, choose him, just see how much better he's made me, offend me and you will see." Yes, I believed, *gra gra,* and I felt better, I had put on weight, I was almost handsome, I wanted to be offended. When we would walk out in tight black rows, in summer, under Grenoble's hot sun, and would meet girls in cotton dresses, *I* didn't look away, I despised them, I waited for them to offend me, and sometimes they would laugh. At such times I would think, Let them strike me and spit in my face, but their laughter, to tell the truth, came to the same thing, bristling with teeth and quips that tore me to shreds, the offense and the suffering were sweet to me! My confessor couldn't understand when I used to heap accusations on myself: "No, no, there's good in you!" Good! There was nothing but sour wine in me, and that was all for the best, how can a man become better if he's not bad, I had grasped that in everything they taught me. That's the only thing I did grasp, a single idea, and, pigheaded bright boy, I carried it to its logical conclusion, I went out of my way for punishments, I groused at the normal, in short I too wanted to be an example in order to be noticed and so that after noticing me people would give credit to what had made me better, through me praise my Lord.

Fierce sun! It's rising, the desert is changing, it has lost its mountain-cyclamen color, O my mountains, and the snow, the soft, enveloping snow, no, it's a rather grayish yellow, the ugly moment before the great resplendence. Nothing, still nothing from here to the horizon over yonder where the plateau disappears in a circle of still soft colors. Behind me, the trail climbs to the dune hiding Taghâsa, whose iron name has been beating in my head for so many years. The first to mention it to me was the half-blind old priest who had retired to our monastery, but why do I say the first, he was the only one, and it wasn't the city of salt, the white walls under the blinding sun, that struck me in his account, but the cruelty of the savage inhabitants and the town closed to all outsiders, only one of those who had tried to get in, one alone, to his knowledge, had lived to relate what he had seen. They had whipped him and driven him out into the desert after having put salt on his wounds and in his mouth, he had met nomads who for once were compassionate, a stroke of luck, and since then I had been dreaming about his tale, about the fire of the salt and the sky, about the House of the Fetish and his slaves, could anything more barbarous, more exciting, be imagined, yes, that was my mission, and I had to go and reveal to them my Lord.

They all expatiated on the subject at the seminary to discourage me, pointing out the necessity of waiting, that it was not missionary country, that I wasn't ready yet, I had to prepare myself specially, know who I was, and even then I had to go through tests, then they would see! But go on waiting, ah, no!—yes, if they insisted, for the special preparation and the tryout, because they took place at Algiers and brought me closer, but for all the rest I shook my pighead and repeated the same thing, to get among the most barbarous and live as they did, to show them at home, and even in the House of the Fetish, through example, that my Lord's truth would prevail. They would offend me, of course, but I was not afraid of offenses, they were essential to the demonstration, and as a result of the way I endured them I'd get the upper hand of those savages like a strong sun. Strong, yes, that was the word I constantly had on the tip of my tongue, I dreamed of absolute power, the kind that makes people kneel down, that forces the adversary to capitulate, converts him, in short, and the blinder, the crueler, he is, the more he's sure of himself, mired in his own conviction, the more his consent establishes the royalty of whoever brought about his collapse. Converting good folk who had strayed somewhat was the shabby ideal of our priests, I despised them for daring so little when they could do so

207

much, they lacked faith and I had it, I wanted to be acknowledged by the torturers themselves, to fling them on their knees and make them say: "O Lord, here is thy victory," to rule, in short, by the sheer force of words over an army of the wicked. Oh, I was sure of reasoning logically on that subject, never quite sure of myself otherwise, but once I get an idea I don't let go of it, that's my strong point, yes, the strong point of the fellow they all pitied!

The sun has risen higher, my forehead is beginning to burn. Around me the stones are beginning to crack open with a dull sound, the only cool thing is the rifle's barrel, cool as the fields, as the evening rain long ago when the soup was simmering, they would wait for me, my father and mother, who would occasionally smile at me, perhaps I loved them. But that's all in the past, a film of heat is beginning to rise from the trail, come on, missionary, I'm waiting for you, now I know how to answer the message, my new masters taught me, and I know they are right, you have to settle accounts with that question of love. When I fled the seminary in Algiers I had a different idea of the savages and only one detail of my imaginings was true, they are cruel. I had robbed the treasurer's office, cast off my habit, crossed the Atlas, the upper plateaus, and the desert, the busdriver of the Trans-Sahara line made fun of me: "Don't go there," he too, what had got into them all, and the gusts of sand for hundreds of windblown kilometers, progressing and backing in the face of the wind, then the mountains again made up of black peaks and ridges sharp as steel, and after them it took a guide to go out on the endless sea of brown pebbles, screaming with heat, burning with the fires of a thousand mirrors, to the spot on the confines of the white country and the land of the blacks, where stands the city of salt. And the money the guide stole from me, ever naïve I had shown it to him, but he left me on the trail—just about here, it so happens—after having struck me: "Dog, there's a way, the honor's all mine, go ahead, go on, they'll show you," and they did show me, oh, yes, they're like the sun that never stops, except at night, beating sharply and proudly, that is beating me hard at this moment, too hard, with a multitude of lances burst from the ground—oh, shelter, yes, shelter, under the big rock, before everything gets muddled.

The shade here is good. How can anyone live in the city of salt, in the hollow of that basin full of dazzling heat? On each of the sharp right-angled walls cut out with a pickax and coarsely planed,

the gashes left by the pickax bristle with blinding scales, pale scattered sand yellows them somewhat except when the wind dusts the
upright walls and terraces, then everything shines with dazzling
whiteness under a sky likewise dusted even to its blue rind. I was
going blind during those days when the stationary fire would crackle
for hours on the surface of the white terraces that all seemed to
meet as if, in the remote past, they had all together tackled a mountain of salt, flattened it first, and then had hollowed out streets, the
insides of houses and windows directly in the mass, or as if—yes,
this is more like it, they had cut out their white, burning hell with a
powerful jet of boiling water just to show that they could live where
no one ever could, thirty days' travel from any living thing, in this
hollow in the middle of the desert where the heat of day prevents
any contact among creatures, separates them by a portcullis of
invisible flames and of searing crystals, where without transition
the cold of night congeals them individually in their rock-salt
shells, nocturnal dwellers in a dried-up ice floe, black Eskimos
suddenly shivering in their cubical igloos. Black because they wear
long black garments and the salt that collects even under their
nails, that they continue tasting bitterly and swallowing during the
sleep of those polar nights, the salt they drink in the water from
the only spring in the hollow of a dazzling groove, often spots
their dark garments with something like the trail of snails after a
rain.

Rain, O Lord, just one real rain, long and hard, rain from your
heaven! Then at last the hideous city, gradually eaten away, would
slowly and irresistibly cave in and, utterly melted in a slimy torrent,
would carry off its savage inhabitants toward the sands. Just one
rain, Lord! But what do I mean, what Lord, they are the lords and
masters! They rule over their sterile homes, over their black slaves
that they work to death in the mines, and each slab of salt that is cut
out is worth a man in the region to the south, they pass by, silent,
wearing their mourning veils in the mineral whiteness of the streets,
and at night, when the whole town looks like a milky phantom, they
stoop down and enter the shade of their homes where the salt walls
shine dimly. They sleep with a weightless sleep, and as soon as they
wake, they give orders, they strike, they say they are a united people, that their god is the true god, and that one must obey. They are
my masters, they are ignorant of pity, and, like masters, they want
to be alone, to progress alone, to rule alone, because they alone had

209

the daring to build in the salt and the sands a cold torrid city. And I . . .

What a jumble when the heat rises, I'm sweating, they never do, now the shade itself is heating up, I feel the sun on the stone above me, it's striking, striking like a hammer on all the stones, and it's the music, the vast music of noon, air and stones vibrating over hundreds of kilometers, *gra,* I hear the silence as I did once before. Yes, it was the same silence, years ago, that greeted me when the guards led me to them, in the sunlight, in the center of the square, whence the concentric terraces rose gradually toward the lid of hard blue sky sitting on the edge of the basin. There I was, thrown on my knees in the hollow of that white shield, my eyes corroded by the swords of salt and fire issuing from all the walls, pale with fatigue, my ear bleeding from the blow given by my guide and they, tall and black, looked at me without saying a word. The day was at its midcourse. Under the blows of the iron sun, the sky resounded at length, a sheet of white-hot tin, it was the same silence, and they stared at me, time passed, they kept on staring at me, and I couldn't face their stares, I panted more and more violently, eventually I wept, and suddenly they turned their backs on me in silence and all together went off in the same direction. On my knees, all I could see, in the red-and-black sandals, was their feet sparkling with salt as they raised the long black gowns, the tip rising somewhat, the heel striking the ground lightly, and when the square was empty I was dragged to the House of the Fetish.

Squatting as I am today in the shelter of the rock and the fire above my head pierces the rock's thickness, I spent several days within the dark of the House of the Fetish, somewhat higher than the others, surrounded by a wall of salt, but without windows, full of a sparkling night. Several days, and I was given a basin of brackish water and some grain that was thrown before me the way chickens are fed, I picked it up. By day the door remained closed and yet the darkness became less oppressive, as if the irresistible sun managed to flow through the masses of salt. No lamp, but by feeling my way along the walls I touched garlands of dried palms decorating the walls and, at the end, a small door, coarsely fitted, of which I could make out the bolt with my fingertips. Several days, long after—I couldn't count the days or the hours, but my handful of grain had been thrown me some ten times and I had dug out a hole for my excrements that I covered up in vain, the stench of an animal den hung on anyway—long after, yes, the door opened wide and they came in.

One of them came toward me where I was squatting in a corner. I felt the burning salt against my cheek, I smelt the dusty scent of the palms, I watched him approach. He stopped a yard away from me, he stared at me with his metallic eyes that shone without expression in his brown horse-face, then he raised his hand. Still impassive, he seized me by the lower lip, which he twisted slowly until he tore my flesh and, without letting go, made me turn around and back up to the center of the room, he pulled on my lip to make me fall on my knees there, mad with pain and my mouth bleeding, then he turned away to join the others standing against the walls. They watched me moaning in the unbearable heat of the unbroken daylight that came in the wide-open door, and in that light suddenly appeared the Sorcerer with his raffia hair, his chest covered with a breastplate of pearls, his legs bare under a straw skirt, wearing a mask of reeds and wire and two square openings for eyes. He was followed by musicians and women wearing heavy motley gowns that revealed nothing of their bodies. They danced in front of the door at the end, but a coarse, scarcely rhythmical dance, they just barely moved, and finally the Sorcerer opened the little door behind me, the masters did not stir, they were watching me, I turned around and saw the Fetish, his double ax-head, his iron nose twisted like a snake.

I was carried before him to the foot of the pedestal, I was made to drink a black, bitter, bitter water, and at once my head began to burn, I was laughing, that's the offense, I am offended. They undressed me, shaved my head and body, washed me in oil, beat my face with cords dipped in water and salt, and I laughed and turned my head away, but, each time, two women would take me by the ears and offer my face to the Sorcerer's blows while I could see only his square eyes, I was still laughing, covered with blood. They stopped, no one spoke but me, the jumble was beginning in my head, then they lifted me up and forced me to raise my eyes toward the Fetish, I had ceased laughing. I knew that I was now consecrated to him to serve him, adore him, no, I was not laughing anymore, fear and pain stifled me. And there, in that white house, between those walls that the sun was assiduously burning on the outside, my face taut, my memory exhausted, yes, I tried to pray to the Fetish, he was all there was, and even his horrible face was less

211

horrible than the rest of the world. Then it was that my ankles were tied with a cord that permitted just one step, they danced again, but this time in front of the Fetish, the masters went out one by one.

The door once closed behind them, the music again, and the Sorcerer lighted a bark fire around which he pranced, his long silhouette broke on the angles of the white walls, fluttered on the flat surfaces, filled the room with dancing shadows. He traced a rectangle in a corner to which the women dragged me, I felt their dry and gentle hands, they set before me a bowl of water and a little pile of grain and pointed to the Fetish, I grasped that I was to keep my eyes fixed on him. Then the Sorcerer called them one after the other over to the fire, he beat some of them, who moaned and who then went and prostrated themselves before the Fetish my god, while the Sorcerer kept on dancing, and he made them all leave the room until only one was left, quite young, squatting near the musicians and not yet beaten. He held her by a shock of hair, which he kept twisting around his wrist, she dropped backward with eyes popping until she finally fell on her back. Dropping her, the Sorcerer screamed, the musicians turned to the wall, while behind the square-eyed mask the scream rose to an impossible pitch, and the woman rolled on the ground in a sort of fit, and, at last on all fours, her head hidden in her locked arms, she too screamed, but with a hollow, muffled sound, and in this position, without ceasing to scream and to look at the Fetish, the Sorcerer took her nimbly and nastily, without the woman's face being visible, for it was covered with the heavy folds of her garment. And, wild as a result of the solitude, *I* screamed too, yes, howled with fright toward the Fetish until a kick hurled me against the wall, biting the salt as I am biting this rock today with my tongueless mouth, while waiting for the man I must kill.

Now the sun has gone a little beyond the middle of the sky. Through the breaks in the rock, I can see the hole it makes in the white-hot metal of the sky, a mouth voluble as mine, constantly vomiting rivers of flame over the colorless desert. On the trail in front of me, nothing, no cloud of dust on the horizon, behind me they must be looking for me, no, not yet, it's only in the late afternoon that they opened the door and I could go out a little, after having spent the day cleaning the House of the Fetish, set out fresh offerings, and in the evening the ceremony would begin, in which I was sometimes beaten, at others not, but always I served the

Fetish, the Fetish whose image is engraved in iron in my memory and now in my hope also. Never had a god so possessed or enslaved me, my whole life day and night was devoted to him, and pain and the absence of pain, wasn't that joy, were due him, and even, yes, desire, as a result of being present, almost every day, at that impersonal and nasty act which I heard without seeing it inasmuch as I now had to face the wall or else be beaten. But my face up against the salt, obsessed by the bestial shadows moving on the wall, I listened to the long scream, my throat was dry, a burning sexless desire squeezed my temples and my belly as in a vise. Thus the days followed one another, I barely distinguished them as if they had liquefied in the torrid heat and the treacherous reverberation from the walls of salt, time had become merely a vague lapping of waves in which there would burst out, at regular intervals, screams of pain or possession, a long, ageless day in which the Fetish ruled as this fierce sun does over my house of rocks, and now as I did then, I weep with unhappiness and longing, a wicked hope consumes me, I want to betray, I lick the barrel of my gun and its soul inside, its soul, only guns have souls—oh, yes! the day they cut out my tongue, I learned to adore the immortal soul of hatred!

What a jumble, what a rage, *gra gra*, drunk with heat and wrath, lying prostrate on my gun. Who's panting here? I can't endure this endless heat, this waiting, I must kill him. Not a bird, not a blade of grass, stone, an arid desire, their screams, this tongue within me talking, and, since they mutilated me, the long, flat, deserted suffering deprived even of the water of night, the night of which I would dream, when locked in with the god, in my den of salt. Night alone with its cool stars and dark fountains could save me, carry me off at last from the wicked gods of mankind, but even locked up I could not contemplate it. If the newcomer tarries more, I shall see it at least rise from the desert and sweep over the sky, a cold golden vine that will hang from the dark zenith and from which I can drink at length, moisten this black dried hole that no muscle of live flexible flesh revives now, forget at last that day when madness took away my tongue.

How hot it was, really hot, the salt was melting or so it seemed to me, the air was corroding my eyes, and the Sorcerer came in without his mask. Almost naked under grayish tatters, a new woman followed him, and her face, covered with a tattoo reproducing the mask of the Fetish, expressed only an idol's ugly stupor. The only thing alive about her was her thin flat body that flopped at the foot of the god when the Sorcerer opened the door of the niche. Then he went out without looking at me, the heat rose, I didn't stir, the Fetish looked at me over that motionless body whose muscles stirred gently, and the woman's idol-face didn't change when I approached. Only her eyes enlarged as she stared at me, my feet touched hers, the heat then began to shriek, and the idol, without a word, still staring at me with her dilated eyes, gradually slipped onto her back, slowly drew her legs up and raised them as she gently spread her knees. But, immediately afterward, *gra,* the Sorcerer was lying in wait for me, they all entered and tore me from the woman, beat me dreadfully on the sinful place, what sin, I'm laughing, where is it and where is virtue, they clapped me against a wall, a hand of steel gripped my jaws, another opened my mouth, pulled on my tongue until it bled, was it I screaming with that bestial scream, a cool cutting caress, yes, cool at last, went over my tongue. When I came to, I was alone in the night, glued to the wall, covered with hardened blood, a gag of strange-smelling dry grasses filled my mouth, it had stopped bleeding, but it was vacant, and in that absence the only living thing was a tormenting pain. I wanted to rise, I fell back, happy, desperately happy to die at last, death too is cool and its shadow hides no god.

I did not die, a new feeling of hatred stood up one day, at the same time I did, walked toward the door of the niche, opened it, closed it behind me, I hated my people, the Fetish was there, and, from the depths of the hole in which I was I did more than pray to him, I believed in him and denied all I had believed up to then. Hail! he was strength and power, he could be destroyed but not converted, he stared over my head with his empty, rusty eyes. Hail! he was the master, the only lord, whose indisputable attribute was malice, there are no good masters. For the first time, as a result of offenses, my whole body crying out a single pain, I surrendered to him and approved his maleficent order, I adored in him the evil principle of the world. A prisoner of his kingdom—the sterile city carved out of a mountain of salt, divorced from nature, deprived of those rare and fleeting flowerings of the desert, preserved from those strokes of chance or marks of affection such as an unexpected cloud or a brief violent downpour that are familiar even to the sun or the sands, the city of order in short, right angles, square rooms, rigid men—I freely became its tortured, hate-filled citizen, I repudiated the long history that had been taught me. I had been misled, solely the reign of malice was devoid of defects, I had been misled, truth is square, heavy, thick, it does not admit distinctions, good is an idle dream, an intention constantly postponed and pursued with exhausting effort, a limit never reached, its reign is impossible. Solely evil can reach its limits and reign absolutely, it must be served to establish its visible kingdom, then we shall see, but what does "then" mean, solely evil is present, down with Europe, reason, honor, and the cross. Yes, I was to be converted to the religion of my masters, yes, indeed, I was a slave, but if I too become vicious I cease to be a slave, despite my shackled feet and my mute mouth. O, this heat is driving me crazy, the desert cries out everywhere under the unbearable light, and he, the Lord of kindness, whose very name revolts me, I disown him, for I know him now. He dreamed and wanted to lie, his tongue was cut out so that his word would no longer be able to deceive the world, he was pierced with nails even in his head, his poor head, like mine now, what a jumble, how weak I am, and the earth didn't tremble, I am sure, it was not a righteous man they had killed, I refuse to believe it, there are no righteous men but only evil masters who bring about the reign of relentless truth. Yes, the Fetish alone has power, he is the sole god of this world, hatred is his commandment, the source of all life, the cool water, cool like mint that chills the mouth and burns the stomach.

Then it was that I changed, they realized it, I would kiss their hands when I met them, I was on their side, never wearying of admiring them, I trusted them, I hoped they would mutilate my people as they had mutilated me. And when I learned that the missionary was to come, I knew what I was to do. That day like all the others, the same blinding daylight that had been going on so long! Late in the afternoon a guard was suddenly seen running along the edge of the basin, and, a few minutes later I was dragged to the House of the Fetish and the door closed. One of them held me on the ground in the dark, under threat of his cross-shaped sword, and the silence lasted for a long time until a strange sound filled the ordinarily peaceful town, voices that it took me some time to recognize because they were speaking my language, but as soon as they rang out the point of the sword was lowered toward my eyes, my guard stared at me in silence. Then two voices came closer, and I can still hear them, one asking why that house was guarded and whether they should break in the door, Lieutenant, the other said:

"No," sharply, then added, after a moment, that an agreement had been reached, that the town accepted a garrison of twenty men on condition that they would camp outside the walls and respect the customs. The private laughed, "They're knuckling under," but the officer didn't know, for the first time in any case they were willing to receive someone to take care of the children, and that would be the chaplain, later on they would see about the territory. The other said they would cut off the chaplain's you know what if the soldiers were not there. "Oh, no!" the officer answered. "In fact, Father Beffort will come before the garrison; he'll be here in two days." That was all I heard, motionless, lying under the sword, I was in pain, a wheel of needles and knives was whirling in me. They were crazy, they were crazy, they were allowing a hand to be laid on the city, on their invincible power, on the true god, and the fellow who was to come would not have his tongue cut out, he would show off his insolent goodness without paying for it, without enduring any offense. The reign of evil would be postponed, there would be doubt again, again time would be wasted dreaming of the impossible good, wearing oneself out in fruitless efforts instead of hastening the realization of the only possible kingdom, and I looked at the sword threatening me, O sole power to rule over the world! O power, and the city gradually emptied of its sounds, the door finally opened, I remained alone, burned and bitter, with the Fetish, and I swore to him to save my new faith, my true masters, my despotic God, to betray well, whatever it might cost me.

Gra, the heat is abating a little, the stone has ceased to vibrate. I can go out of my hole, watch the desert gradually take on yellow and ochre tints that will soon be mauve. Last night I waited until they were asleep, I had blocked the lock on the door, I went out with the same step as usual, measured by the cord, I knew the streets, I knew where to get the old rifle, what gate wasn't guarded, and I reached here just as the night was beginning to fade around a handful of stars while the desert was getting a little darker. And now it seems days and days that I have been crouching in these rocks. Soon, soon, I hope he comes soon! In a moment they'll begin to look for me, they'll speed over the trails in all directions, they won't know that I left for them and to serve them better, my legs are weak, drunk with hunger and hate. O! over there, *gra,* at the end of the trail, two camels are growing bigger, ambling along, already multiplied by short shadows, they are running with that lively and dreamy gait they always have. Here they are, here at last!

Quick, the rifle, and I load it quickly. O Fetish, my god over yonder, may your power be preserved, may the offense be multiplied, may hate rule pitilessly over a world of the damned, may the wicked forever be masters, may the kingdom come, where in a single city of salt and iron black tyrants will enslave and possess without pity! And now, *gra gra*, fire on pity, fire on impotence and its charity, fire on all that postpones the coming of evil, fire twice, and there they are toppling over, falling, and the camels flee toward the horizon, where a geyser of black birds has just risen in the unchanged sky. I laugh, I laugh, the fellow is writhing in his detested habit, he is raising his head a little, he sees me—me, his all-powerful shackled master, why does he smile at me, I'll crush that smile! How pleasant is the sound of a rifle butt on the face of goodness, today, today at last, all is consummated, and everywhere in the desert, even hours away from here, jackals sniff the nonexistent wind, then set out in a patient trot toward the feast of carrion awaiting them. Victory! I raise my arms to a heaven moved to pity, a lavender shadow is just barely suggested on the opposite side, O nights of Europe, home, childhood, why must I weep in the moment of triumph?

He stirred, no, the sound comes from somewhere else, and from the other direction, here they come rushing like a flight of dark birds, my masters, who fall upon me, seize me, ah, yes! strike, they fear their city sacked and howling, they fear the avenging soldiers I called forth, and this is only right, upon the sacred city. Defend yourselves now, strike! strike me first, you possess the truth! O my masters, they will then conquer the soldiers, they'll conquer the word and love, they'll spread over the deserts, cross the seas, fill the light of Europe with their black veils—strike the belly, yes, strike the eyes—sow their salt on the continent, all vegetation, all youth will die out, and dumb crowds with shackled feet will plod beside me in the worldwide desert under the cruel sun of the true faith, I'll not be alone. Ah! the pain, the pain they cause me, their rage is good, and on this cross-shaped war saddle where they are now quartering me, pity! I'm laughing, I love the blow that nails me down crucified.

217

How silent the desert is! Already night and I am alone, I'm thirsty. Still waiting, where is the city, those sounds in the distance, and the soldiers perhaps the victors, no, it can't be, even if the soldiers are victorious, they're not wicked enough, they won't be able to rule, they'll still say one must become better, and still millions of men between evil and good, torn, bewildered, O Fetish, why hast thou forsaken me? All is over, I'm thirsty, my body is burning, a darker night fills my eyes.

This long, this long dream, I'm awakening, no, I'm going to die, dawn is breaking, the first light, daylight for the living, and for me the inexorable sun, the flies. Who is speaking, no one, the sky is not opening up, no, no, God doesn't speak in the desert, yet whence comes that voice saying: "If you consent to die for hate and power, who will forgive us?" Is it another tongue in me or still that other fellow refusing to die, at my feet, and repeating: "Courage! courage! courage!"? Ah! supposing I were wrong again! Once fraternal men, sole recourse, O solitude, forsake me not! Here, here, who are you, torn, with bleeding mouth, is it you, Sorcerer, the soldiers defeated you, the salt is burning over there, it's you, my beloved master! Cast off that hate-ridden face, be good now, we were mistaken, we'll begin all over again, we'll rebuild the city of mercy, I want to go back home. Yes, help me, that's right, give me your hand. . . .

A handful of salt fills the mouth of the garrulous slave.

Boris Pasternak

(1890–1960)

Prize awarded 1958 (prize declined) "for his important achievement in both

contemporary lyrical poetry and in the field of the great Russian epic

tradition." ★ *Despite notoriety surrounding the Western publication of his*

Soviet-censured novel Dr. Zhivago *(1956), and the subsequent pressure on him*

to decline the Nobel Prize in 1958, Boris Pasternak is remembered primarily as

a poet. The poems in his first books, The Twin in the Clouds *(1914) and*

Over the Barricades *(1917), are both romantic and futuristic (he was influ-*

enced in this latter respect by his friend Mayakovsky), but by 1922, in the lyrical

collection My Sister, Life, *he had established a more individual style.*

Pasternak may have survived the Stalinist purges because of his lack of

interest in immediate political issues. Still, he was attacked by the regime and, in

reaction, undertook translations of von Kleist, Ben Jonson, Goethe, Shelley, and

Shakespeare, all highly regarded. In 1948 Pasternak began work on Dr.

Zhivago, *set in the Russia of 1903–29. After the furor surrounding its pub-*

lication and the Nobel Prize, he was forced to apologize publicly for his ideo-

logical errors in order to be allowed to live out his last few years in Russia.

219

THE NOBEL PRIZE

I've fallen beast-like in a snare:
Light, people, freedom, somewhere bide:
But at my back I hear the chase
And there is no escape outside.

Darkest wood and lakeside shore,
Gaunt trunk of a levelled tree,
My way is cut off on all sides:
Let what may, come; all's one to me.

Is there some ill I have committed?
Am I a murderer, miscreant?
For I have made the whole world weep
Over the beauty of my land.

But even at the very grave
I trust the time shall come to be
When over malice, over wrong,
The good will win its victory.

ivo Andrić

(1892–1975)

Prize awarded 1961 "for the epic force with which he has traced themes and depicted human destinies from his country's history." ★ *The Yugoslavian Andrić drew heavily on experiences in his native Serbia for his richly philosophical and psychologically sensitive prose. His career began in 1911, and by 1918 his literary reputation was firmly established with the first collection of his poems,* Ex Ponto. *In 1914, while imprisoned by the Austrians for his strong nationalistic sentiments, he wrote* Nemri *(Anxieties), a diary in lyrical prose reflecting on World War I and his incarceration.*

Just after the war, Andrić began a second career in the diplomatic service, which culminated in his appointment as ambassador to Germany on the eve of World War II. During this period between the wars, he published three volumes entitled Stories *(1924, 1931, 1936), which, for the most part, portrayed life in Bosnia and experiences of Turkish oppression.*

With the German invasion of 1941, Andrić was placed under house arrest in Belgrade for the duration, and once again he used his imprisonment to produce important literature, the Bosnian trilogy: The Bridge on the Drina, Bosnian Story, *and* The Woman from Sarajevo *(1945). This epic trilogy, which chronicled the culture clashes of East and West in the Balkans over several generations, was specifically cited by the Nobel committee.*

In later works, including New Stories *(1948), Andrić used psychological portraits to describe the impact of the new postwar socialism on an old "class" society. In his last book* Devil's Yard *(1954), he returned to historical and patriotic depictions of Ottoman rule in Yugoslavia.*

221

THIRST

IMMEDIATELY AFTER THE AUSTRIAN OCCUPA-
tion, a gendarme barracks was built in the highland village of
Sokolac. The commander of the station brought a pretty blond wife
along with him, with large blue eyes that had a glassy look. With her
frail beauty, with her European dress and fashion, she looked like
a small treasure, which had been lost by travelers journeying over
this mountain summit on the way from one big town to another.

The village had not recovered from its first wonder, nor had the
young wife arranged her marriage room, full of small cushions,
embroideries, and ribbons, when highwaymen appeared in this region. A platoon of gendarmes arrived at the barracks, doubling the
staff. The commander spent his days and nights up and down the
countryside supervising and arranging patrols. The young wife lived
confused and scared, in the company of the village women, just so
that she would not be considered to be living alone. Her time passed
in waiting. Her sleeping and eating turned into mere expectation
with nothing to sustain and strengthen her. The village women
begged and urged her to eat and, urging, ate and drank everything
themselves. At night, they told her stories and personal experiences
in order to put her to sleep. Finally the women, tired of talking,
would fall asleep on the red rug, and she would look at them from
the bed, wide awake, bothered by the heavy smell of milk and wool
that rose from the sleeping housewives. And when the commander
would arrive after many days of waiting, even then she was neither
more joyful nor consoled. The man returned home thoroughly
tired from walking and lack of sleep, bearded, dirty, and wet. Boots

that he had not taken off for several days would become tight from moisture and mud; two aides strained to take them off with woolen stockings, tearing the skin from the swollen and sore feet. He was worried and distraught because of his lack of success, continually planning in his thoughts a new chase. His worry and zeal made him thin, his lips became chapped, and face darkened from sun, wind, and the mountain air. During these short rest periods at home, his wife treated him like a wounded man, and after two or three days she would send him back again at dawn to the mountain. Because of this, all her thoughts and prayers had only one aim, that these highwaymen be caught as soon as possible, and that this horrible life be ended.

One day, her greatest desire was realized. The most important and cleverest highwayman, Lazar Zelenović, was caught. After him, according to the talk in the barracks and the village, it would be easier to catch or to chase away the less important, less skillful, and less experienced highwaymen.

Lazar was caught accidentally. A patrol that was chasing another, younger highwayman, stumbled onto him. Two months earlier, when he came over from Herzegovina, Lazar had been wounded by a bullet in the chest. No one knew this. To cure himself, Lazar, with the help of younger highwaymen, had made a shelter of dry branches, flooded mud, and parts of a fallen tree located near a brook, under a big log. He managed to live in this hole, hidden from view from the paths high above the brook, and was able to reach for water with his hand. He washed the wound on his chest all day long, while the patrols were looking for him everywhere, uphill and downhill. Perhaps he would have recovered had he dared to look for a better hiding place and had it not been for the early hot weather, which aggravated the wound. He was defending himself from flies and mosquitoes as well as he could, but the wound broadened and deepened, where water could not reach it, and the infection spread. His fever rose.

Such was his condition when his younger friend tried to bring some wax and whiskey as medicine. The patrol noticed the young man as he left a shepherd's hut and went to the brook in the mountain. Having noticed the patrol at the last moment, the young man ran away along the brook and disappeared without a trace.

The commander, who had left his horse in the pasture and on foot run ahead of the gendarmes after the young highwayman, fell up to his waist in mud and sediment and with his leg hit something soft and immovable. Perhaps he would have continued farther, were it not difficult to get himself out; and he would not even have noticed Lazar's small and skullfully hidden shelter, had he not smelled the awful stench of the highwayman's wound. After getting his legs out, the commander looked through the gap in the branches and noticed sheepskin. Having sensed that a man was hiding in the hole below him, it did not even occur to him that it might be Lazar himself; he thought that it was the younger highwayman or one of his friends. In order to deceive the hidden highwayman, the commander loudly ordered the gendarmes:

"He must have gone along the brook farther away. Run after him, and I will follow you shortly, because I hurt my leg on this thorn."

While shouting the order, he gave his men a sign with one hand to keep quiet and, with the other, to gather around him. When the three of them had gathered, they threw themselves simultaneously on the hiding place and caught the highwayman from behind, like a badger. Since he had only a long rifle and a big knife, he could neither shoot nor swing. They chained his hands and tied his feet with rope and carried him like a log through the backwoods to the meadow, where the commander's horse was waiting. On the way to the meadow they smelled the heavy stench, and, when they placed him on the grass, they saw the big wound in his bear chest. A certain Živan from Goražde, who worked as a jailor and an informer, recognized Lazar at once. They were from the same village; both celebrated the same patron's day, Saint John.

The highwayman rolled his large gray eyes, clear from living in the open, near water, though inflamed by the fever. The commander asked Živan to verify once again that it was really Lazar. Everybody leaned over the highwayman. Živan told him for the second time:

"It is you, Lazar!"

"I see that you know me better than I know you."

"You know me, too, Lazar. How would you not know me?"

"Ah, had I never known you, I would have recognized now who you were and what you did. All the villages, Serbian and Turkish, would recognize you from here to Goražde. If you were to bring the stupidest child, who had never seen us, and if the child saw us the way we are, it would have said: 'The one who is bound and wounded is Lazar, and the wicked man who is leaning over him—that is Živan!' "

The highwayman had a feverish need to speak, as if in that way he was prolonging his life, and Živan wanted to show his power and defend his reputation in front of the others. Who knows for how long these two would have argued in this way, had they not been interrupted by the commander? But the highwayman would not answer any other questions. He did not want to say anything about his friends and accomplices. He excused himself because of his wound and sickness. The commander, after consulting with the sergeant-major of the gendarmes, a husky man from Lika, ordered sharply that the highwayman should not be given even a drop of water, no matter how much he begged for it, but to tell him to address himself to the commander.

While they were preparing what was necessary for the transportation of the wounded highwayman, the young commander sat off to one side to rest and compose himself. He put an elbow on his knee and his head on his wrist, looking at the mountain as large as the sea, which only recently had become green. He wanted to think of his success, of the recognition that was awaiting him, of returning to his wife. But his thought could not attach itself to anything. He felt only a leaden tiredness he had to fight, as a man who has to sleep overnight in the snow must resist sleep and freezing. Rising painfully from the ground, he got up and ordered them to move. The other patrol caught up with them. Now there were nine of them. The stretcher that they had made for the highwayman was rough and knotty. One of the gendarmes threw his raincoat over it, turning his face away while doing it, as if he were throwing it into an abyss.

They were traveling slowly. The sun became hotter. The commander, who had been riding behind the stretcher, had to move up to the front because the odor from the wounded man was unbearable. But in the afternoon, when they descended to the plain of Glasinac, they took a wagon and oxen from a peasant. So, they appeared on the plain before Sokolac just before sunset. They looked like a returning hunting party, except that the hunters were thoughtful and the quarry was unusual. 225

In the meadow in front of the barracks the village women and children gathered. Among them was also the commander's wife. At the beginning she did not even think of the highwayman; she was only waiting for her husband, as always. But as the women talked more and more about the highwayman who was being carried, and as their stories became more fantastic with the approaching column stretched and slow like a funeral, she felt full of apprehension and expectation. Finally they arrived. The people noisily were opening the left wing of the gate, normally opened only when they brought in wood or hay. The column entered directly in front of the barracks' door. Here the commander got off his horse, hitting the ground heavily as a tired man dismounts. The young woman felt his sharp beard of several days' growth on her face and smelled the sweat, earth, and rain that he always brought from his official expeditions.

While the commander was giving orders, his wife cast a glance at the highwayman, who was lying tied and still all the time. Only his head was elevated a bit since it rested on a piece of wood against some hay. His eyes looked at no one. A sharp stench was spreading from him as from a wounded animal.

When the commander had ordered what was to be done, he took his wife by the hand and led her into the house so that she would not see them taking him off the stretcher and untying him. After washing and changing himself, the commander went out once more to see where they had put Lazar and if they had tied him. The highwayman was confined in the basement under the commander's lodging, which was supposed to serve as a temporary prison. The door was weak, with an iron bar in the upper half, and the lock was a common one. Because of this, a guard was posted for the whole night.

The commander ate little but talked to his wife continually. He talked about little things, lively and joyful as a child. He was content. He had caught the most important and the most dangerous highwayman, after five months of wandering and effort and undeserved reproaches from his superiors in Rogatica and the headquarters in Sarajevo. He would learn from Lazar about the highwaymen and their hideouts and the names of their accomplices, and in this way he would be able to rest fully and win recognition.

"And what if he does not want to betray others?" asked his wife fearfully.

"He will do it, he will have to," answered the commander, not talking further about it with his wife.

The commander felt sleepy. Fatigue was overcoming him, and it was even stronger than his joy, hunger, and desire for his wife. The freshness of the bed was intoxicating him. He made himself talk further and tried to show that he was not sleepy, but the words stopped in his mouth, he stuttered, and the distance between words became ever longer. He fell asleep in the middle of a sentence, holding his wife's small, white, round shoulder with the fingers of his left hand. His wife was not sleepy. She was pleased and excited, scared and sad. For a long time she looked at the sleeping man, whose right cheek sank in the softness of the featherbedding, with his mouth open a little, as if he were eagerly drinking the pillow. A cold and large distance is always created between a person wide awake and the one asleep, a coldness that grows with every minute and is filled more and more with misunderstanding and with a strange feeling of abandonment and intense loneliness. The woman herself tried to fall asleep. She closed her eyes and breathed evenly. But the change of the guard in front of the basement door woke her up from her first dream. Her thoughts returned to the highwayman, as if she had not slept and as if she had thought of nothing else.

The same Živan, Lazar's countryman, was on guard. Now, she realized that she was not awakened by the change of the guard as much as by Lazar's calling. The highwayman asked for water.

"Who is on guard?"

"Silence."

"Is it you, Živan?"

"Yes, it is me. Keep quiet!"

"Well, how am I to keep quiet, you traitor, when I am dying of thirst and fever? But give me some water, Živan, for the sake of St. John, our patron, so that I will not die like this—as an animal."

Živan pretended not to hear anything and did not answer in the hope that the highwayman would get weary of begging. But the highwayman kept calling him with his quiet, hoarse voice.

"If you know what suffering and prison are, do not turn a deaf ear to me, Živan, for the sake of the life of your children!"

"Do not swear by my children. You know that I am obeying orders and that this is my job. Keep quiet. You are going to wake up the commander."

"Let him sleep in misery! He is worse than a Turk, for he tortures me with thirst, in spite of all my evil luck! But hand me over some water if you are a brother of mine in God."

227

From their hushed conversation, the wife determined that by the commander's order they were not giving him water, because they wanted to force him, by thirst, to betray his comrades and accomplices. The highwayman, tortured by unbearable thirst and fever, had apparently found some relief in swearing at God, in a string of harsh words and curses and in the constant repetition of the word "water." He would keep quiet for several moments, and then he would let out a long, deep, manly sigh, followed by a torrent of words.

"Eh, Živan, Živan, may you get leprosy from my bread and salt for torturing me in a way such as nobody has ever tortured anybody. Give me a jug of water and then kill me at once, and may you be forgiven in this world and the next."

But Živan stopped answering him.

"Živan . . . Živan, I beg you as if you were God . . . I am burning!"

Silence. The last quarter of the scorched moon appeared late. Živan hid himself in a shadow, and now when he spoke, his voice was not as clear. The highwayman was calling the commander loudly.

"Oh, Commander, please do not torture me anymore, for the sake of the tsar's bread, without need."

After each of his calls, the silence was deeper. In that depth, the highwayman was grunting heavily and growling hoarsely, neither lowering his voice nor paying attention to what he said.

"Oooh, you filthy bitches, may God let you drink blood all your lives and never quench your thirst. Let your blood gush out through your noses. Where are you, Commander? May dogs have your mother!"

He yelled the last words with a choking, feeble voice that was faltering in the dried-out throat. Again Živan started to hush him up and kept promising that at sunrise he would call the commander and that he would surely give him some water; he only had to confess to them what they asked him, and until that time he should have to endure. But the highwayman, in his fever, forgot about everything after several moments and again whined:

"Živan, for God's sake, I am burning! Water!"

He was repeating this word for the hundredth time the way a child would, changing with his unequal feverish breath the strength of his voice and pronunciation.

Awake and trembling, the wife listened to all of this—the

highwayman's screaming, Živan's whispered orders for silence coming in hisses, and her husband's heavy and deep sleeping beside her—sitting on the edge of the bed and not feeling her body or the room around her, losing herself in the hitherto unknown horror.

During her childhood, in her parents' home, it happened some nights in the autumn or spring that she could not sleep, and she would listen to something all night alone, to some oppressive and monotonous noise from outside: the wind turning the tin weather vane or tapping the little garden gate, which they forgot to lock. As a child, she attached particular meaning to those noises, imagining that they were living beings who were fighting, groaning, and sobbing. Life in its wider scope often makes the imaginations and the fears of our childhood real, and the little, imaginative fears create the great and true ones. Would it not be wonderful if the innocent horrors, which sometimes tore her girlish dreams, were real and if this night in the wild village, in her marriage bed, above the horrible highwayman's conversation and screams, if this were only imagination and a dream.

And during all that time, just as with the tin weather vane or the dry board in the little open garden gate under the wind, the man's heavy, even breathing was coming as regularly as did the exhausted human voice, which was passing through a dry, wide-open mouth, over the burnt, immovable tongue.

"Water, water! Oooh!"

Živan was replaced on guard duty by another gendarme, but the highwayman's cry for water did not stop but became weaker and more tired. The woman was still sitting, stiffly, listening to every murmur from below. She thought constantly about one and the same thing without end and conclusion. How can one comprehend and understand this life and these people? She sees only that there are gendarmes and the others, the highwaymen (two faces of one and the same misfortune), chasing each other without mercy, and that one has to pine away among them from grief and compassion.

A lot of things had been said long ago about his Lazar in Sokolac. She heard stories of his cruelty. She had heard how he tortured in the most horrible way the peasants who did not submit to him; how he killed gendarmes from ambush, stripping them naked and leaving them thus on the road. Well, see how here the gendarmes are now paying him back their debt. But can it go on forever this way? It seemed to her that they were recklessly leaping into an abyss and

229

that all of them would perish in this night without sunrise, in blood, in thirst, and in unknown fears.

From time to time she thought of waking her husband, to ask him to scatter this horrible dream with one word and one smile. But she did not move from her place; neither did she wake her husband. Instead she sat immovable, as if a dead body were beside her, listening to the voice from the basement, alone with her fears and her questions. She even thought about the prayers that they taught her in childhood, but these were the prayers of another, forgotten and sunken life, and they could give her neither solace nor help. As with her own death, she was reconciled to the thought that the one who was screaming would beg and howl forever, and this one, beside her, would go on sleeping and breathing like this eternally.

The oppressive night was becoming even thicker and heavier. It was no longer a common night, one of the innumerable ones in a series of days and nights, but the only one, an eternal and endless desert of darkness in which the last living man was howling and begging, asking for a drop of water, without any hope of help. But in all of God's big world, with waters, rains, and dews, there was not even a drop of water, and there was not even one hand out of all living human beings to offer help. The waters have dried up, and the people have grieved to death. Only her little flame of awareness lives, as the lone witness of it all.

Nevertheless, the dawn came. The wife looked unbelievingly as the wall became white, in the same place as at previous dawns, and the dawn, first gray and then rosy, conquered the room and separated and brought to life the things in it.

Straining her hearing, she could still distinguish the highwayman's voice, but as if it came from far away. There was no swearing or cursing, only the hoarse and less frequent:

"Ooooooo, ooooooo, oo!"

Even that she guessed at more than heard.

Although the dawn was conquering, the wife had no strength to move. All stiff, bent with her head in her palms, she sat on the edge of the bed and did not even notice when the commander woke up.

The man opened his rested eyes and looked, and his eyes fell on his wife's bent back and her pale neck. Then, after the first hesitation, an awareness of this joyful reality passed through him like a soft and sweeping wave. He felt like calling his wife, shouting her name, but he changed his mind. Smiling, he raised himself a bit, noiselessly supporting himself on his left elbow, and with his free right hand, silently, suddenly embraced her shoulders, drew her to him, and pushed her under him.

The wife struggled shortly and in vain. This sudden and irresistible embrace seemed horrible to her. It seemed to her impossible and sacrilegious that she could betray the world of night in which she had lived and suffered until that moment, alone with her suffering, that she could do it so quickly and easily, without a word of explanation. She wanted to resist and to convince him that it would not be, that there are difficult and painful things that she had to tell him, which cannot be so easily overlooked before the return to everyday life. Bitter words gushed out of her, but she could not utter even one. She only choked, and the man did not notice this sign of her resistance: a sound that did not even succeed in becoming a single word. She wanted to push him away, but her movements hardly matched the strength of her bitterness or the quickness of her thoughts. The very warmth of this rested and alert body oppressed her like a burden. The bones and muscles in her young frame yielded like an obedient machine. Her mouth was sealed by his lips. She felt him on her like a huge stone to which she was bound, falling with it like an arrow without a place to stop.

Losing consciousness, not only of last night but of life itself, she sank into a desolate, gloomy sea of the familiar but always new sweetness. Above her remained the last traces of her nocturnal thoughts, decisions, and of all human compassion, which were disappearing one after another, like water bubbles over a drowning man.

The white, decorated room was rapidly becoming full of the living light of day.

John steinbeck

(1902–1968)

Prize awarded 1962 "for his realistic as well as imaginative writings, distinguished by a sympathetic humor and a keen social perception." ★ *A journalist as well as a novelist, Steinbeck combined social realism with an easy narrative approach reminiscent of American predecessors Frank Norris and Theodore Dreiser. Like them, Steinbeck chronicled the lives and times of Californians and was critical of the political policies that heightened their difficulties.* The Grapes of Wrath (*1939*), *Steinbeck's poignant saga of uprooted rural victims of the Great Depression, set a standard for social consciousness in American literature for generations. This tour de force stands in contrast with his fond, often humorous depictions of Sausalito Valley life in* Tortilla Flat (*1935*) *and* Cannery Row (*1944*). *And although* In Dubious Battle (*1936*) *deals seriously with the problems of organizing rural labor* (*the plight of migratory workers was one of Steinbeck's lifelong concerns*), The Short Reign of Pippin IV (*1957*) *is pure fun.*

Despite a lack of psychological complexity, Steinbeck's works often contain moving, bittersweet characterizations, as in The Red Pony (*1945*) *or the novella* Of Mice and Men (*written in 1937 and later turned into a play*). *His simple, occasionally sentimental prose clearly reflects a sincere, sympathetic understanding of the natural and social causes of suffering. Steinbeck is the author of several nonfiction works, including* The Sea of Cortez (*1941, with E. F. Ricketts*), A Russian Journal (*1948, with photos by Robert Capa*), *and the original screenplay for* Viva Zapata! (*1952*).

THE CHRYSANTHEMUMS

HE HIGH GRAY-FLANNEL FOG OF WINTER closed off the Salinas Valley from the sky and from all the rest of the world. On every side it sat like a lid on the mountains and made of the great valley a closed pot. On the broad, level land floor the gang plows bit deep and left the black earth shining like metal where the shares had cut. On the foothill ranches across the Salinas River, the yellow stubble fields seemed to be bathed in pale cold sunshine, but there was no sunshine in the valley now in December. The thick willow scrub along the river flamed with sharp and positive yellow leaves.

It was a time of quiet and of waiting. The air was cold and tender. A light wind blew up from the southwest so that the farmers were mildly hopeful of a good rain before long; but fog and rain do not go together.

Across the river, on Henry Allen's foothill ranch there was little work to be done, for the hay was cut and stored and the orchards were plowed up to receive the rain deeply when it should come. The cattle on the higher slopes were becoming shaggy and rough-coated.

Elisa Allen, working in her flower garden, looked down across the yard and saw Henry, her husband, talking to two men in business suits. The three of them stood by the tractor shed, each man with one foot on the side of the little Fordson. They smoked cigarettes and studied the machine as they talked.

Elisa watched them for a moment and then went back to her work. She was thirty-five. Her face was lean and strong and her eyes were as clear as water. Her figure looked blocked and heavy in her gardening costume, a man's black hat pulled low down over her eyes, clodhopper shoes, a figured print dress almost completely covered by a big corduroy apron with four big pockets to hold the snips, the trowel and scratcher, the seeds and the knife she worked with. She wore heavy leather gloves to protect her hands while she worked.

She was cutting down the old year's chrysanthemum stalks with a pair of short and powerful scissors. She looked down toward the men by the tractor shed now and then. Her face was eager and mature and handsome; even her work with the scissors was overeager, overpowerful. The chrysanthemum stems seemed too small and easy for her energy.

She brushed a cloud of hair out of her eyes with the back of her glove, and left a smudge of earth on her cheek in doing it. Behind her stood the neat white farm house with red geraniums close-banked around it as high as the windows. It was a hard-swept-looking little house, with hard-polished windows and a clean mud-mat on the front steps.

Elisa cast another glance toward the tractor shed. The strangers were getting into their Ford coupe. She took off a glove and put her strong fingers down into the forest of new green chrysanthemum sprouts that were growing around the old roots. She spread the leaves and looked down among the close-growing stems. No aphids were there, no sowbugs or snails or cutworms. Her terrier fingers destroyed such pests before they could get started.

Elisa started at the sound of her husband's voice. He had come near quietly, and he leaned over the wire fence that protected her flower garden from cattle and dogs and chickens.

"At it again," he said. "You've got a strong new crop coming."

Elisa straightened her back and pulled on the gardening glove again. "Yes. They'll be strong this coming year." In her tone and on her face there was a little smugness.

"You've got a gift with things," Henry observed. "Some of those yellow chrysanthemums you had this year were ten inches across. I wish you'd work out in the orchard and raise some apples that big."

Her eyes sharpened. "Maybe I could do it, too. I've a gift with things, all right. My mother had it. She could stick anything into the ground and make it grow. She said it was having planters' hands that knew how to do it."

"Well, it sure works with flowers," he said.

"Henry, who were those men you were talking to?"

"Why, sure, that's what I came to tell you. They were from the Western Meat Company. I sold those thirty head of three-year-old steers. Got nearly my own price, too."

"Good," she said. "Good for you."

"And I thought," he continued, "I thought how it's Saturday afternoon, and we might go into Salinas for dinner at a restaurant, and then to a picture show—to celebrate, you see."

"Good," she repeated. "Oh, yes. That will be good."

Henry put on his joking tone. "There's fights tonight. How'd you like to go to the fights?"

"Oh, no," she said breathlessly. "No, I wouldn't like fights."

"Just fooling, Elisa. We'll go to a movie. Let's see. It's two now. I'm going to take Scotty and bring down those steers from the hill. It'll take us maybe two hours. We'll go in town about five and have dinner at the Cominos Hotel. Like that?"

"Of course I'll like it. It's good to eat away from home."

"All right, then. I'll go get up a couple of horses."

She said, "I'll have plenty of time to transplant some of these sets, I guess."

She heard her husband calling Scotty down by the barn. And a little later she saw the two men ride up the pale yellow hillside in search of the steers.

There was a little square sandy bed kept for rooting the chrysanthemums. With her trowel she turned the soil over and over, and smoothed it and patted it firm. Then she dug ten parallel trenches to receive the sets. Back at the chrysanthemum bed she pulled out the little crisp shoots, trimmed off the leaves of each one with her scissors and laid it on a small orderly pile.

A squeak of wheels and plod of hoofs came from the road. Elisa looked up. The country road ran along the dense bank of willows and cottonwoods that bordered the river, and up this road came a curious vehicle, curiously drawn. It was an old spring-wagon, with a round canvas top on it like the cover of a prairie schooner. It was drawn by an old bay horse and a little gray-and-white burro. A big stubble-bearded man sat between the cover flaps and drove the crawling team. Underneath the wagon, between the hind wheels, a lean and rangy mongrel dog walked sedately. Words were painted on the canvas, in clumsy, crooked letters. "Pots, pans, knives, sisors,

235

lawn mores, Fixed." Two rows of articles, and the triumphantly definitive "Fixed" below. The black paint had run down in little sharp points beneath each letter.

Elisa, squatting on the ground, watched to see the crazy, loose-jointed wagon pass by. But it didn't pass. It turned into the farm road in front of her house, crooked old wheels skirling and squeaking. The rangy dog darted from between the wheels and ran ahead. Instantly the two ranch shepherds flew out at him. Then all three stopped, and with stiff and quivering tails, with taut straight legs, with ambassadorial dignity, they slowly circled, sniffing daintily. The caravan pulled up to Elisa's wire fence and stopped. Now the newcomer dog, feeling outnumbered, lowered his tail and retired under the wagon with raised hackles and bared teeth.

The man on the wagon seat called out, "That's a bad dog in a fight when he gets started."

Elisa laughed. "I see he is. How soon does he generally get started?"

The man caught up her laughter and echoed it heartily. "Sometimes not for weeks and weeks," he said. He climbed stiffly down, over the wheel. The horse and the donkey drooped like unwatered flowers.

Elisa saw that he was a very big man. Although his hair and beard were graying, he did not look old. His worn black suit was wrinkled and spotted with grease. The laughter had disappeared from his face and eyes the moment his laughing voice had ceased. His eyes were dark, and they were full of brooding that gets in the eyes of teamsters and of sailors. The callused hands he rested on the wire fence were cracked, and every crack was a black line. He took off his battered hat.

"I'm off my general road, ma'am," he said. "Does this dirt road cut over across the river to the Los Angeles highway?"

Elisa stood up and shoved the thick scissors in her apron pocket. "Well, yes, it does, but it winds around and then fords the river. I don't think your team could pull through the sand."

He replied with some asperity, "It might surprise you what them beasts can pull through."

"When they get started?" she asked.

He smiled for a second. "Yes. When they get started."

"Well," said Elisa, "I think you'll save time if you go back to the Salinas road and pick up the highway there."

He drew a big finger down the chicken wire and made it sing. "I ain't in any hurry, ma'am. I go from Seattle to San Diego and back every year. Takes all my time. About six months each way. I aim to follow nice weather."

Elisa took off her gloves and stuffed them in the apron pocket with the scissors. She touched the under edge of her man's hat, searching for fugitive hairs. "That sounds like a nice kind of a way to live," she said.

He leaned confidentially over the fence. "Maybe you noticed the writing on my wagon. I mend pots and sharpen knives and scissors. You got any of them things to do?"

"Oh, no," she said quickly. "Nothing like that." Her eyes hardened with resistance.

"Scissors is the worst thing," he explained. "Most people just ruin scissors trying to sharpen 'em, but I know how. I got a special tool. It's a little bobbit kind of thing, and patented. But it sure does the trick."

"No. My scissors are all sharp."

"All right, then. Take a pot," he continued earnestly, "a bent pot, or a pot with a hole. I can make it like new so you don't have to buy no new ones. That's a saving for you."

"No," she said shortly. "I tell you I have nothing like that for you to do."

His face fell to an exaggerated sadness. His voice took on a whining undertone. "I ain't had a thing to do today. Maybe I won't have no supper tonight. You see I'm off my regular road. I know folks on the highway clear from Seattle to San Diego. They save their things for me to sharpen up because they know I do it so good and save them money."

"I'm sorry," Elisa said irritably. "I haven't anything for you to do."

His eyes left her face and fell to searching the ground. They roamed about until they came to the chrysanthemum bed where she had been working. "What's them plants, ma'am?"

The irritation and resistance melted from Elisa's face. "Oh, those are chrysanthemums, giant whites and yellows. I raise them every year, bigger than anybody around here."

"Kind of a long-stemmed flower? Looks like a quick puff of colored smoke?" he asked.

"That's it. What a nice way to describe them."

237

"They smell kind of nasty till you get used to them," he said.

"It's a good bitter smell," she retorted, "not nasty at all."

He changed his tone quickly. "I like the smell myself."

"I had ten-inch blooms this year," she said.

The man leaned farther over the fence. "Look. I know a lady down the road a piece, has got the nicest garden you ever seen. Got nearly every kind of flower but no chrysantheums. Last time I was mending a copper-bottom washtub for her (that's a hard job but I do it good), she said to me, 'If you ever run acrost some nice chrysantheums I wish you'd try to get me a few seeds.' That's what she told me."

Elisa's eyes grew alert and eager. "She couldn't have known much about chrysanthemums. You *can* raise them from seed, but it's much easier to root the little sprouts you see there."

"Oh," he said. "I s'pose I can't take none to her, then."

"Why, yes, you can," Elisa cried. "I can put some in damp sand, and you can carry them right along with you. They'll take root in the pot if you keep them damp. And then she can transplant them."

"She'd sure like to have some, ma'am. You say they're nice ones?"

"Beautiful," she said. "Oh, beautiful." Her eyes shone. She tore off the battered hat and shook out her dark pretty hair. "I'll put them in a flower pot, and you can take them right with you. Come into the yard."

While the man came through the picket gate Elisa ran excitedly along the geranium-bordered path to the back of the house. And she returned carrying a big red flower pot. The gloves were forgotten now. She kneeled on the ground by the starting bed and dug up the sandy soil with her fingers and scooped it into the bright new flower pot. Then she picked up the little pile of shoots she had prepared. With her strong fingers she pressed them into the sand and tamped around them with her knuckles. The man stood over her. "I'll tell you what to do," she said. "You remember so you can tell the lady."

"Yes, I'll try to remember."

"Well, look. These will take root in about a month. Then she must set them out, about a foot apart in good rich earth like this, see?" She lifted a handful of dark soil for him to look at. "They'll grow fast and tall. Now remember this: In July tell her to cut them down, about eight inches from the ground."

"Before they bloom?" he asked.

"Yes, before they bloom." Her face was tight with eagerness. "They'll grow right up again. About the last of September the buds will start."

She stopped and seemed perplexed. "It's the budding that takes the most care," she said hesitantly. "I don't know how to tell you." She looked deep into his eyes, searchingly. Her mouth opened a little, and she seemed to be listening. "I'll try to tell you," she said. "Did you ever hear of planting hands?"

"Can't say I have, ma'am."

"Well, I can only tell you what it feels like. It's when you're picking off the buds you don't want. Everything goes right down into your fingertips. You watch your fingers work. They do it themselves. You can feel how it is. They pick and pick the buds. They never make a mistake. They're with the plant. Do you see? Your fingers and the plant. You can feel that, right up your arm. They know. They never make a mistake. You can feel it. When you're like that you can't do anything wrong. Do you see that? Can you understand that?"

She was kneeling on the ground looking up at him. Her breast swelled passionately.

The man's eyes narrowed. He looked away self-consciously. "Maybe I know," he said. "Sometimes in the night in the wagon there—"

Elisa's voice grew husky. She broke in on him, "I've never lived as you do, but I know what you mean. When the night is dark—why the stars are sharp-pointed, and there's quiet. Why, you rise up and up! Every pointed star gets driven into your body. It's like that. Hot and sharp and—lovely."

Kneeling there, her hand went out toward his legs in the greasy black trousers. Her hesitant fingers almost touched the cloth. Then her hand dropped to the ground. She crouched low like a fawning dog.

He said, "It's nice, just like you say. Only when you don't have no dinner, it ain't."

She stood up then, very straight, and her face was ashamed. She held the flower pot out to him and placed it gently in his arms. "Here. Put it in your wagon, on the seat, where you can watch it. Maybe I can find something for you to do."

At the back of the house she dug in the can pile and found two

239

old and battered aluminum saucepans. She carried them back and gave them to him. "Here, maybe you can fix these."

His manner changed. He became professional. "Good as new I can fix them." At the back of his wagon he set a little anvil, and out of an oily tool box dug a small machine hammer. Elisa came through the gate to watch him while he pounded out the dents in the kettles. His mouth grew sure and knowing. At a difficult part of the work he sucked his underlip.

"You sleep right in the wagon?" Elisa asked.

"Right in the wagon, ma'am. Rain or shine I'm dry as a cow in there."

"It must be nice," she said. "It must be very nice. I wish women could do such things."

"It ain't the right kind of a life for a woman."

Her upper lip raised a little, showing her teeth. "How do you know? How can you tell?" she said.

"I don't know, ma'am," he protested. "Of course I don't know. Now here's your kettles, done. You don't have to buy no new ones."

"How much?"

"Oh, fifty cents'll do. I keep my prices down and my work good. That's why I have all them satisfied customers up and down the highway."

Elisa brought him a fifty-cent piece from the house and dropped it in his hand. "You might be surprised to have a rival some time. I can sharpen scissors, too. And I can beat the dents out of little pots. I could show you what a woman might do."

He put his hammer back in the oily box and shoved the little anvil out of sight. "It would be a lonely life for a woman, ma'am, and a scary life, too, with animals creeping under the wagon all night." He climbed over the singletree, steadying himself with a hand on the burro's white rump. He settled himself in the seat, picked up the lines. "Thank you kindly, ma'am," he said. "I'll do like you told me; I'll go back and catch the Salinas road."

"Mind," she called, "if you're long in getting there, keep the sand damp."

"Sand, ma'am? . . . Sand? Oh, sure. You mean around the chrysantheums. Sure I will." He clucked his tongue. The beasts leaned luxuriously into their collars. The mongrel dog took his place between the back wheels. The wagon turned and crawled out the entrance road and back the way it had come, along the river.

Elisa stood in front of her wire fence watching the slow progress of the caravan. Her shoulders were straight, her head thrown back, her eyes half-closed, so that the scene came vaguely into them. Her lips moved silently, forming the words, "Good-bye—good-bye." Then she whispered, "That's a bright direction. There's a glowing there." The sound of her whisper startled her. She shook herself free and looked about to see whether anyone had been listening. Only the dogs had heard. They lifted their heads toward her from their sleeping in the dust, and then stretched out their chins and settled asleep again. Elisa turned and ran hurriedly into the house.

In the kitchen she reached behind the stove and felt the water tank. It was full of hot water from the noonday cooking. In the bathroom she tore off her soiled clothes and flung them into the corner. And then she scrubbed herself with a little block of pumice, legs and thighs, loins and chest and arms, until her skin was scratched and red. When she had dried herself she stood in front of a mirror in the bedroom and looked at her body. She tightened her stomach and threw out her chest. She turned and looked over her shoulder at her back.

After a while she began to dress, slowly. She put on her newest underclothing and her nicest stockings and the dress which was the symbol of her prettiness. She worked carefully on her hair, penciled her eyebrows and rouged her lips.

Before she was finished she heard the little thunder of hoofs and the shouts of Henry and his helper as they drove the red steers into the corral. She heard the gate bang shut and set herself for Henry's arrival.

His step sounded on the porch. He entered the house calling, "Elisa, where are you?"

"In my room, dressing. I'm not ready. There's hot water for your bath. Hurry up. It's getting late."

When she heard him splashing in the tub, Elisa laid his dark suit on the bed, and shirt and socks and tie beside it. She stood his polished shoes on the floor beside the bed. Then she went to the porch and sat primly and stiffly down. She looked toward the river road where the willow-line was still yellow with frosted leaves so that under the high gray fog they seemed a thin band of sunshine. This was the only color in the gray afternoon. She sat unmoving for a long time. Her eyes blinked rarely.

Henry came banging out of the door, shoving his tie inside his

241

vest as he came. Elisa stiffened and her face grew tight. Henry stopped short and looked at her. "Why—why, Elisa. You look so nice!"

"Nice? You think I look nice? What do you mean by 'nice'?"

Henry blundered on. "I don't know. I mean you look different, strong and happy?"

"I am strong? Yes, strong. What do you mean 'strong'?"

He looked bewildered. "You're playing some kind of a game," he said helplessly. "It's a kind of a play. You look strong enough to break a calf over your knee, happy enough to eat it like a watermelon."

For a second she lost her rigidity. "Henry! Don't talk like that. You didn't know what you said." She grew complete again. "I'm strong," she boasted. "I never knew before how strong."

Henry looked down toward the tractor shed, and when he brought his eyes back to her, they were his own again. "I'll get out the car. You can put on your coat while I'm starting."

Elisa went into the house. She heard him drive to the gate and idle down his motor, and then she took a long time to put on her hat. She pulled it here and pressed it there. When Henry turned the motor off she slipped into her coat and went out.

The little roadster bounced along on the dirt road by the river, raising the birds and driving the rabbits into the brush. Two cranes flapped heavily over the willow-line and dropped into the river-bed.

Far ahead on the road Elisa saw a dark speck. She knew.

She tried not to look as they passed it, but her eyes would not obey. She whispered to herself sadly, "He might have thrown them off the road. That wouldn't have been much trouble, not very much. But he kept the pot," she explained. "He had to keep the pot. That's why he couldn't get them off the road."

The roadster turned a bend and she saw the caravan ahead. She swung full around toward her husband so she could not see the little covered wagon and the mismatched team as the car passed them.

In a moment it was over. The thing was done. She did not look back.

She said loudly, to be heard above the motor. "It will be good, tonight, a good dinner."

"Now you're changed again," Henry complained. He took one hand from the wheel and patted her knee. "I ought to take you in to dinner oftener. It would be good for both of us. We get so heavy out on the ranch."

"Henry," she asked, "could we have wine at dinner?"

"Sure we could. Say! That will be fine."

She was silent for a while; then she said, "Henry, at those prize-fights, do the men hurt each other very much?"

"Sometimes a little, not often. Why?"

"Well, I've read how they break noses, and blood runs down their chests. I've read how the fighting gloves get heavy and soggy with blood."

He looked around at her. "What's the matter, Elisa? I didn't know you read things like that." He brought the car to a stop, then turned to the right over the Salinas River bridge.

"Do any women ever go to the fights?" she asked.

"Oh sure, some. What's the matter, Elisa? Do you want to go? I don't think you'd like it, but I'll take you if you really want to go."

She relaxed limply in the seat. "Oh, no. No. I don't want to go. I'm sure I don't." Her face was turned away from him. "It will be enough if we can have wine. It will be plenty." She turned up her coat collar so he could not see that she was crying weakly—like an old woman.

S. Y. Agnon

(1888–1970)

Prize awarded 1966 "for his profoundly characteristic narrative art with motifs

from the life of the Jewish people." ★ *Agnon was born Shmuel Czackes in*

eastern Galicia (Austro-Hungary) into a long line of Jewish scholars. His ed-

ucation included not only the Bible and Talmudic and Midrashic commentaries,

but also the great rabbinical dissertations and Hasidic folklore. While in Ger-

many (1913–24), he coauthored with Martin Buber a definitive collection of

Hasidic tales. Agnon carried on the rich storytelling tradition of Eastern Eu-

ropean Jews, creating detailed pictures of the simple religious life-style of earlier

generations in The Bridal Canopy *(1931) and* In the Heart of Seas *(1935).*

Yet he chose not to confine himself to historic or nostalgic genres, but went on to

address some of the major questions of the twentieth century, including the

ominous implications of its shattered faith in A Simple Story *(1935) and* A

Guest for the Night *(1939).* Yesterday *(1945), written with a distinctive*

modern perspective, reflects Agnon's experiences as a young pioneer in Palestine.

And in Whole Loaf *(1958),* Edo and Enam *(1965), and* Betrothed *(1966),*

244

he adopted postsurrealist and symbolic literary devices. Beneath his evolving

vision and understanding of contemporary life, however, may be found constant

allusions to Jewish tradition and mysticism and to the Midrash.

THE KERCHIEF

E

¹

VERY YEAR MY FATHER, OF BLESSED MEM-
ory, used to visit the Lashkowitz fair to do business with the merchants. Lashkowitz is a small town of no more consequence than any
of the other small towns in the district, except that once a year
merchants gather together there from everywhere and offer their
wares for sale in the town's marketplace; and whoever needs goods
comes and buys them. In earlier times, two or three generations
ago, more than a hundred thousand people used to gather together
there; and even now, when Lashkowitz is in its decline, they come to
it from all over the country. You will not find a single merchant in
the whole of Galicia who does not keep a stall in Lashkowitz during
the fair.

²

For us the week in which my father went to the market was just like
the week of the Ninth of Ab. During those days there was not a
smile to be seen on Mother's lips, and the children also refrained
from laughing. Mother, peace be with her, used to cook light meals
with milk and vegetables and all sorts of things that children do not
dislike. If we caused her trouble, she would quiet us and did not
rebuke us even for things that deserved a beating. I often used to
find her sitting at the window with moist eyelids. And why should
my mother sit at the window; did she wish to watch the passersby?
Why, she, peace be with her, never concerned herself with other
people's affairs and would only half hear the stories her neighbors

might tell her; but it was her custom, ever since the first year in which my father went to Lashkowitz, to stand at the window and look out.

When my father, of blessed memory, went to the fair at Lashkowitz for the first time, my mother was once standing at the window when she suddenly cried out, "Oh, they're strangling him!" Folk asked her, "What are you saying?" She answered, "I see a robber taking him by the throat"; and before she had finished her words she had fainted. They sent to the fair and found my father injured, for at the very time that my mother had fainted, somebody had attacked my father for his money and taken him by the throat; and he had been saved by a miracle. In later years, when I found in the Book of Lamentations the words "She is become as a widow," and I read Rashi's explanation, "As a woman whose husband has gone to a distant land and who intends to return to her," it brought to mind my mother, peace be with her, as she used to sit at the window with her tears upon her cheeks.

3

All the time that Father was in Lashkowitz I used to sleep in his bed. As soon as I had said the night prayer I used to undress and stretch my limbs in his long bed, cover myself up to my ears, and keep them pricked up and ready so that in case I heard the trumpet of the Messiah I might rise at once. It was a particular pleasure for me to meditate on Messiah the King. Sometimes I used to laugh to myself when I thought of the consternation that would come about in the whole world when our just Messiah would reveal himself. Only yesterday he was binding his wounds and his bruises, and today he's a king! Yesterday he sat among the beggars and they did not recognize him but sometimes even abused him and treated him with disrespect; and now suddenly the Holy One, Blessed be He, has remembered the oath He swore to redeem Israel, and given him permission to reveal himself to the world. Another in my place might have been angered at the beggars who treated Messiah the King with disrespect; but I honored and revered them, since Messiah the King had desired to dwell in their quarters. In my place another might have treated the beggars without respect, as they eat black bread even on the Sabbaths, and wear dirty clothes. But I honored and revered them, since among them were those who had dwelt together with the Messiah.

4

Those were fine nights in which I used to lie on my bed and think of Messiah the King, who would reveal himself suddenly in the world. He would lead us to the Land of Israel, where we would dwell, every man under his own vine and his own fig tree. Father would not go to fairs, and I would not go to school but would walk about all day long in the courts of the House of our God. And while lying and meditating thus, my eyes would close of their own accord; and before they closed entirely I would take my fringed garment and count the knots I had made in the fringes, indicating the number of days my father stayed in Lashkowitz. Then all sorts of lights, green, white, black, red, and blue, used to come toward me, like the lights seen by wayfarers in fields and woods and valleys and streams, and all kinds of precious things would be gleaming and glittering in them; and my heart danced for joy at all the good stored away for us in the days to come, when our just Messiah would reveal himself, may it be speedily and in our days, Amen.

While I rejoiced so, a great bird would come and peck at the light. Once I took my fringed garment and tied myself to his wings and said, "Bird, bird, take me to Father." The bird spread its wings and flew with me to a city called Rome. I looked down and saw a group of poor men sitting at the gates of the city and one beggar among them binding his wounds. I turned my eyes away from him in order not to see his sufferings. When I turned my eyes away there grew a great mountain with all kinds of thorns and thistles upon it and evil beasts grazing there, and impure birds and ugly creeping things crawling about it, and a great wind blew all of a sudden and flung me onto the mountain, and the mountain began quaking under me, and my limbs felt as though they would fall asunder; but I feared to cry out lest the creeping things should enter my mouth and the impure birds should peck at my tongue. Then Father came and wrapped me in his prayer shawl and brought me back to my bed. I opened my eyes to gaze at his face and found that it was day. At once I knew that the Holy One, blessed be He, had rolled away another night of the nights of the fair. I took my fringes and made a fresh knot.

247

5

Whenever Father returned from the fair he brought us many gifts. He was very clever, knowing what each of us would want most and bringing it to us. Or maybe the Master of Dreams used to tell Father what he showed us in dream, and he would bring it for us.

There were not many gifts that survived long. As is the way of the valuables of this world, they were not lasting. Yesterday we were playing with them, and today they were already thrown away. Even my fine prayerbook was torn, for whatever I might have had to do, I used to open it and ask its counsel; and finally nothing was left of it but a few dogeared scraps.

But one present that Father brought Mother remained whole for many years. And even after it was lost it was not lost from my heart, and I still think of it as though it were yet there.

6

That day, when Father returned from the fair, it was Friday, after the noon hour, when the children are freed from school. This fact should not be mentioned to children. Those Friday-afternoon hours were the best time of the week, because all the week around a child is bent over his book, and his eyes and heart are not his own; as soon as he raises his head he is beaten. On Friday afternoon he is freed from study, and even if he does whatever he wants to, nobody objects. Were it not for the noon meal the world would be like Paradise. But Mother had already summoned me to eat, and I had no heart to refuse.

Almost before we had begun eating my little sister put her right hand to her ear and set her ear to the table. "What are you doing?" Mother asked her. "I'm trying to listen," she answered. Mother asked, "Daughter, what are you trying to listen to?" Then she began clapping her hands with joy and crying, "Father's coming, Father's coming." And in a little while we heard the wheels of a wagon. Very faint at first, then louder and louder. At once we threw our spoons down while they were still half-full, left our plates on the table, and ran out to meet Father coming back from the fair. Mother, peace be with her, also let her apron fall and stood erect, her arms folded on her bosom, until Father entered the house.

How big Father was then! I knew my father was bigger than all the other fathers. All the same I used to think there must be some-

248

one taller than he—but now even the chandelier hanging from the ceiling in our house seemed to be lower.

Suddenly Father bent down, caught me to him, kissed me, and asked me what I had learned. Is it likely that Father did not know which portion of the week was being read? But he only asked to try me out. Before I could answer he had caught my brother and sisters, raised them on high, and kissed them.

I look about me now to try and find something to which to compare my father when he stood together with his tender children on his return from afar, and I can think of many comparisons, each one finer than the next; yet I can find nothing pleasant enough. But I hope that the love haloing my father, of blessed memory, may wrap us around whenever we come to embrace our little children, and the joy that possessed us then will be possessed by our children all their lives.

7

The wagoner entered, carrying two trunks, one large, and the other neither large nor small but medium. Father looked with one eye at us and with the other at the medium trunk; and that second trunk, too, seemed to have eyes and smile with them.

Father took his bunch of keys from his pocket and said, "We'll open the trunk and take out my prayer shawl and phylacteries." Father was just speaking for fun, since who needs phylacteries on Friday afternoon, and even if you think of the prayer shawl, my father had a special one for Sabbath, but he only said it in order that we should not be too expectant and not be too anxious for presents.

But we went and undid the straps of the trunk and watched his every movement while he took one of the keys and examined it, smiling affectionately. The key also smiled at us; that is, gleams of light sparkled on the key, and it seemed to be smiling.

Finally he pressed the key into the lock, opened the trunk, put his hand inside, and felt among possessions. Suddenly he looked at us and became silent. Had Father forgotten to place the presents there? Or had he been lodging at an inn where the inn people rose and took out the presents? As happened with the sage by whose hands they sent a gift to the emperor, a chest full of jewels and pearls, and when he lodged one night at the inn, the inn folk opened the chest and took out everything that was in it and filled it with dust. Then I prayed that just as a miracle was done to that sage so that that dust should be the dust of Abraham our father, which turned into swords when it was thrown into the air, so should the Holy One, blessed be He, perform a miracle with us in order that the things with which the innkeepers had filled Father's trunk should be better than all presents. Before my prayer was at an end Father brought out all kinds of fine things. There was not a single one among his gifts that we had not longed for all the year around. And that is why I said that the Master of Dreams must have revealed to Father what he had shown us in dream.

The gifts of my father deserve to be praised at length, but who is going to praise things that will vanish and be lost? All the same, one fine gift that my father brought my mother on the day that he returned from the fair deserves to be mentioned in particular.

8

It was a silk-brocaded kerchief adorned with flowers and blossoms. On the one side it was brown and they were white, while on the other they were brown and it was white. That was the gift that Father, of blessed memory, brought to Mother, peace be with her.

Mother opened up the kerchief, stroked it with her fingers, and gazed at Father; he gazed back at her, and they were silent. Finally she folded it again, rose, put it in the cupboard, and said to Father, "Wash your hands and have a meal." As soon as Father sat down to his meal I went out to my friends in the street and showed them the presents I had received and was busy outside with them until the Sabbath began and I went to pray with Father.

How pleasant that Sabbath eve was when we returned from the House of Prayer! The skies were full of stars, the houses full of lamps and candles, people were wearing their Sabbath clothes and walking quietly beside Father in order not to disturb the Sabbath angels who accompany one home from the House of Prayer on Sabbath eves: candles were alight in the house and the table prepared and the fine smell of white bread and a white tablecloth spread and two Sabbath loaves on it, covered by a small cloth out of respect so that they should not feel ashamed when the blessing is said first over the wine.

Father bowed and entered and said, "A peaceful and blessed Sabbath," and Mother answered, "Peaceful and blessed." Father looked at the table and began singing, "Peace be unto you, angels of peace," while Mother sat at the table, her prayerbook in hand, and

the big chandelier with the ten candles—one for each of the Ten
Commandments—hanging from the ceiling, gave light. They were
answered back by the rest of the candles, one for Father, one for
Mother, one for each of the little ones; and although we were smaller
than Father and Mother, all the same our candles were as big as
theirs.

Then I looked at Mother and saw that her face had changed and
her forehead had grown smaller because of the kerchief wound
around her head and covering her hair, while her eyes seemed
much larger and were shining toward Father, who went on singing,
"A woman of valor who shall find?"; and the ends of her kerchief,
which hung down below her chin, were quivering very gently because the Sabbath angels were moving their wings and making the
wind. It must have been so, for the windows were closed, and where
could the wind have come from if not from the wings of the angels?
As it says in the Psalms, "He maketh the winds His messengers." I
held back my breath in order not to confuse the angels and looked
at my mother, peace be with her, who stood at such a lofty rung,
and wondered at the Sabbath day, which is given us for an honor
and a glory. Suddenly I felt how my cheeks were being patted. I do
not know whether the wings of the angels or the corners of the
kerchief were caressing me. Happy is he who merits to have good
angels hovering over his head, and happy is he whose mother has
stroked his head on the Sabbath eve.

9

When I awakened from sleep it was already day. The whole world
was full of the Sabbath morning. Father and Mother were about to
go out, he to his little prayer room and she to the House of Study
of my grandfather, peace be with him. Father was wearing a black
satin robe and a round shtreimel of sable on his head, and Mother
wore a black dress and a hat with feathers. In the House of Study of
my grandfather, where Mother used to pray, they did not spend too
much time singing, and so she could return early. When I came
back with Father from the small prayer room she was already seated
at the table wearing her kerchief, and the table was prepared with
wine and cakes, large and small, round and doubled over. Father
entered, said, "A Sabbath of peace and blessing," put his prayer
shawl on the bed, sat down at the head of the table, said, "The Lord
is my shepherd, I shall not want," blessed the wine, tasted the cake,

251

and began, "A Psalm of David: The earth is the Lord's and the fullness thereof."

When the Ark is opened on the eve of the New Year and this psalm is said, the soul's awakening can be felt in the air. There was a similar stirring in my heart then. Had my mother not taught me that you do not stand on chairs and do not clamber onto the table and do not shout, I would have climbed onto the table and shouted out, "The earth is the Lord's and the fullness thereof," like that child in the Talmud who used to be seated in the middle of a gold table that was a load for sixteen men, with sixteen silver chains attached, and dishes and glasses and bowls and platters fitted, and with all kinds of food and sweetmeats and spices of all that was created in the six days of creation; and he used to proclaim, "The earth is the Lord's and the fullness thereof."

Mother cut the cake, giving each his or her portion; and the ends of her kerchief accompanied her hands. While doing so a cherry fell out of the cake and stained her apron; but it did not touch her kerchief, which remained as clean as it had been when Father took it out of his trunk.

10

A woman does not put on a silken kerchief every day or every Sabbath. When a woman stands at the oven, what room is there for ornament? Every day is not Sabbath, but on the other hand there are festivals. The Holy One, blessed be He, took pity on His creatures and gave them times of gladness, holidays and appointed seasons. On festivals Mother used to put on a feather hat and go to the House of Prayer, and at home she would don her kerchief. But on the New Year and the Day of Atonement she kept the kerchief on all day long; similarly on the morning of Hoshana Rabbah, the seventh day of Tabernacles. I used to look at Mother on the Day of Atonement, when she wore her kerchief and her eyes were bright with prayer and fasting. She seemed to me like a prayerbook bound in silk and presented to a bride.

The rest of the time the kerchief lay folded in the cupboard, and on the eves of the Sabbaths and festivals Mother would take it out. I never saw her washing it, although she was very particular about cleanliness. When Sabbaths and festivals are properly kept, they themselves preserve the clothes. But for me she would have kept the kerchief all her life long and would have left it as an heirloom.

What happened was as follows. On the day I became thirteen years old and a member of the congregation, my mother, peace be with her, bound her kerchief around my neck. Blessed be God, who has given His world to guardians. There was not a spot of dirt to be found on the kerchief. But sentence had already been passed on the kerchief, that it was to be lost through me. This kerchief, which I had observed so much and so long, would vanish because of me.

1 1

Now I shall pass from one theme to another until I return to my original theme. At that time there came a beggar to our town who was sick with running sores; his hands were swollen, his clothes were rent and tattered, his shoes were cracked, and when he showed himself in the street the children threw earth and stones at him. And not only the children but even the grown-ups and household-ers turned angry faces on him. Once when he went to the market to buy bread or onions the shopwomen drove him away in anger. Not that the shopwomen in our town were cruel; indeed, they were tender-hearted. Some would give food from their mouths to or-phans, others went to the forest, gathered twigs, made charcoal of them, and shared them free among the beggars and poor folk. But every beggar has his own luck. When he fled from them and en-tered the House of Study, the beadle shouted at him and pushed him out. And when on the Sabbath eve he crept into the House of Study, nobody invited him to come home with them and share the Sabbath meal. God forbid that the sons of our father Abraham do not perform works of charity; but the ministers of Satan used to accompany that beggar and pull a veil over Jewish eyes so that they could not perceive his dire needs. As to where he heard the blessing over wine, and where he ate his three Sabbath meals—if he was not sustained by humankind, he must have been sustained by the grace of God.

Hospitality is a great thing, since buildings are erected and ad-ministrators appointed for the sake of it and to support the poor. But I say it in praise of our townsfolk, that although they did not establish any poorhouse or elect any administrators, every man who could do so used to find a place for a poor man in his own house, thus seeing the troubles of his brother and aiding him and support-ing him at the hour of his need; and his sons and daughters who saw this would learn from his deeds. When trouble befell a man he

253

would groan; the walls of his house would groan with him because of the mighty groaning of the poor; and he would know that there are blows even greater than that which had befallen him. And as he comforted the poor, so would the Holy One, blessed be He, in the future comfort him.

1 2

Now I leave the beggar and shall tell only of my mother's kerchief, which she tied around my neck when I entered the age of Commandments and was to be counted a member of the congregation. On that day, when I returned from the House of Study to eat the midday meal, I was dressed like a bridegroom and was very happy and pleased with myself because I was now putting on phylacteries. On the way I found that beggar sitting on a heap of stones, changing the bandages of his sores, his clothes rent and tattered, nothing but a bundle of rags that did not even hide his sores. He looked at me as well. The sores on his face seemed like eyes of fire. My heart stopped, my knees began shaking, my eyes grew dim, and everything seemed to be in a whirl. But I took my heart in my hand, nodded to the beggar, and greeted him, and he returned my greeting.

Suddenly my heart began thumping, my ears grew hot, and a sweetness such as I had never experienced in all my days took possession of all my limbs; my lips and my tongue were sweet with it, my mouth fell agape, my two eyes were opened, and I stared before me as a man who sees in waking what has been shown him in dream. And so I stood staring in front of me. The sun stopped still in the sky, not a creature was to be seen in the street; but He in His mercy sat in Heaven and looked down upon the earth and let His light shine bright on the sores of the beggar. I began loosening my kerchief to breathe more freely, for tears stood in my throat. Before I could loosen it, my heart began racing in strong emotion, and the sweetness, which I had already felt, doubled and redoubled. I took off the kerchief and gave it to the beggar. He took it and wound it around his sores. The sun came and stroked my neck.

I looked around. There was not a creature in the market, but a pile of stones lay there and reflected the sun's light. For a little while I stood there without thinking. Then I moved my feet and returned home.

13

When I reached the house I walked around it on all four sides. Suddenly I stopped at Mother's window, the one from which she used to look out. The place was strange; the sun's light upon it did not dazzle but warmed, and there was perfect rest there. Two or three people passing slowed their paces and lowered their voices; one of them wiped his brow and sighed deeply. It seems to me that that sigh must still be hanging there.

I stood there awhile, a minute or two minutes or more. Finally I moved from thence and entered the house. When I entered I found Mother sitting in the window as was her way. I greeted her, and she returned my greeting. Suddenly I felt that I had not treated her properly; she had had a fine kerchief which she used to bind around her head on Sabbaths and festivals, and I had taken it and given it to a beggar to bind up his feet with. Ere I had ended asking her to forgive me she was gazing at me with love and affection. I gazed back at her, and my heart was filled with the same gladness as I had felt on that Sabbath when my mother had set the kerchief about her head for the first time.

The end of the story of the kerchief of my mother, peace be with her.

......

samuel Beckett

(1906–   )

Prize awarded 1969 "for his writing, which—in new forms for the novel and drama—in the destitution of modern man acquires its elevation." ★ *Born outside of Dublin and educated at Trinity College, Dublin, Beckett left Ireland in 1928 and made his way to Paris, where he became a friend of James Joyce. After a period of peacetime wandering, then wartime activity in the Resistance, dislocation, and finally service as an interpreter in a French military hospital, he settled down in Paris. Beckett's earliest published work was* Whoroscope *(1930), a long poem about Descartes, whose assertion "I think, therefore I am" set the tone for existentialism. Other early works, the novels* Murphy *(1930) and* Watt *(1942–44) and the short-story collection* More Pricks Than Kicks *(1934), mined his Irish heritage.*

After the war, Beckett began writing in French, producing the prose narratives Molloy *(1951),* Malone Dies *(1955), and* The Unnamable *(1958), which he translated into English himself. He also wrote the play* Waiting for Godot *(1948–49), which, when it was finally produced in Paris in 1953, brought him international fame. As his concerns grew more fundamental—the relationship between the physical and spiritual worlds, the primary questions of being—he developed minimalist forms to express them.* Come and Go *(1967) is composed of 121 words for three characters, and other plays have only two characters (*Endgame, *1958, about servant and master) or even one (in* Krapp's Last Tape, *1961, an old man listens to a tape of his young self speaking of love; the brief* Rockabye, *1981, has a single female character).*

256

Even at a distance, Beckett is very involved in the productions of his plays, even directing one over transcontinental telephone, bringing suit when he heard one staging included music he had not called for and altered his lighting plan. Beckett has also written for radio and television, and all his works, no matter how bleak and despairing, are infused with black humor.

THE CALMATIVE

I DON'T KNOW WHEN I DIED. IT ALWAYS SEEMED to me I died old, about ninety years old, and what years, and that my body bore it out, from head to foot. But this evening, alone in my icy bed, I have the feeling I'll be older than the day, the night, when the sky with all its lights fell upon me, the same I had so often gazed on since my first stumblings on the distant earth. For I'm too frightened this evening to listen to myself rot, waiting for the great red lapses of the heart, the tearings at the caecal walls, and for the slow killings to finish in my skull, the assaults on unshakable pillars, the fornications with corpses. So I'll tell myself a story, I'll try and tell myself another story, to try and calm myself, and it's there I feel I'll be old, old, even older than the day I fell, calling for help, and it came. Or is it possible that in this story I have come back to life, after my death? No, it's not like me to come back to life, after my death.

What possessed me to stir when I wasn't with anybody? Was I being thrown out? No, I wasn't with anybody. I see a kind of den littered with empty tins. And yet we are not in the country. Perhaps it's just ruins, a ruined folly, on the skirts of the town, in a field, for the fields come right up to our walls, their walls, and the cows lie down at night in the lee of the ramparts. I have changed refuge so often, in the course of my rout, that now I can't tell between dens and ruins. But there was never any city but the one. It is true you often move along in a dream, houses and factories darken the air, trams go by, and under your feet wet from the grass there are suddenly cobbles. I only know the city of my childhood, I must have seen the other, but unbelieving. All I say cancels out, I'll have said nothing. Was I hungry itself? Did the weather tempt me? It was cloudy and cool, I insist, but not to the extent of luring me out. I couldn't get up at the first attempt, nor let us say at the second, and once up, propped against the wall, I wondered if I could go on, I mean up, propped against the wall. Impossible to go out and walk. I speak as though it all happened yesterday. Yesterday indeed is recent, but not enough. For what I tell this evening is passing this evening, at this passing hour. I'm no longer with these assassins, in this bed of terror, but in my distant refuge, my hands twined together, my head bowed, weak, breathless, calm, free, and older than I'll have ever been, if my calculations are correct. I'll tell my story in the past none the less, as though it were a myth, or an old fable, for this evening I need another age, that age to become another age in which I became what I was.

But little by little I got myself out and started walking with short steps among the trees, oh look, trees! The paths of other days were rank with tangled growth. I leaned against the trunks to get my breath and pulled myself forward with the help of boughs. Of my last passage no trace remained. They were the perishing oaks immortalized by d'Aubigné. It was only a grove. The fringe was near, a light less green and kind of tattered told me so, in a whisper. Yes, no matter where you stood, in this little wood, and were it in the furthest recess of its poor secrecies, you saw on every hand the gleam of this pale light, promise of God knows what fatuous eternity. Die without too much pain, a little, that's worth your while. Under the blind sky close with your own hands the eyes soon sockets, then quick into carrion not to mislead the crows. That's the advantage of death by drowning, one of the advantages, the crabs never get there too soon. But here a strange thing, I was no sooner free of the wood at last, having crossed unminding the ditch that girdles it, than thoughts came to me of cruelty, the kind that smiles. A lush pasture lay before me, nonsuch perhaps, who cares, drenched in evening dew or recent rain. Beyond this meadow to my certain knowledge a path, then a field and finally the ramparts, closing the prospect. Cyclopean and crenellated, standing out faintly against a sky scarcely less sombre, they did not seem in ruins, viewed from mine, but were, to my certain knowledge. Such was the scene offered to me, in vain, for I knew it well and loathed it. What I saw was a bald man in a brown suit, a comedian. He was telling a funny story about a fiasco. Its point escaped me. He used the word snail, or slug, to the delight of all present. The women seemed even more entertained than their escorts, if that were possible. Their shrill laughter pierced the clapping and, when this had subsided, broke out still here and there in sudden peals even after the next story had begun, so that part of it was lost. Perhaps they had in mind the reigning penis sitting who knows by their side and from that sweet shore launched their cries of joy towards the comic vast, what a talent. But it's to me this evening something has to happen, to my body as in myth and metamorphosis, this old body to which nothing ever happened, or so little, which never met with anything, loved anything, wished for anything, in its tarnished universe, except for the mirrors to shatter, the plane, the curved, the magnifying, the minifying, and to vanish in the havoc of its images. Yes, this evening it has to be as in the story my father used to read to me, evening after evening, when I was small, and he had all his health, to calm me, evening after evening, year after year it seems to me this evening, which I don't remember much about, except that it was the adventures of one Joe Breem, or Breen, the son of a lighthouse-keeper, a strong muscular lad of fifteen, those were the words, who swam for miles in the night, a knife between his teeth, after a shark, I forget why, out of sheer heroism. He might have simply told me the story, he knew it by heart, so did I, but that wouldn't have calmed me, he had to read it to me, evening after evening, or pretend to read it to me, turning the pages and explaining the pictures that were of me already, evening after evening the same pictures, till I dozed off on his shoulder. If he had skipped a single word I would have hit him, with my little fist, in his big belly bursting out of the old cardigan and unbuttoned trousers that rested him from his office canonicals. For me now the setting forth, the struggle and perhaps the return, for the old man I am this evening, older than my father ever was, older than I shall ever be. I crossed the meadow with little stiff steps at the same time limp, the best I could manage. Of my last passage no trace remained, it was long ago. And the little bruised stems soon straighten up again, having need of air and light, and so for the broken their place is soon taken. I entered the town by what they call the Shepherds' Gate without having seen a soul, only the first bats like flying crucifixions, nor heard a sound except my steps, my heart in my breast and then, as I went under the arch, the hoot of an owl, that cry at once so soft and fierce which

259

in the night, calling, answering, through my little wood and those nearby, sounded in my shelter like a tocsin. The further I went into the city the more I was struck by its deserted air. It was lit as usual, brighter than usual, although the shops were shut. But the lights were on in their windows with the object no doubt of attracting customers and prompting them to say, I say, I like that, not dear either, I'll come back tomorrow, if I'm still alive. I nearly said, Good God it's Sunday. The trams were running, the buses too, but few, slow, empty, noiseless, as if under water. I didn't see a single horse! I was wearing my long green greatcoat with the velvet collar, such as motorists wore about 1900, my father's, but that day it was sleeveless, a vast cloak. But on me it was still the same great dead weight, with no warmth to it, and the tails swept the ground, scraped it rather, they had grown so stiff, and I so shrunken. What would, what could happen to me in this empty place? But I felt the houses packed with people, lurking behind the curtains they looked out into the street or, crouched far back in the depths of the room, head in hands, were sunk in dream. Up aloft my hat, the same as always, I reached no further. I went right across the city and came to the sea, having followed the river to its mouth. I kept saying, I'll go back, unbelieving. The boats at anchor in the harbour, tied up to the jetty, seemed no less numerous than usual, as if I knew anything about what was usual. But the quays were deserted and there was no sign or stir of arrival or departure. But all might change from one moment to the next and be transformed like magic before my eyes. Then all the bustle of the people and things of the sea, the masts of the big craft gravely rocking and of the small more jauntily, I insist, and I'd hear the gulls' terrible cry and perhaps the sailors' cry. And I might slip unnoticed aboard a freighter outward bound and get far away and spend far away a few good months, perhaps even a year or two, in the sun, in peace, before I died. And without going that far it would be a sad state of affairs if in that unscandalizable throng I couldn't achieve a little encounter that would calm me a little, or exchange a few words with a navigator, for example, words to carry away with me to my refuge, to add to my collection. I waited sitting on a kind of topless capstan, saying, The very capstans this evening are out of order. And I gazed out to sea, out beyond the breakwaters, without sighting the least vessel. I could see lights flush with the water. And the pretty beacons at the harbour mouth I could see too, and others in the distance, flashing from the coast, the islands, the headlands. But seeing still no sign or stir I made ready to go, to turn away sadly from this dead haven, for there are scenes that call for strange farewells. I had merely to bow my head and look down at my feet, for it is in this attitude I always drew the strength to, how shall I say, I don't know, and it was always from the earth, rather than from the sky, notwithstanding its reputation, that my help came in time of trouble. And there, on the flagstone, which I was not focussing, for why focus it, I saw haven afar, where the black swell was most perilous, and all about me storm and wreck. I'll never come back here, I said. But when with the thrust of both hands against the rim of the capstan I heaved myself up I found facing me a young boy holding a goat by a horn. I sat down again. He stood there silent looking at me without visible fear or revulsion. Admittedly the light was poor. His silence seemed natural to me, it befitted me as the elder to speak first. He was barefoot and in rags. Haunter of the waterfront he had stepped aside to see what the dark hulk could be abandoned on the quayside. Such was my train of thought. Close up to me now with his little guttersnipe's eye there could be no doubt left in his mind. And yet he stayed. Can this base thought be mine? Moved, for after all that is what I must have come out for, in a way, and with little expectation of advantage from what might follow, I resolved to speak to him. So I marshalled the words and opened my mouth, thinking I would hear them. But all I heard was a kind of rattle, unintelligible even to me who knew what was intended. But it was nothing, mere speechlessness due to long silence, as in the wood that darkens the mouth of hell, do you remember, I only just. Without letting go of his goat he moved right up against me and offered me a sweet out of a twist of paper such as you could buy for a penny. I hadn't been offered a sweet for eighty years at least, but I took it eagerly and put it in my mouth, the old gesture came back to me, more and more moved since that is what I wanted. The sweets were stuck together and I had my work cut out to separate the top one, a green one, from the others, but he helped me and his hand brushed mine. And a moment later as he made to move away, hauling his goat after him, with a great gesticulation of my whole body I motioned him to stay and I said, in an impetuous murmur, Where are you off to, my little man, with your nanny? The words were hardly out of my mouth when for shame I covered my face. And yet they were the same I had tried to utter but a moment before. Where are you off to, my little man, with your

nanny! If I could have blushed I would have, but there was not
enough blood left in my extremities. If I had had a penny in my
pocket I would have given it to him, for him to forgive me, but I did
not have a penny in my pocket, nor anything resembling it. Nothing
that could give pleasure to a little unfortunate at the mouth of life.
I suspect I had nothing with me but my stone, that day, having gone
out as it were without premeditation. Of his little person I was fated
to see no more than the black curly hair and the pretty curve of the
long bare legs all muscle and dirt. And the hand, so fresh and keen,
I would not forget in a hurry either. I looked for better words to say
to him, I found them too late, he was gone, oh not far, but far. Out
of my life too he went without a care, not one of his thoughts would
ever be for me again, unless perhaps when he was old and, delving
in his boyhood, would come upon that gallows night and hold the
goat by the horn again and linger again a moment by my side, with
who knows perhaps a touch of tenderness, even of envy, but I have
my doubts. Poor dear dumb beasts, how you will have helped me.
What does your daddy do? that's what I would have said to him if
he had given me the chance. Soon they were no more than a single
blur which if I hadn't known I might have taken for a young cen-
taur. I was nearly going to have the goat dung, then pick up a
handful of the pellets so soon cold and hard, sniff and even taste
them, no, that would not help me this evening. I say this evening as
if it were always the same evening, but are there two evenings? I
went, intending to get back as fast as I could, but it would not be
quite empty-handed, repeating, I'll never come back here. My legs
were paining me, every step would gladly have been the last, but the
glances I darted towards the windows, stealthily, showed me a great
cylinder sweeping past as though on rollers on the asphalt. I must
indeed have been moving fast, for I overhauled more than one
pedestrian, there are the first men, without extending myself, I who
in the normal way was left standing by cripples, and then I seemed
to hear the footfalls die behind me. And yet each little step would
gladly have been the last. So much so that when I emerged on a
square I hadn't noticed on the way out, with a cathedral looming on
the far side, I decided to go in, if it was open, and hide, as in the
Middle Ages, for a space. I say cathedral, it may not have been, I
don't know, all I know is it would vex me in this story that aspires to
be the last, to have taken refuge in a common church. I remarked
the Saxon Stützenwechsel. Charming effect, but it didn't charm me.

The brilliantly lit nave appeared deserted. I walked round it several times without seeing a soul. They were hiding perhaps, under the choirstalls, or dodging behind the pillars, like woodpeckers. Suddenly close to where I was, and without my having heard the long preliminary rumblings, the organ began to boom. I sprang up from the mat on which I lay before the altar and hastened to the far end of the nave as if on my way out. But it was a side aisle and the door I disappeared through was not the exit. For instead of being restored to the night I found myself at the foot of a spiral staircase which I began to climb at top speed, mindless of my heart, like one hotly pursued by a homicidal maniac. This staircase faintly lit by I know not what means, slits perhaps, I mounted panting as far as the projecting gallery in which it culminated and which, separated from the void by a cynical parapet, encompassed a smooth round wall capped by a little dome covered with lead or verdigrised copper, phew, if that's not clear. People must have come here for the view, those who fall die on the way. Flattening myself against the wall I started round, clockwise. But I had hardly gone a few steps when I met a man revolving in the other direction, with the utmost circumspection. How I'd love to push him, or him to push me, over the edge. He gazed at me wild-eyed for a moment and then, not daring to pass me on the parapet side and surmising correctly that I would not relinquish the wall just to oblige him, abruptly turned his back on me, his head rather, for his back remained glued to the wall, and went back the way he had come so that soon there was nothing left of him but a left hand. It lingered a moment, then slid out of sight. All that remained to me was the vision of two burning eyes starting out of their sockets under a check cap. Into what nightmare thingness am I fallen? My hat flew off, but did not get far thanks to the string. I turned my head towards the staircase and lent an eye. Nothing. Then a little girl came into view followed by a man holding her by the hand, both pressed against the wall. He pushed her into the stairway, disappeared after her, turned and raised towards me a face that made me recoil. I could only see his bare head above the top step. When they were gone I called. I completed in haste the round of the gallery. No one. I saw on the horizon, where sky, sea, plain and mountain meet, a few low stars, not to be confused with the fires men light, at night, or that go alight alone. Enough. Back in the street I tried to find my way in the sky, where I knew the Bears so well. If I had seen someone I would have stopped him to ask, the most ferocious aspect would not have daunted me. I would have said, touching my hat, Pardon me, your honour, the Shepherds' Gate for the love of God. I thought I could go no further, but no sooner had the impetus reached my legs than on I went, believe it or not, at a very fair pace. I wasn't returning empty-handed, not quite, I was taking back with me the virtual certainty that I was still of this world, of that world too, in a way. But I was paying the price. I would have done better to spend the night in the cathedral, on the mat before the altar, I would have continued on my way at first light, or they would have found me stretched out in the rigor of death, the genuine bodily article, under the blue eyes fount of so much hope, and put me in the evening papers. But suddenly I was descending a wide street, vaguely familiar, but in which I could never have set foot, in my lifetime. But soon realizing I was going downhill I turned about and set off in the other direction. For I was afraid if I went downhill of returning to the sea where I had sworn never to return. When I say I turned about I mean I wheeled round in a wide semicircle without slowing down, for I was afraid if I stopped of not being able to start again, yes, I was afraid of that too. And this evening too I dare not stop. I was struck more and more by the contrast between the brightly lit streets and their deserted air. To say it distressed me, no, but I say it all the same, in the hope of calming myself. To say there was no one abroad, no, I would not go that far, for I remarked a number of shapes, male and female, strange shapes, but not more so than usual. As to what hour it might have been I had no idea, except that it must have been some hour of the night. But it might have been three or four in the morning just as it might have been ten or eleven in the evening, depending no doubt on whether one wondered at the scarcity of passersby or at the extraordinary radiance shed by the street-lamps and traffic-lights. For at one or other of these no one could fail to wonder, unless he was out of his mind. Not a single private car, but admittedly from time to time a public vehicle, slow sweep of light silent and empty. It is not my wish to labour these antinomies, for we are needless to say in a skull, but I have no choice but to add the following few remarks. All the mortals I saw were alone and as if sunk in themselves. It must be a common sight, but mixed with something else I imagine. The only couple was two men grappling, their legs intertwined. I only saw one cyclist! He was going the same way as I was. All were going the same way as I was, vehicles too, I have only just realized it. He was pedalling slowly in the middle of the street, reading a newspaper which he held with both hands spread open before his eyes. Every now and then he rang his bell without interrupting his reading. I watched him recede till he was no more than a dot on the horizon. Suddenly a young woman perhaps of easy virtue, dishevelled and her dress in disarray, darted across the street like a rabbit. That is all I had to add. But here a strange thing, yet another, I had no pain whatever, not even in my legs. Weakness. A good night's nightmare and a tin of sardines would restore my sensitivity. My shadow, one of my shadows, flew before me, dwindled, slid under my feet, trailed behind me the way shadows will. This degree of opacity appeared to me conclusive. But suddenly ahead of me a man on the same side of the street and going the same way, to keep harping on the same thing lest I forget. The distance between us was considerable, seventy paces at least, and fearing he might escape me I quickened my step with the result I swept forward as if on rollers. This is not me, I said, let us make the most of it. Finding myself in an instant a bare ten paces in his rear I slowed down so as not to burst in on him and so heighten the aversion my person inspired even in its most abject and obsequious attitudes. And a moment later, keeping humbly in step with him, Excuse me, your honour, the Shepherds' Gate for the love of God! At close quarters he appeared normal apart from that air already noted of ebbing inward. I drew a few steps ahead, turned, cringed, touched my hat and said, The right time for mercy's sake! I might as well not have existed. But what about the sweet? A light! I cried. Given my need of help I can't think why I did not bar his path. I couldn't have, that's all, I couldn't have touched him. Seeing a stone seat by the kerb I sat down and crossed my legs, like Walther. I must have dozed off, for the next thing was a man sitting beside me. I was still taking him in when he opened his eyes and set them on me, as if for the first time, for he shrank back unaffectedly. Where did you spring from? he said. To hear myself addressed again so soon impressed me greatly. What's the matter with you? he said. I tried to look like one with whom that only is the matter which is native to him. Forgive me, your honour, I said, gingerly lifting my hat and rising a fraction from the seat, the right time for the love of God! He said a time, I don't remember which, a time that explained nothing, that's all I remember, and did not calm me. But what time could have done that? Oh I know, I know, one will come that will.

265

But in the meantime? What's that you said? he said. Unfortunately I had said nothing. But I wriggled out of it by asking him if he could help me find my way which I had lost. No, he said, for I am not from these parts and if I am sitting on this slab it is because the hotels were full or would not let me in, I have no opinion. But tell me the story of your life, then we'll see. My life! I cried. Why yes, he said, you know, that kind of—what shall I say? He brooded for a time, no doubt trying to think of what life could well be said to be a kind. In the end he went on, testily, Come now, everyone knows that. He jogged me in the ribs. No details, he said, the main drift, the main drift. But as I remained silent he said, Shall I tell you mine, then you'll see what I mean. The account he then gave was brief and dense, facts, without comment. That's what I call a life, he said, do you follow me now? It wasn't bad, his story, positively fairylike in places. But that Pauline, I said, are you still with her? I am, he said, but I'm going to leave her and set up with another, younger and plumper. You travel a lot, I said. Oh, widely, widely, he said. Words were coming back to me, and the way to make them sound. All that's a thing of the past for you no doubt, he said. Do you think of spending some time among us? I said. This sentence struck me as particularly well turned. If it's not a rude question, he said, how old are you? I don't know, I said. You don't know! he cried. Not exactly, I said. Are thighs much in your thoughts, he said, arses, cunts and environs. I didn't follow. No more erections naturally, he said. Erections? I said. The penis, he said, you know what the penis is, there, between the legs. Ah that, I said. It thickens, lengthens, stiffens and rises, he said, does it not? I assented, though they were not the terms I would have used. That is what we call an erection, he said. He pondered, then exclaimed, Phenomenal! No? Strange right enough, I said. And there you have it all, he said. But what will become of her? I said. Who? he said. Pauline, I said. She will grow old, he said with tranquil assurance, slowly at first, then faster and faster, in pain and bitterness, pulling the devil by the tail. The face was not full, but I eyed it in vain, it remained clothed in its flesh instead of turning all chalky and channelled as with a gouge. The very vomer kept its cushion. It is true discussion was always bad for me. I longed for the tender nonsuch, I would have trodden it gently, with my boots in my hand, and for the shade of my wood, far from this terrible light. What are you grinning and bearing? he said. He held on his knees a big black bag, like a midwife's

I imagine. It was full of glittering phials. I asked him if they were all alike. Oho no, he said, for every taste. He took one and held it out to me, saying, One and six. What did he want? To sell it to me? Proceeding on this hypothesis I told him I had no money. No money! he cried. All of a sudden his hand came down on the back of my neck, his sinewy fingers closed and with a jerk and a twist he had me up against him. But instead of dispatching me he began to murmur words so sweet that I went limp and my head fell forward in his lap. Between the caressing voice and the fingers rowelling my neck the contrast was striking. But gradually the two things merged in a devastating hope, if I dare say so, and I dare. For this evening I have nothing to lose that I can discern. And if I have reached this point (in my story) without anything having changed, for if anything had changed I think I'd know, the fact remains I have reached it, and that's something too. It's no excuse for rushing matters. No, it must cease gently, as gently cease on the stairs the steps of the loved one, who could not love and will not come back, and whose steps say so, that she could not love and will not come back. He suddenly shoved me away and showed me the phial again. There you have it all, he said. It can't have been the same all as before. Want it? he said. No, but I said yes, so as not to vex him. He proposed an exchange. Give me your hat, he said. I refused. What vehemence! he said. I haven't a thing, I said. Try in your pockets, he said. I haven't a thing, I said, I came out without a thing. Give me a lace, he said. I refused. Long silence. And if you gave me a kiss, he said finally. I knew there were kisses in the air. Can you take off your hat? he said. I took it off. Put it back, he said, you look nicer with it on. I put it on. Come on, he said, give me a kiss and let there be an end to it. Did it not occur to him I might turn him down? No, a kiss is not a bootlace, he must have seen from my face that all passion was not quite spent. Come, he said. I wiped my mouth in its tod of hair and advanced it towards his. Just a moment, he said. My mouth stood still. You know what a kiss is? he said. Yes yes, I said. If it's not a rude question, he said, when was your last? Some time ago, I said, but I can still do them. He took off his hat, a bowler, and tapped the middle of his forehead. There, he said, and there only. He had a noble brow, white and high. He leaned forward, closing his eyes. Quick, he said. I pursed up my lips as mother had taught me and brought them down where he had said. Enough, he said. He raised his hand towards the spot, but left the gesture unfinished

267

......

and put on his hat. I turned away and looked across the street. It was then I noticed we were sitting opposite a horse-butcher's. Here, he said, take it. I had forgotten. He rose. Standing he was quite short. One good turn, he said, with radiant smile. His teeth shone. I listened to his steps die away. How tell what remains. But it's the end. Or have I been dreaming, am I dreaming? No no, none of that, for dream is nothing, a joke, and significant what is worse. I said, Stay where you are till day breaks, wait sleeping till the lamps go out and the streets come to life. But I stood up and moved off. My pains were back, but with something untoward which prevented my wrapping them round me. But I said, Little by little you are coming to. From my gait alone, slow, stiff and which seemed at every step to solve a statodynamic problem never posed before, I would have been known again, if I had been known. I crossed over and stopped before the butcher's. Behind the grille the curtains were drawn, rough canvas curtains striped blue and white, the colours of the Virgin, and stained with great pink stains. They did not quite meet in the middle, and through the chink I could make out the dim carcasses of the gutted horses hanging from hooks head downwards. I hugged the walls, famished for shadow. To think that in a moment all will be said, all to do again. And the city clocks, what was wrong with them, whose great chill clang even in my wood fell on me from the air? What else? Ah yes, my spoils. I tried to think of Pauline, but she eluded me, gleamed an instant and was gone, like the young woman in the street. So I went in the atrocious brightness, buried in my old flesh, straining towards an issue and passing them by to left and right, and my mind panting after this and that and always flung back to where there was nothing. I succeeded however in fastening briefly on the little girl, long enough to see her a little more clearly than before, so that she wore a kind of bonnet and clasped in her hand a book, of common prayer perhaps, and to try and have her smile, but she did not smile, but vanished down the staircase without having yielded me her little face. I had to stop. At first nothing, then little by little, I mean rising up out of the silence till suddenly no higher, a kind of massive murmur coming perhaps from the house that was propping me up. That reminded me that the houses were full of people, besieged, no, I don't know. When I stepped back to look at the windows I could see, in spite of shutters, blinds and muslins, that many of the rooms were lit. The light was so dimmed by the brilliancy flooding the boulevard that short of knowing or suspecting it was not so one might have supposed everyone sleeping. The sound was not continuous, but broken by silences possibly of consternation. I thought of ringing at the door and asking for shelter and protection till morning. But suddenly I was on my way again. But little by little, in a slow swoon, darkness fell about me. I saw a mass of bright flowers fade in an exquisite cascade of paling colours. I found myself admiring, all along the housefronts, the gradual blossoming of squares and rectangles, casement and sash, yellow, green, pink, according to the curtains and blinds, finding that pretty. Then at last, before I fell, first to my knees, as cattle do, then on my face, I was in a throng. I didn't lose consciousness, when I lose consciousness it will not be to recover it. They paid no heed to me, though careful not to walk on me, a courtesy that must have touched me, it was what I had come out for. It was well with me, sated with dark and calm, lying at the feet of mortals, fathom deep in the grey of dawn, if it was dawn. But reality, too tired to look for the right word, was soon restored, the throng fell away, the light came back and I had no need to raise my head from the ground to know I was back in the same blinding void as before. I said, Stay where you are, down on the friendly stone, or at least indifferent, don't open your eyes, wait for morning. But up with me again and back on the way that was not mine, on uphill along the boulevard. A blessing he was not waiting for me, poor old Breem, or Breen. I said, The sea is east, it's west I must go, to the left of north. But in vain I raised without hope my eyes to the sky to look for the Bears. For the light I stepped in put out the stars, assuming they were there, which I doubted, remembering the clouds.

Aleksandr Solzhenitsyn

(1918–   )

Prize awarded 1970 (accepted by letter, 1970; in person 1974) "for the ethical force with which he has pursued the indespensable tradition of Russian literature." ★ *Born one year after the Russian Revolution, Aleksandr Solzhenitsyn, teacher of mathematics and physics, political activist, and prolific author of historical novels, has emerged as the archetypal dissident Russian.*

Like Dostoyevsky, Solzhenitsyn endured imprisonment, exile, and censorship. For criticizing Stalin in a letter to a friend, he served eight years of forced labor in an arctic camp and then three years in detention. It was after this period that he started to write. One Day in the Life of Ivan Denisovitch (*1962*), *based on the labor camp experience, was published in the Soviet Union during the brief period of liberalization under Khrushchev, but only one other of his works, the short story "Zakhar-Kalita," was published in the USSR.*

In all Solzhenitsyn's work there is strong criticism of the Soviet system. World-wide recognition came to him with the publication of the Samizdat (*illegally self-published and clandestinely distributed*), *versions of* The Cancer Ward (*1968*), *an emotional, personal work based on Solzhenitsyn's bout with cancer, and* The First Circle (*1968*), *which satirically describes the labors of jailed scientists forced to develop wiretapping and voice-print technologies for Stalin, similar to work Solzhenitsyn did in detention. As important as his criticism of the Soviet system is the understanding gained through his art of how it is possible to retain one's humanity, one's inner freedom, under adverse circumstances.*

Much of Solzhenitsyn's work emulates classical nineteenth-century Russian novels in style and substance (if not in length). His later books include August 1918 (*1972*), *the first novel of a projected trilogy, which analyzes the corrupt and inept czarist regime;* The Gulag Archipelago 1918–1956 (*vols. I and II, 1973*), *a devastating documentary tour de force exposing tyrannical Soviet "justice"; and* Lenin in Zurich (*1976*), *which covers the month just before Lenin's triumphant return to Russia.*

Solzhenitsyn's continual inference in all his works that socialism itself is tyranny removes him from the dissident mainstream as represented by Osip Mandelstam and Andrei Sakharov, with whom he was implicated in a treason trial in 1968. Promising to complete his treatment of the Russian Revolution and its aftermath, Solzhenitsyn goes on writing and speaking out on behalf of human rights from his home in Vermont.

IN YESENIN COUNTRY

FOUR MONOTONOUS VILLAGES STRUNG OUT one after another along the road. Dust. No gardens, and no woods nearby. Rickety fences. Here and there some garishly painted shutters. A pig scratching itself against the pump in the middle of the road. As the shadow of a bicycle flashes past them, a flock of geese in single file turn their heads in unison and give it a cheerfully aggressive honk. Chickens scratch busily in the roadway and the yards, searching for food.

Even the village general store of Konstantinovo looks like a rickety henhouse. Salted herrings. Several brands of vodka. Sticky boiled sweets of a kind people stopped eating fifteen years ago. Round loaves of black bread, twice as heavy as the ones you buy in town, looking as if they are meant to be sliced with an axe rather than a knife.

Inside the Yesenins' cottage, wretched little partitions that do not reach the ceiling divide it up into what are more like cupboards or loose boxes than rooms. Outside is a little fenced-in yard; here there used to be a bathhouse, where Sergey would shut himself in the dark and compose his first poems. Beyond the fence is the usual little paddock.

I walked around this village, which is exactly like so many others, where the villagers' main concerns are still the crops, how to make money, how to keep up with the neighbors, and I am moved: the divine fire once scorched this piece of countryside, and I can feel it burning my cheeks to this day. Walking along the steep banks of the Oka, I stare into the distance with wonderment—was

271

it really that far-off strip of Khvorostov wood that inspired the evocative line:

The forest clamorous with a wood-grouse's lament . . .

And is this the same peaceful Oka, meandering through water meadows, of which he wrote:

Hayricks of sun stacked in the waters' depth . . .

What a thunderbolt of talent the Creator must have hurled into that cottage, into the heart of that quick-tempered country boy, for the shock of it to have opened his eyes to so much beauty—by the stove, in the pigsty, on the threshing floor, in the fields; beauty that for a thousand years others had simply trampled on and ignored.

THE ASHES OF A POET

WHERE NOW THERE IS A VILLAGE called L'govo, the ancient town of Ol'gov once stood on this cliff above the river Oka. When the Russians of those days chose a site, next in importance after good, drinkable, running water was its beauty.

Saved by a miracle from murder at his brothers' hands, Ingvar Igorevich founded the Monastery of the Assumption here as a thanks offering.

From this place, on a clear day you can see far across the water meadows to where, thirty-five versts away, on another such eminence stands the tall belfry of the Monastery of St. John the Divine.

Both were spared by the superstitious Khan Bahty.

From all others, Yakov Petrovich Polonsky chose this place as his own and gave instructions that he was to be buried here. Man, it seems, has always been prone to the belief that his spirit will hover over his grave and gaze down on the peaceful countryside around it.

But the domed churches have gone; the half of the stone walls that is left has been made up in height by a plank fence with barbed wire, and the whole of this ancient place is dominated by those sickeningly familiar monsters: watchtowers. There is a guardhouse in the monastery gateway, and a poster that says "Peace among Nations," with a Russian workman holding a little black girl in his arms.

We pretend ignorance. Among the huts where the guards live, an off-duty warder, dressed in a singlet, explains to us:

"There was a monastery here, in the second world. They say the first world was Rome, and Moscow is the third. It used to be a children's colony once, too, but the kids didn't know what the place was, so they messed up the walls and smashed the icons. Then a collective farm bought the two churches for forty thousand rubles—for the bricks, to build a big cowshed with six rows of stalls. Worked on it myself. We were paid fifty kopecks for a whole one, twenty kopecks for a half brick. But they never came out clean—always had lumps of mortar stuck to them. They found a vault under the church with a bishop in it. He was just a skeleton, but his robe was still all right. A couple of us tried to pull the robe in two, but the stuff was that good it wouldn't tear. . . ."

"Tell me—according to the map, there's a poet called Polonsky buried here. Where is his grave?"

"You can't see Polonsky. He's inside the perimeter."

So Polonsky was out of bounds. What else was there to see? A crumbling ruin? Wait, though—the warder was turning to his wife: "Didn't they dig Polonsky up?"

"Mm. Took him to Ryazan." The woman nodded from the porch as she cracked sunflower seeds with her teeth.

The warder thought this was a great joke: "Seems he'd done his time—so they let him out. . . ."

THE OLD BUCKET

YES, KARTUN FOREST IS A DEPRESSING place for an ex-soldier to explore. There is a place in it where the traces of eighteen years ago are still preserved. Partly collapsed, it hardly looks like a line of trenches or the firing position of a troop of field guns but was most likely an infantry platoon strong point where an anonymous band of hefty Russian soldiers, in their tattered greatcoats, had dug themselves in. Over the years the roof beams of the dugout have been removed, of course, but the trenches are still quite plain to see.

Although I never fought here, I was in action in another wood like it nearby. I walked from dugout to dugout trying to reconstruct the position. Suddenly, coming out of one dugout, I stumbled on an old bucket that had already seen better days when it had been left lying there eighteen years ago.

Even then, in that first wartime winter, it had been broken. Maybe some quick-witted soldier had picked it up in a burnt-out village, had battered the lower half of the sides into a cone and used it to connect his tin stove to a flue. Here, in this same dugout, for the ninety or perhaps hundred and fifty days that the front line was stabilized in this sector, smoke had poured through this broken bucket. It had glowed hellishly hot, men had warmed their hands over it, you could light a cigarette on it and toast bread in front of it. As much smoke had passed through that bucket as all the unspoken thoughts and unwritten letters of the men there—men, alas, probably long since dead.

Then one bright morning the tactical position changed, the dug-

275

out was abandoned, and as the officer urged them on—"Come on,
get moving!"—an orderly doused the stove, packed it into the back
of the truck until everything was stowed away, except that there was
no room for the broken bucket.

"Chuck the filthy thing away!" shouted the sergeant major. "You'll
find another one in the new place."

They had a long way to go, and in any case the warmer spring
weather was not far off; the orderly stood there with the broken
bucket, and with a sigh he dropped it by the entrance to the dugout.

Everybody laughed.

Since then the logs have been pulled off the roof, the bunks and
the table removed from inside, but that faithful bucket has stayed
there beside its dugout.

As I stood over it, tears started to my eyes. How splendid they
were, those friends of wartime days. The spirit that kept us going,
our hopes, even that selfless friendship of ours—it has all vanished
like smoke, and there will never again be a use for that rusty, forgotten . . .

A Journey Along the Oka

TRAVELING ALONG COUNTRY ROADS IN
central Russia, you begin to understand why the Russian countryside has such a soothing effect.

It is because of its churches. They rise over ridge and hillside,
descending toward wide rivers like red-and-white princesses, towering above the thatch and wooden huts of everyday life with their
slender, carved, and fretted belfries. From far away they greet each
other; from distant, unseen villages they rise toward the same sky.

Wherever you may wander, over field or pasture, many miles
from any homestead, you are never alone: above the wall of trees,
above the hayricks, even above the very curve of the earth itself, the
dome of a belfry is always beckoning to you, from Borki Lovetskie,
Lyubichi, or Gavrilovskoe.

But as soon as you enter a village you realize that the churches
that welcomed you from afar are no longer living. Their crosses
have long since been bent or broken off; the dome with its peeling
paint reveals its rusty ribcage; weeds grow on the roofs and in the
cracks of the walls; the cemetery is hardly ever cared for, its crosses
knocked over and its graves ransacked; the icons behind the altar
have faded from a decade of rain and are scrawled with obscene
graffiti.

277

In the porch there are barrels of salt, and a tractor is swinging
round toward them, or a lorry is backing up to the vestry door to
collect some sacks. In one church, machine tools are humming away;
another stands silent, simply locked up. Others have been turned
into clubs where propaganda meetings are held ("We Will Achieve

High Yields of Milk!") or films shown: *Poem about the Sea, The Great Adventure.*

People have always been selfish and often evil. But the Angelus used to toll, and its echo would float over village, field, and wood. It reminded man that he must abandon his trivial earthly cares and give up one hour of his thoughts to life eternal. The tolling of the eventide bell, which now survives for us only in a popular song, raised man above the level of a beast.

Our ancestors put their best into these stones and these belfries— all their knowledge and all their faith.

Come on, Vitka, buck up and stop feeling sorry for yourself! The film starts at six, and the dance is at eight. . . .

REFLECTIONS

N THE SURFACE OF A SWIFT-FLOWING
stream the reflections of things near or far are always indistinct;
even if the water is clear and has no foam, reflections in the constant
stream of ripples, the restless kaleidoscope of water, are still uncertain, vague, incomprehensible.

Only when the water has flowed down river after river and reaches
a broad, calm estuary or comes to rest in some backwater or a small,
still lake—only then can we see in its mirrorlike smoothness every
leaf of a tree on the bank, every wisp of a cloud, and the deep blue
expanse of the sky.

It is the same with our lives. If so far we have been unable to see
clearly or to reflect the eternal lineaments of truth, is it not because
we, too, are still moving toward some end—because we are still alive?

Pablo Neruda

(1904–1973)

Prize awarded 1971 "for a poetry that with the action of an elemental force

brings alive a continent's destiny and dreams." ★ *Chilean poet Pablo Neruda's*

works encompassed twenty volumes and were translated into eighty languages.

Neruda also had a distinguished career in politics, serving in the Chilean

Senate, on the Communist Central Committee, and as consul in Rangoon,

Colombo, Madrid, Buenos Aires, and Barcelona. Neruda was befriended and

encouraged by García Lorca, the Spanish playwright whose martyrdom at the

hands of the fascists deeply influenced Neruda's literary and political develop-

ment. He formally became a Marxist in 1975. Under the auspices of his close

friend Salvador Allende, he served as ambassador to France.

Neruda was increasingly concerned with social realities in his art as well as

his political life, yet the lyricism and earthy celebration of real people in his often

erotic and surreal poetry transcended the literature of rigid social realism. His

activism and political affiliations distracted his critics for many years from an

objective appreciation of his literary worth; this might (in part) explain why he

was not awarded the Nobel Prize in the first twenty years his name was submitted

as a nominee. His best-known collections are the graceful Twenty Poems of

Love and One Song of Despair *(1924),* Canto General *(1950), and the*

moving and evocative Macchu Picchu *(1945).*

GENTLEMAN ALONE

The young homosexuals and languishing girls,
the tall widows frantic with sleeplessness,
the matrons still tender in years, now thirty hours pregnant,
the gravel-voiced tomcats that cross in the night of my
     garden
like a necklace of sensual oysters, atremble,
encircle my lonely environs—
antagonists stalking my soul,
schemers in nightgowns,
exchanging long kisses, packed in like a countersign.

The luminous summer leads on: formations
of lovers identically sad,
deploying in twos: the lean with the plump, the merry and
     mournful:
under elegant coconut palms, near the moon and the ocean,
the bustle of trousers and petticoat-hoops is unending,
a sound of silk hosiery fondled,
and the feminine nipple blazing out like an eye.

At long last, the petty employee, delivered from weekly
routine, after bedding himself for the night with a novel,
seduces his neighbor conclusively.
They go on to a villainous movie
where all of the heroes are horses or passionate princes,
and he dandles a fleecy pubescence of legs
with his sweltering fingers still rank with tobacco.

All the twilight seducers, the night of the wedded,
close over like bed sheets and bury me:
all those hours after luncheon, when the green undergraduate,
the boys and the girls, and the ministers, masturbate,
and the beasts couple openly;
when the bee sniffs a blood-smell, the choleric fly
buzzes, the cousin plays games with his girl-cousin

queerly; when the doctor keeps furious watch on the mate
  of the lady
malingerer; the matutinal hour when the schoolteacher
absentmindedly renders his conjugal due and sits down to
  his breakfast;
above all, the adulterers making love with unfalsified
ardor, on bedspreads like boats, high and trim on the waters:
so, tautly, eternally,
that big, breathing forest encircles me
with its raddle of towering blossoms, like mouths with
  their teeth:
it is black at the root; it is shaped like a shoe and a fingernail.

Isaac Bashevis Singer

(1904–   )

Prize awarded 1978 "for his impassioned narrative art, which, with roots in a Polish-Jewish cultural tradition, brings universal human conditions to life." ★ *Isaac Bashevis Singer was born in Poland and in 1935 emigrated to New York, where he worked as a journalist. Singer is well versed in Hasidic traditions; in his folkloric and nostalgic chronicles of the central European Jewish experience, theological and psychological themes interweave with the surreal and the grotesque. He writes in Yiddish but works closely with his translators (often his son) to preserve linguistic subtleties, which contribute to the charm of his stories. His semiautobiographical first novel,* The Family Moskat *(1950) realistically portrayed a range of characters from Orthodox to nonbelievers in Warsaw in the fifty years before the Holocaust. The novel* Satan in Goray *(1955) takes place in a shtetl in medieval Poland.*

Many of Singer's books are compilations of novellas and stories, as in The Dybbuk and the Golem *(1955) amd* Gimpel the Fool *(1957). Some of these works reflect a nineteenth-century provincialism, while others, like the novel* The Magician of Lublin *(1960), are concerned with modern man's relation to tradition. The eleven stories in* The Spinoza of Market Street *(1961) occur after World War II, and* Enemies, A Love Story *(1972), a lusty modern comedy with Holocaust overtones, takes place in New York City. With his masterful prose style and vivid narrative, Singer can bestow even simple rural village personalities with an overlay of modern psychological understanding.*

283

SHORT FRIDAY

IN THE VILLAGE OF LAPSCHITZ LIVED A TAILOR named Shmul-Leibele with his wife, Shoshe. Shmul-Leibele was half tailor, half furrier, and a complete pauper. He had never mastered his trade. When filling an order for a jacket or a gaberdine, he inevitably made the garment either too short or too tight. The belt in the back would hang either too high or too low, the lapels never matched, the vent was off center. It was said that he had once sewn a pair of trousers with the fly off to one side. Shmul-Leibele could not count the wealthy citizens among his customers. Common people brought him their shabby garments to have patched and turned, and the peasants gave him their old pelts to reverse. As is usual with bunglers, he was also slow. He would dawdle over a garment for weeks at a time. Yet despite his shortcomings, it must be said that Shmul-Leibele was an honorable man. He used only strong thread and none of his seams ever gave. If one ordered a lining from Shmul-Leibele, even one of common sackcloth or cotton, he bought only the very best material, and thus lost most of his profit. Unlike other tailors who hoarded every last bit of remaining cloth, he returned all scraps to his customers.

Had it not been for his competent wife, Shmul-Leibele would certainly have starved to death. Shoshe helped him in whatever way she could. On Thursdays she hired herself out to wealthy families to knead dough, and on summer days went off to the forest to gather berries and mushrooms, as well as pinecones and twigs for the stove. In winter she plucked down for brides' featherbeds. She was also a better tailor than her husband, and when he began to sigh, or dally and mumble to himself, an indication that he could no longer muddle through, she would take the chalk from his hand and show him how to continue. Shoshe had no children, but it was common knowledge that it wasn't she who was barren, but rather her husband who was sterile, since all of her sisters had borne children, while his only brother was likewise childless. The townswomen repeatedly urged Shoshe to divorce him, but she turned a deaf ear, for the couple loved one another with a great love.

Shmul-Leibele was small and clumsy. His hands and feet were too large for his body, and his forehead bulged on either side as is common in simpletons. His cheeks, red as apples, were bare of whiskers, and but a few hairs sprouted from his chin. He had scarcely any neck at all; his head sat upon his shoulders like a snowman's. When he walked, he scraped his shoes along the ground so that every step could be heard far away. He hummed continuously and there was always an amiable smile on his face. Both winter and summer he wore the same caftan and sheepskin cap with earlaps. Whenever there was any need for a messenger, it was always Shmul-Leibele who was pressed into service, and however far away he was sent, he always went willingly. The wags saddled him with a variety of nicknames and made him the butt of all sorts of pranks, but he never took offense. When others scolded his tormentors, he would merely observe: "What do I care? Let them have their fun. They're only children, after all. . . ."

Sometimes he would present one or another of the mischief makers with a piece of candy or a nut. This he did without any ulterior motive, but simply out of goodheartedness.

Shoshe towered over him by a head. In her younger days she had been considered a beauty, and in the households where she worked as a servant they spoke highly of her honesty and diligence. Many young men had vied for her hand, but she had selected Shmul-Leibele because he was quiet and because he never joined the other town boys who gathered on the Lublin road at noon Saturdays to flirt with the girls. His piety and retiring nature pleased her. Even as a girl Shoshe had taken pleasure in studying the Pentateuch, in nursing the infirm at the almshouse, in listening to the tales of the old women who sat before their houses darning stockings. She would fast on the last day of each month, the Minor Day of Atonement, and often attended the services at the women's synagogue. The other servant girls mocked her and thought her old-fashioned. Im-

285

mediately following her wedding she shaved her head and fastened a kerchief firmly over her ears, never permitting a stray strand of hair from her matron's wig to show as did some of the other young women. The bath attendant praised her because she never frolicked at the ritual bath, but performed her ablutions according to the laws. She purchased only indisputably kosher meat, though it was a half-cent more per pound, and when she was in doubt about the dietary laws she sought out the rabbi's advice. More than once she had not hesitated to throw out all the food and even to smash the earthen crockery. In short, she was a capable, God-fearing woman, and more than one man envied Shmul-Leibele his jewel of a wife.

Above all of life's blessings the couple revered the Sabbath. Every Friday noon Shmul-Leibele would lay aside his tools and cease all work. He was always among the first at the ritual bath, and he immersed himself in the water four times for the four letters of the Holy Name. He also helped the beadle set the candles in the chandeliers and the candelabra. Shoshe scrimped throughout the week, but on the Sabbath she was lavish. Into the heated oven went cakes, cookies and the Sabbath loaf. In winter, she prepared puddings made of chicken's neck stuffed with dough and rendered fat. In summer she made puddings with rice or noodles, greased with chicken fat and sprinkled with sugar or cinnamon. The main dish consisted of potatoes and buckwheat, or pearl barley with beans, in the midst of which she never failed to set a marrowbone. To insure that the dish would be well cooked, she sealed the oven with loose dough. Shmul-Leibele treasured every mouthful, and at every Sabbath meal he would remark: "Ah, Shoshe love, it's food fit for a king! Nothing less than a taste of Paradise!" to which Shoshe replied, "Eat hearty. May it bring you good health."

Although Shmul-Leibele was a poor scholar, unable to memorize a chapter of the Mishnah, he was well versed in all the laws. He and his wife frequently studied *The Good Heart* in Yiddish. On half-holidays, holidays and on each free day, he studied the Bible in Yiddish. He never missed a sermon, and though a pauper, he bought from peddlers all sorts of books of moral instructions and religious tales, which he then read together with his wife. He never wearied of reciting sacred phrases. As soon as he arose in the morning he washed his hands and began to mouth the preamble to the prayers. Then he would walk over to the study house and worship as one of the quorum. Every day he recited a few chapters of the Psalms, as well as those prayers which the less serious tended to skip over. From his father he had inherited a thick prayer book with wooden covers, which contained the rites and laws pertaining to each day of the year. Shmul-Leibele and his wife heeded each and every one of these. Often he would observe to his wife: "I shall surely end up in Gehenna, since there'll be no one on earth to say Kaddish over me." "Bite your tongue, Shmul-Leibele," she would counter. "For one, everything is possible under God. Secondly, you'll live until the Messiah comes. Thirdly, it's just possible that I will die before you and you will marry a young woman who'll bear you a dozen children." When Shoshe said this, Shmul-Leibele would shout: "God forbid! You must remain in good health. I'd rather rot in Gehenna!"

Although Shmul-Leibele and Shoshe relished every Sabbath, their greatest satisfaction came from the Sabbaths in wintertime. Since the day before the Sabbath evening was a short one, and since Shoshe was busy until late Thursday at her work, the couple usually stayed up all of Thursday night. Shoshe kneaded dough in the trough, covering it with cloth and a pillow so that it might ferment. She heated the oven with kindling-wood and dry twigs. The shutters in the room were kept closed, the door shut. The bed and bench-bed remained unmade, for at daybreak the couple would take a nap. As long as it was dark Shoshe prepared the Sabbath meal by the light of a candle. She plucked a chicken or a goose (if she had managed to come by one cheaply), soaked it, salted it and scraped the fat from it. She roasted a liver for Shmul-Leibele over the glowing coals and baked a small Sabbath loaf for him. Occasionally she would inscribe her name upon the loaf with letters of dough, and then Shmul-Leibele would tease her: "Shoshe, I am eating you up. Shoshe, I have already swallowed you." Shmul-Leibele loved warmth, and he would climb up on the oven and from there look down as his spouse cooked, baked, washed, rinsed, pounded and carved. The Sabbath loaf would turn out round and brown. Shoshe braided the loaf so swiftly that it seemed to dance before Shmul-Leibele's eyes. She bustled about efficiently with spatulas, pokers, ladles and goosewing dusters, and at times even snatched up a live coal with her bare fingers. The pots perked and bubbled. Occasionally a drop of soup would spill and the hot tin would hiss and squeal. And all the while the cricket continued its chirping. Although Shmul-Leibele had finished his supper by this time, his appetite would be whetted afresh, and Shoshe would throw

287

him a knish, a chicken gizzard, a cookie, a plum from the plum stew or a chunk of the pot-roast. At the same time she would chide him, saying that he was a glutton. When he attempted to defend himself she would cry: "Oh, the sin is upon me, I have allowed you to starve. . . ."

At dawn they would both lie down in utter exhaustion. But because of their efforts Shoshe would not have to run herself ragged the following day, and she could make the benediction over the candles a quarter of an hour before sunset.

The Friday on which this story took place was the shortest Friday of the year. Outside, the snow had been falling all night and had blanketed the house up to the windows and barricaded the door. As usual, the couple had stayed up until morning, then had lain down to sleep. They had arisen later than usual, for they hadn't heard the rooster's crow, and since the windows were covered with snow and frost, the day seemed as dark as night. After whispering, "I thank Thee," Shmul-Leibele went outside with a broom and shovel to clear a path, after which he took a bucket and fetched water from the well. Then, as he had no pressing work, he decided to lay off for the whole day. He went to the study house for the morning prayers, and after breakfast wended his way to the bathhouse. Because of the cold outside, the patrons kept up an eternal plaint: "A bucket! A bucket!" and the bath attendant poured more and more water over the glowing stones so that the steam grew constantly denser. Shmul-Leibele located a scraggly willow-broom, mounted to the highest bench and whipped himself until his skin glowed red. From the bathhouse, he hurried over to the study house where the beadle had already swept and sprinkled the floor with sand. Shmul-Leibele set the candles and helped spread the tablecloths over the tables. Then he went home again changed into his Sabbath clothes. His boots, resoled but a few days before, no longer let the wet through. Shoshe had done her washing for the week, and had given him a fresh shirt, underdrawers, a fringed garment, even a clean pair of stockings. She had already performed the benediction over the candles, and the spirit of the Sabbath emanated from every corner of the room. She was wearing her silk kerchief with the silver spangles, a yellow-and-gray dress, and shoes with gleaming, pointed tips. On her throat hung the chain that Shmul-Leibele's mother, peace be with her, had given her to celebrate the signing of the wedding contract. The marriage band sparkled on her index finger. The candlelight reflected in the window panes, and Shmul-Leibele fancied that there was a duplicate of this room outside and that another Shoshe was out there lighting the Sabbath candles. He yearned to tell his wife how full of grace she was, but there was no time for it, since it is specifically stated in the prayer book that it is fitting and proper to be amongst the first ten worshipers at the synagogue; as it so happened, going off to prayers he was the tenth man to arrive. After the congregation had intoned the Song of Songs, the cantor sang, "Give thanks," and "O come, let us exult." Shmul-Leibele prayed with fervor. The words were sweet upon his tongue, they seemed to fall from his lips with a life of their own, and he felt that they soared to the eastern wall, rose above the embroidered curtain of the Holy Ark, the gilded lions, and the tablets, and floated up to the ceiling with its painting of the twelve constellations. From there, the prayers surely ascended to the Throne of Glory.

2

The cantor chanted, "Come, my beloved," and Shmul-Leibele trumpeted along in accompaniment. Then came the prayers, and the men recited "It is our duty to praise . . ." to which Shmul-Leibele added a "Lord of the Universe." Afterwards, he wished everyone a good Sabbath: the rabbi, the ritual slaughterer, the head of the community, the assistant rabbi, everyone present. The *cheder* lads shouted, "Good Sabbath, Shmul-Leibele," while they mocked him with gestures and grimaces, but Shmul-Leibele answered them all with a smile, even occasionally pinched a boy's cheek affectionately. Then he was off for home. The snow was piled high so that one could barely make out the contours of the roofs, as if the entire settlement had been immersed in white. The sky, which had hung low and overcast all day, now grew clear. From among white clouds a full moon peered down, casting a daylike brilliance over the snow. In the west, the edge of a cloud still held the glint of sunset. The stars on this Friday seemed larger and sharper, and through some miracle Lapschitz seemed to have blended with the sky. Shmul-Leibele's hut, which was situated not far from the synagogue, now hung suspended in space, as it is written: "He suspendeth the earth on nothingness." Shmul-Leibele walked slowly since, according to law, one must not hurry when coming from a holy place. Yet he longed to be home. "Who knows?" he thought. "Perhaps Shoshe has become ill? Maybe she's gone to fetch water and, God forbid, has fallen into the well? Heaven save us, what a lot of troubles can befall a man."

On the threshold he stamped his feet to shake off the snow, then opened the door and saw Shoshe. The room made him think of Paradise. The oven had been freshly whitewashed, the candles in the brass candelabras cast a Sabbath glow. The aromas coming from the sealed oven blended with the scents of the Sabbath supper. Shoshe sat on the bench-bed apparently awaiting him, her cheeks shining with the freshness of a young girl's. Shmul-Leibele wished her a happy Sabbath and she in turn wished him a good year. He began to hum, "Peace upon ye minstering angels . . ." and after he had said his farewells to the invisible angels that accompany each Jew leaving the synagogue, he recited: "That worthy woman." How well he understood the meaning of these words, for he had read them often in Yiddish, and each time reflected anew on how aptly they seemed to fit Shoshe.

Shoshe was aware that these holy sentences were being said in her honor, and thought to herself, "Here am I, a simple woman, an orphan, and yet God has chosen to bless me with a devoted husband who praises me in the holy tongue."

Both of them had eaten sparingly during the day so that they would have an appetite for the Sabbath meal. Shmul-Leibele said the benediction over the raisin wine and gave Shoshe the cup so that she might drink. Afterwards, he rinsed his fingers from a tin dipper, then she washed hers, and they both dried their hands with a single towel, each at either end. Shmul-Leibele lifted the Sabbath loaf and cut it with the bread knife, a slice for himself and one for his wife.

He immediately informed her that the loaf was just right, and she countered: "Go on, you say that every Sabbath."

"But it happens to be the truth," he replied.

Although it was hard to obtain fish during the cold weather, Shoshe had purchased three-fourths of a pound of pike from the fishmonger. She had chopped it with onions, added an egg, salt and pepper and cooked it with carrots and parsley. It took Shmul-Leibele's breath away, and after it he had to drink a tumbler of whiskey. When he began the table chants, Shoshe accompanied him quietly. Then came the chicken soup with noodles and tiny circlets of fat which glowed on the surface like golden ducats. Between the soup and the main course, Shmul-Leibele again sang Sabbath hymns.

290

Since goose was cheap at this time of year, Shoshe gave Shmul-Leibele an extra leg for good measure. After the dessert, Shmul-Leibele washed for the last time and made a benediction. When he came to the words: "Let us not be in need either of the gifts of flesh and blood nor of their loans," he rolled his eyes upward and brandished his fists. He never stopped praying that he be allowed to continue to earn his own livelihood and not, God forbid, become an object of charity.

After grace, he said yet another chapter of the Mishnah, and all sorts of other prayers which were found in his large prayer book. Then he sat down to read the weekly portion of the Pentateuch twice in Hebrew and once in Aramaic. He enunciated every word and took care to make no mistake in the difficult Aramaic paragraphs of the Onkelos. When he reached the last section, he began to yawn and tears gathered in his eyes. Utter exhaustion overcame him. He could barely keep his eyes open and between one passage and the next he dozed off for a second or two. When Shoshe noticed this, she made up the bench-bed for him and prepared her own featherbed with clean sheets. Shmul-Leibele barely managed to say the retiring prayers and began to undress. When he was already lying on his bench-bed he said: "A good Sabbath, my pious wife. I am very tired. . . ." and turning to the wall, he promptly began to snore.

Shoshe sat a while longer gazing at the Sabbath candles which had already begun to smoke and flicker. Before getting into bed, she placed a pitcher of water and a basin at Shmul-Leibele's bedstead so that he would not rise the following morning without water to wash with. Then she, too, lay down and fell asleep.

They had slept an hour or two or possibly three—what does it matter, actually?—when suddenly Shoshe heard Shmul-Leibele's voice. He waked her and whispered her name. She opened one eye and asked, "What is it?"

"Are you clean?" he mumbled.

She thought for a moment and replied, "Yes."

He rose and came to her. Presently he was in bed with her. A desire for her flesh had roused him. His heart pounded rapidly, the blood coursed in his veins. He felt a pressure in his loins. His urge was to mate with her immediately, but he remembered the law which admonished a man not to copulate with a woman until he had first spoken affectionately to her, and he now began to speak of his

291

love for her and how this mating could possibly result in a male-child.

"And a girl you wouldn't accept?" Shoshe chided him, and he replied, "Whatever God deigns to bestow would be welcome."

"I fear this privilege isn't mine anymore," she said with a sigh.

"Why not?" he demanded. "Our mother Sarah was far older than you."

"How can one compare oneself to Sarah? Far better you divorce me and marry another."

He interrupted her, stopping her mouth with his hand. "Were I sure that I could sire the twelve tribes of Israel with another, I still would not leave you. I cannot even imagine myself with another woman. You are the jewel of my crown."

"And what if I were to die?" she asked.

"God forbid! I would simply perish from sorrow. They would bury us both on the same day."

"Don't speak blasphemy. May you outlive my bones. You are a man. You would find somebody else. But what would I do without you?"

He wanted to answer her, but she sealed his lips with a kiss. He went to her then. He loved her body. Each time she gave herself to him, the wonder of it astonished him anew. How was it possible, he would think, that he, Shmul-Leibele, should have such a treasure all to himself? He knew the law, one dared not surrender to lust for pleasure. But somewhere in a sacred book he had read that it was permissible to kiss and embrace a wife to whom one had been wed according to the laws of Moses and Israel, and he now caressed her face, her throat and her breasts. She warned him that this was frivolity. He replied, "So I'll lie on the torture rack. The great saints also loved their wives." Nevertheless, he promised himself to attend to ritual bath the following morning, to intone psalms and to pledge a sum to charity. Since she loved him also and enjoyed his caresses, she let him do his will.

After he had satiated his desire, he wanted to return to his own bed, but a heavy sleepiness came over him. He felt a pain in his temples. Shoshe's head ached as well. She suddenly said, "I'm afraid something is burning in the oven. Maybe I should open the flue?"

"Go on, you're imagining it," he replied. "It'll become too cold in here."

And so complete was his weariness that he fell asleep, as did she.

That night Shmul-Leibele suffered an eerie dream. He imagined that he had passed away. The Burial-Society brethren came by, picked him up, lit candles by his head, opened the windows, intoned the prayer to justify God's ordainment. Afterwards, they washed him on the ablution board, carried him on a stretcher to the cemetery. There they buried him as the gravedigger said Kaddish over his body.

"That's odd," he thought, "I hear nothing of Shoshe lamenting or begging forgiveness. Is it possible that she would so quickly grow unfaithful? Or has she, God forbid, been overcome by grief?"

He wanted to call her name, but he was unable to. He tried to tear free of the grave, but his limbs were powerless. All of a sudden he awoke.

"What a horrible nightmare!" he thought. "I hope I come out of it all right."

At that moment Shoshe also awoke. When he related his dream to her, she did not speak for a while. Then she said, "Woe is me. I had the very same dream."

"Really? You too?" asked Shmul-Leibele, now frightened. "This I don't like."

He tried to sit up, but he could not. It was as if he had been shorn of all his strength. He looked towards the window to see if it were day already, but there was no window visible, nor any windowpane. Darkness loomed everywhere. He cocked his ears. Usually he would be able to hear the chirping of a cricket, the scurrying of a mouse, but this time only a dead silence prevailed. He wanted to reach out to Shoshe, but his hand seemed lifeless.

"Shoshe," he said quietly. "I've grown paralyzed."

"Woe is me, so have I," she said. "I cannot move a limb."

They lay there for a long while, silently, feeling their numbness. Then Shoshe spoke: "I fear that we are already in our graves for good."

"I'm afraid you're right," Shmul-Leibele replied in a voice that was not of the living.

"Pity me, when did it happen? How?" Shoshe asked. "After all, we went to sleep hale and hearty."

"We must have been asphyxiated by the fumes from the stove," Shmul-Leibele said.

"But I said I wanted to open the flue."

"Well, it's too late for that now."

293

"God have mercy upon us, what do we do now? We were still young people. . . ."

"It's no use. Apparently it was fated."

"Why? We arranged a proper Sabbath. I prepared such a tasty meal. An entire chicken neck and tripe."

"We have no further need of food."

Shoshe did not immediately reply. She was trying to sense her own entrails. No, she felt no appetite. Not even for a chicken neck and tripe. She wanted to weep, but she could not.

"Shmul-Leibele, they've buried us already. It's all over."

"Yes, Shoshe, praised be the true Judge! We are in God's hands."

"Will you be able to recite the passage attributed to your name before the Angel Dumah?"

"Yes."

"It's good that we are lying side by side," she muttered.

"Yes, Shoshe," he said, recalling a verse: *Lovely and pleasant in their lives, and in their death they were not divided.*

"And what will become of our hut? You did not even leave a will."

"It will undoubtedly go to your sister."

Shoshe wished to ask something else, but she was ashamed. She was curious about the Sabbath meal. Had it been removed from the oven? Who had eaten it? But she felt that such a query would not be fitting of a corpse. She was no longer Shoshe the dough-kneader, but a pure, shrouded corpse with shards covering her eyes, a cowl over her head and myrtle twigs between her fingers. The Angel Dumah would appear at any moment with his fiery staff, and she would have to be ready to give an account of herself.

Yes, the brief years of turmoil and temptation had come to an end. Shmul-Leibele and Shoshe had reached the true world. Man and wife grew silent. In the stillness they heard the flapping of wings, a quiet singing. An angel of God had come to guide Shmul-Leibele the tailor and his wife, Shoshe, into Paradise.

Gabriel García Márquez

(1928–   )

Prize awarded 1982 "for his novels and short stories, in which the fantastic and realistic are combined in a richly composed world of imagination." ★ García Márquez, who was born into a poor family in Aracataca, Colombia, studied both law and journalism at universities in his native land. A career in journalism took him to Europe, Cuba, Mexico, and New York City; he was also a screenwriter and publicist. Yet almost from the start he wrote fiction. His stories were collected and published in The Leaf Storm *(1955) and* No One Writes to the Colonel *(1968), which introduced his imaginary jungle village city of Macondo. The rise and fall of Macondo is related in the poetic, epic novel* One Hundred Years of Solitude *(1967), which brought García Márquez international fame—it has been translated into thirty-two languages. (Despite his fame, his travels in both Colombia and the United States were restricted in the early 1980s because of his liberal politics.) His novels have a vivid sense of place, and his skillful blend of an idealized past with the present is expressed in fantasy, rich phantasmagorical imagery, and lyric mysticism.*

Innocent Erendira and Other Stories *(1972) further explores some of the themes and characters of* One Hundred Years of Solitude. The Autumn of the Patriarch *(1973) portrays the long finale of an archetypal Latin American dictator, characterized by historical futility and tragedy.* Chronicle of a Death Foretold *(1983) is about a murder committed for honor. Always, along with the abstractions and surrealism, there is in the works of García Márquez a strong narrative, told with humor, color, and deep feeling.*

EVA IS INSIDE HER CAT

ALL OF A SUDDEN SHE NOTICED THAT her beauty had fallen all apart on her, that it had begun to pain her physically like a tumor or a cancer. She still remembered the weight of the privilege she had borne over her body during adolescence, which she had dropped now—who knows where?—with the weariness of resignation, with the final gesture of a declining creature. It was impossible to bear that burden any longer. She had to drop that useless attribute of her personality somewhere; as she turned a corner, somewhere in the outskirts. Or leave it behind on the coatrack of a second-rate restaurant like some old useless coat. She was tired of being the center of attention, of being under siege from men's long looks. At night, when insomnia stuck its pins into her eyes, she would have liked to be an ordinary woman, without any special attraction. Everything was hostile to her within the four walls of her room. Desperate, she could feel her vigil spreading out under her skin, into her head, pushing the fever upward toward the roots of her hair. It was as if her arteries had become peopled with hot, tiny insects who, with the approach of dawn, awoke each day and ran about on their moving feet in a rending subcutaneous adventure in that place of clay made fruit where her anatomical beauty had found its home. In vain she struggled to chase those terrible creatures away. She couldn't. They were part of her own organism. They'd been there, alive, since much before her physical existence. They came from the heart of her father, who had fed them painfully during the nights of desperate solitude. Or maybe they had poured into her arteries through the cord that linked her to her mother ever since the beginning of the world. There was no doubt that those insects had not been born spontaneously inside her body. She knew that they came from back there, that all who bore her surname had to bear them, had to suffer them as she did when insomnia held unconquerable sway until dawn. It was those very insects who painted that bitter expression, the inconsolable sadness on the faces of her forebears. She had seen them looking out of their extinguished existence, out of their ancient portraits, victims of that same anguish. She still remembered the disquieting face of the great-grandmother who, from her aged canvas, begged for a minute of rest, a second of peace from those insects who there, in the channels of her blood, kept on martyrizing her, pitilessly beautifying her. No. Those insects didn't belong to her. They came, transmitted from generation to generation, sustaining with their tiny armor all the prestige of a select caste, a painfully select group. Those insects had been born in the womb of the first woman who had had a beautiful daughter. But it was necessary, urgent, to put a stop to that heritage. Someone must renounce the eternal transmission of that artificial beauty. It was no good for women of her breed to admire themselves as they came back from their mirrors if during the night those creatures did their slow, effective, ceaseless work with the constancy of centuries. It was no longer beauty, it was a sickness that had to be halted, that had to be cut off in some bold and radical way.

She still remembered the endless hours spent on that bed sown with hot needles. Those nights when she tried to speed time along so that with the arrival of daylight the beasts would stop hurting her. What good was beauty like that? Night after night, sunken in her desperation, she thought it would have been better for her to have been an ordinary woman, or a man. But that useless virtue was denied her, fed by insects of remote origin who were hastening the irrevocable arrival of her death. Maybe she would have been happy if she had had the same lack of grace, that same desolate ugliness, as her Czechoslovakian friend who had a dog's name. She would have been better off ugly, so that she could sleep peacefully like any other Christian.

She cursed her ancestors. They were to blame for her insomnia. They had transmitted that exact, invariable beauty, as if after death mothers shook and renewed their heads in order to graft them onto the trunks of their daughters. It was as if the same head, a single head, had been continuously transmitted, with the same ears, the same nose, the identical mouth, with its weighty intelligence, to all the women who were to receive it irremediably like a painful inheritance of beauty. It was there, in the transmission of the head, that the eternal microbe that came through across generations had been accentuated, had taken on personality, strength, until it became an invincible being, an incurable illness, which upon reaching her after having passed through a complicated process of judgment, could no longer be borne and was bitter and painful . . . just like a tumor or a cancer.

It was during those hours of wakefulness that she remembered the things disagreeable to her fine sensibility. She remembered the objects that made up the sentimental universe where, as in a chemical stew, those microbes of despair had been cultivated. During those nights, with her big round eyes open and frightened, she bore the weight of the darkness that fell upon her temples like molten lead. Everything was asleep around her. And from her corner, in order to bring on sleep, she tried to go back over her childhood memories.

But that remembering always ended with a terror of the unknown. Always, after wandering through the dark corners of the house, her thoughts would find themselves face to face with fear. Then the struggle would begin. The real struggle against three unmovable enemies. She would never—no, she would never—be able to shake the fear from her head. She would have to bear it as it clutched at her throat. And all just to live in that ancient mansion, to sleep alone in that corner, away from the rest of the world.

Her thoughts always went down along the damp, dark passageways, shaking the dry, cobweb-covered dust off the portraits. That disturbing and fearsome dust that fell from above, from the place where the bones of her ancestors were falling apart. Invariably she remembered the "boy." She imagined him there, sleepwalking under the grass in the courtyard beside the orange tree, a handful of wet earth in his mouth. She seemed to see him in his clay depths, digging upward with his nails, his teeth, fleeing the cold that bit into his back, looking for the exit into the courtyard through that small tunnel where they had placed him along with the snails. In winter she would hear him weeping with his tiny sob, mud-covered, drenched with rain. She imagined him intact. Just as they had left him five years before in that water-filled hole. She couldn't think of

298

him as having decomposed. On the contrary, he was probably most handsome sailing along in that thick water as on a voyage with no escape. Or she saw him alive but frightened, afraid of feeling himself alone, buried in such a somber courtyard. She herself had been against their leaving him there, under the orange tree, so close to the house. She was afraid of him. She knew that on nights when insomnia hounded her he would sense it. He would come back along the wide corridors to ask her to stay with him, ask her to defend him against those other insects, who were eating at the roots of his violets. He would come back to have her let him sleep beside her as he did when he was alive. She was afraid of feeling him beside her again after he had leaped over the wall of death. She was afraid of stealing those hands that the "boy" would always keep closed to warm up his little piece of ice. She wished, after she saw him turned into cement, like the statue of fear fallen in the mud, she wished that they would take him far away so that she wouldn't remember him at night. And yet they had left him there, where he was imperturbable now, wretched, feeding his blood with the mud of earthworms. And she had to resign herself to seeing him return from the depths of his shadows. Because always, invariably, when she lay awake she began to think about the "boy," who must be calling her from his piece of earth to help him flee that absurd death.

But now, in her new life, temporal and spaceless, she was more tranquil. She knew that outside her world there, everything would keep going on with the same rhythm as before; that her room would still be sunken in early-morning darkness, and her things, her furniture, her thirteen favorite books, all in place. And that on her unoccupied bed, the body aroma that filled the void of what had been a whole woman was only now beginning to evaporate. But how could "that" happen? How could she, after being a beautiful woman, her blood peopled by insects, pursued by the fear of the total night, have the immense, wakeful nightmare now of entering a strange, unknown world where all dimensions had been eliminated? She remembered. That night—the night of her passage—had been colder than usual and she was alone in the house, martyrized by insomnia. No one disturbed the silence, and the smell that came from the garden was a smell of fear. Sweat broke out on her body as if the blood in her arteries were pouring out its cargo of insects. She wanted someone to pass by on the street, someone who would shout, would shatter that halted atmosphere. For something to move in nature, for the earth to move around the sun again. But it was useless. There was no waking up even for those imbecilic men who had fallen asleep under her ear, inside the pillow. She, too, was motionless. The walls gave off a strong smell of fresh paint, that thick, grand smell that you don't smell with your nose but with your stomach. And on the table the single clock, pounding on the silence with its mortal machinery. "Time . . . oh, time!" she sighed, remembering death. And there in the courtyard, under the orange tree, the "boy" was still weeping with his tiny sob from the other world.

She took refuge in all her beliefs. Why didn't it dawn right then and there, or why didn't she die once and for all? She had never thought that beauty would cost her so many sacrifices. At that moment—as usual—it still pained her on top of her fear. And underneath her fear those implacable insects were still martyrizing her. Death had squeezed her into life like a spider, biting her in a rage, ready to make her succumb. But the final moment was taking its time. Her hands, those hands that men squeezed like imbeciles with manifest animal nervousness, were motionless, paralyzed by fear, by that irrational terror that came from within, with no motive, just from knowing that she was abandoned in that ancient house. She tried to react and couldn't. Fear had absorbed her completely and remained there, fixed, tenacious, almost corporeal, as if it were some invisible person who had made up his mind not to leave her room. And the most upsetting part was that the fear had no justification at all, that it was a unique fear, without any reason, a fear just because.

The saliva had grown thick on her tongue. That hard gum that stuck to her palate and flowed because she was unable to contain it was bothersome between her teeth. It was a desire that was quite different from thirst. A superior desire that she was feeling for the first time in her life. For a moment she forgot about her beauty, her insomnia, and her irrational fear. She didn't recognize herself. For an instant she thought that the microbes had left her body. She felt that they'd come out stuck to her saliva. Yes, that was all very fine. It was fine that the insects no longer occupied her and that she could sleep now, but she had to find a way to dissolve that resin that dulled her tongue. If she could only get to the pantry and . . . But what was she thinking about? She gave a start of surprise. She'd never felt "that desire." The urgency of the acidity had debilitated her, rendering useless the discipline that she had faithfully followed for so many years ever since the day they had buried the "boy." It was foolish, but she felt revulsion about eating an orange. She knew that the "boy" had climbed up to the orange blossoms and that the fruit of next autumn would be swollen with his flesh, cooled by the coolness of his death. No. She couldn't eat them. She knew that under every orange tree in the world there was a boy buried, sweetening the fruit with the lime of his bones. Nevertheless, she had to eat an orange now. It was the only thing for that gum that was smothering her. It was foolishness to think that the "boy" was inside a fruit. She would take advantage of that moment in which beauty had stopped paining her to get to the pantry. But wasn't that strange? It was the first time in her life that she'd felt a real urge to eat an orange. She became happy, happy. Oh, what pleasure! Eating an orange. She didn't know why, but she'd never had such a demanding desire. She would get up, happy to be a normal woman again, singing merrily until she got to the pantry, singing merrily like a new woman, newborn. She would even get to the courtyard and—

Her memory was suddenly cut off. She remembered that she had tried to get up and that she was no longer in her bed, that her body had disappeared, that her thirteen favorite books were no longer there, that she was no longer she, now that she was bodiless, floating, drifting over an absolute nothingness, changed into an amorphous dot, tiny, lacking direction. She was able to pinpoint what had happened. She was confused. She just had the sensation that someone had pushed her into space from the top of a precipice. She felt changed into an abstract, imaginary being. She felt changed into an incorporeal woman, something like her suddenly having entered that high and unknown world of pure spirits.

She was afraid again. But it was a different fear from what she had felt a moment before. It was no longer the fear of the "boy"'s weeping. It was a terror of the strange, of what was mysterious and unknown in her new world. And to think that all of it had happened so innocently, with so much naiveté on her part. What would she tell her mother when she told her what had happened when she got home? She began to think about how alarmed the neighbors would be when they opened the door to her bedroom and discovered that the bed was empty, that the locks had not been touched, that no one had been able to enter or to leave, and that, nonetheless, she wasn't there. She imagined her mother's desperate movements as she searched through the room, conjecturing, wondering "what could have become of that girl?" The scene was clear to her. The neighbors would arrive and begin to weave comments together—some of them malicious—concerning her disappearance. Each would think according to his own and particular way of thinking. Each would try to offer the most logical explanation, the most acceptable, at least, while her mother would run along all the corridors in the big house, desperate, calling her by name.

And there she would be. She would contemplate the moment, detail by detail, from a corner, from the ceiling, from the chinks in the wall, from anywhere; from the best angle, shielded by her bodiless state, in her spacelessness. It bothered her, thinking about it. Now she realized her mistake. She wouldn't be able to give any explanation, clear anything up, console anybody. No living being could be informed of her transformation. Now—perhaps the only time that she needed them—she wouldn't have a mouth, arms, so that everybody could know that she was there, in her corner, separated from the three-dimensional world by an unbridgeable distance. In her new life she was isolated, completely prevented from grasping emotions. But at every moment something was vibrating in her, a shudder that ran through her, overwhelming her, making her aware of that other physical universe that moved outside her world. She couldn't hear, she couldn't see, but she *knew* about that sound and that sight. And there, in the heights of her superior world, she began to know that an environment of anguish surrounded her.

Just a moment before—according to our temporal world—she had made the passage, so that only now was she beginning to know the peculiarities, the characteristics, of her new world. Around her an absolute, radical darkness spun. How long would that darkness last? Would she have to get used to it for eternity? Her anguish grew from her concentration as she saw herself sunken in that thick impenetrable fog: could she be in limbo? She shuddered. She remembered everything she had heard about limbo. If she really was there, floating beside her were other pure spirits, those of children who had died without baptism, who had been dying for a thousand years. In the darkness she tried to find next to her those beings who must have been much purer, ever so much simpler, than she. Completely isolated from the physical world, condemned to a sleepwalking and eternal life. Maybe the "boy" was there looking for an exit that would lead him to his body.

But no. Why should she be in limbo? Had she died, perhaps? No. It was simply a change in state, a normal passage from the physical world to an easier, uncomplicated world, where all dimensions had been eliminated.

Now she would not have to bear those subterranean insects. Her beauty had collapsed on her. Now, in that elemental situation, she could be happy. Although—oh!—not completely happy, because now her greatest desire, the desire to eat an orange, had become impossible. It was the only thing that might have caused her still to want to be in her first life. To be able to satisfy the urgency of the acidity that still persisted after the passage. She tried to orient herself so as to reach the pantry and feel, if nothing else, the cool and sour company of the oranges. It was then that she discovered a new characteristic of her world: she was everywhere in the house, in the courtyard, on the roof, even in the "boy"'s orange tree. She was in the whole physical world there beyond. And yet she was nowhere. She became upset again. She had lost control over herself. Now she was under a superior will, she was a useless being, absurd, good for nothing. Without knowing why, she began to feel sad. She almost began to feel nostalgia for her beauty: for the beauty that had foolishly ruined her.

But one supreme idea reanimated her. Hadn't she heard, perhaps, that pure spirit can penetrate any body at will? After all, what harm was there in trying? She attempted to remember what inhabitant of the house could be put to the proof. If she could fulfill her aim she would be satisfied: she could eat the orange. She remembered. At that time the servants were usually not there. Her mother still hadn't arrived. But the need to eat an orange, joined now to the curiosity of seeing herself incarnate in a body different from her own, obliged her to act at once. And yet there was no one there in whom she could incarnate herself. It was a desolating bit of reason: there was nobody in the house. She would have to live eternally isolated from the outside world, in her undimensional world, unable to eat the first orange. And all because of a foolish thing. It would have been better to go on bearing up for a few more years under that hostile beauty and not wipe herself out forever, making herself useless, like a conquered beast. But it was too late.

303

She was going to withdraw, disappointed, into a distant region of the universe, to a place where she could forget all her earthly desires. But something made her suddenly hold back. The promise of a better future had opened up in her unknown region. Yes, there was someone in the house in whom she would reincarnate herself: the cat! Then she hesitated. It was difficult to resign herself to live inside an animal. She would have soft, white fur, and a great energy for a leap would probably be concentrated in her muscles. And she would feel her eyes glow in the dark like two green coals. And she would have white, sharp teeth to smile at her mother from her feline heart with a broad and good animal smile. But no! It couldn't be. She imagined herself quickly inside the body of the cat, running through the corridors of the house once more, managing four uncomfortable legs, and that tail would move on its own, without rhythm, alien to her will. What would life look like through those green and luminous eyes? At night she would go to mew at the sky so that it would not pour its moonlight cement down on the face of the "boy," who would be on his back drinking in the dew. Maybe in her status as a cat she would also feel fear. And maybe, in the end, she would be unable to eat the orange with that carnivorous mouth. A coldness that came from right then and there, born of the very roots of her spirit, quivered in her memory. No. It was impossible to incarnate herself in the cat. She was afraid of one day feeling in her palate, in her throat, in all her quadruped organism, the irrevocable desire to eat a mouse. Probably when her spirit began to inhabit the cat's body she would no longer feel any desire to eat an orange but the repugnant and urgent desire to eat a mouse. She shuddered on thinking about it, caught between her teeth after the chase. She felt it struggling in its last attempts to escape, trying to free itself to get back to its hole again. No. Anything but that. It was preferable to stay there for eternity, in that distant and mysterious world of pure spirits.

But it was difficult to resign herself to live forgotten forever. Why did she have to feel the desire to eat a mouse? Who would rule in the synthesis of woman and cat? Would the primitive animal instinct of the body rule, or the pure will of the woman? The answer was crystal clear. There was no reason to be afraid. She would incarnate herself in the cat and would eat her desired orange. Besides, she would be a strange being, a cat with the intelligence of a beautiful woman. She would be the center of all attention. . . . It was then, for the first time, that she understood that above all her virtues what was in command was the vanity of a metaphysical woman.

Like an insect on the alert that raises its antennae, she put her energy to work throughout the house in search of the cat. It must still be on top of the stove at that time, dreaming that it would wake up with a sprig of heliotrope between its teeth. But it wasn't there. She looked for it again, but she could no longer find the stove. The kitchen wasn't the same. The corners of the house were strange to her; they were no longer those dark corners full of cobwebs. The cat was nowhere to be found. She looked on the roof, in the trees, in the drains, under the bed, in the pantry. She found everything confused. Where she expected to find the portraits of her ancestors again, she found only a bottle of arsenic. From there on she found arsenic all through the house, but the cat had disappeared. The house was no longer the same as before. What had happened to her things? Why were her thirteen favorite books now covered with a thick coat of arsenic? She remembered the orange tree in the courtyard. She looked for it, and tried to find the "boy" again in his pit of water. But the orange tree wasn't in its place, and the "boy" was nothing now but a handful of arsenic mixed with ashes underneath a heavy concrete platform. Now she really was going to sleep. Everything was different. And the house had a strong smell of arsenic that beat on her nostrils as if from the depths of a pharmacy.

Only then did she understand that three thousand years had passed since the day she had had a desire to eat the first orange.

Jaroslav siefert

(1901–1986)

Prize awarded 1984 "for the astonishing clarity, musicality, and sensuality of his poems . . . and for his unembellished but deeply felt identification with his country and its traditions." ★ *Jaroslav Siefert began his career as an avant-garde poet and political radical, then went on to become one of Czechoslovakia's most admired cultural and political figures. Although his working-class background prevented him from completing his formal education, Siefert joined the Communist party in 1921 and became editor of its newspaper,* Rude Pravo, *for the next two years. In 1929 he left the party, still drawn to the ideals of the Communist revolution but disillusioned by its excesses; his feelings toward the party would remain ambivalent for the rest of his life.*

In 1926 he wrote The Nightingale Sings Badly, *in which he repudiated the idea that revolution was a cure-all for society's ills. After World War II, he wrote one of his best-known works,* Helmet Full of Soil. *And in 1948 he published* The Kremlin Wall, *a book of poetry praising the USSR.*

Siefert proved to be a durable poet, withstanding repression, war, and even obscurity over more than six decades of writing. By the end of his life he had made peace with the party as well as with its dissidents. His last major work, All the Beauty in the World *(1982), recalled the days of his youth, with love and nature emerging as his favorite themes. Shortly before his death he declared, "I am being laughed at for being old and still writing love poems, but I shall write them to the end."*

306

"You Are Asking . . ."

You are asking, what more can women accomplish?
Evidently everything.

Place three pieces of straw
across a precipice,
They'll walk over with a light foot.
How? I can't explain these things.
But remember
it was they who invented the dance.

In their easy moments
they will go to the Black Forest
to dig up ferns.
And if they linger until night
they will boldly place the morning candles
on the pathway so that the lonely traveler who comes
will not fear the dark morass.

Even the shy flowers are advised
to fill their chalices
with authentic scent.
They'll prove how to deal with accents,
    sword in hand,
much more dangerous
than the scorpion's poison.

Oh, the female breast
is the Chateau of Loire,
but more beautiful,
and their children suckling
to the passionate lullabies
are born to the songs that come
from their brief sleep in the castle.

Still, when women want to fall in love,
they tie their webs around someone,
(often in the heat of Indian summer).

Jaroslav siefert

They tie him so securely
that his blood will pour
and they create such a
profound depression in their love
that you too will be drowned.
I won't even mention it all.
Masked passions control their caresses,
silently crying to lull evil thoughts to sleep;
yet they wake the sleeping man again with their kisses.
(But that is delight!)
They will draw the curtains together
with just one breath,
easily pulling it up and letting it fall again,
because, right then (as we watch from across the street)
they are taking their clothes off,
just to cover later, at will,
their nakedness.
And not even the gala dresses of Dior
sewn with golden spangles
can match that.

But what do men accomplish?
Not much of anything.
They invented war,
misery, despair and the cry of the wounded.
They can foment vain ideas,
turn cities to rubble
and thereby exhibit
stinking male bravery.

They invented gas pumps
and equal rights for women.

ORANGEADE

At the surrealists' exhibit in Paris
they were selling female breasts
made from soft elastic rubber.
  I don't know why, nor do I know the cup sizes.
They were real!
    All nightingales, strutting feather and flute,
sing the same melody.
    The old hard-working fishermen
    Used to say: something's wrong with him,
Something's definitely wrong with him.

That was a happy, carefree time
and I've already forgotten the last digit of the year.
The Sacre Coeur was floating quietly in a spring storm
like a big whale . . .
a shimmering tower of fountain,
and war was far away from this place,
    keeping its battle for another time.

I was breakfasting at a cafe under the canvas
at the Boulevard Montparnasse
and a black woman, smiling,
sat down next to my little table:
a thick, white, knitted sweater covered her bare body.
She was drowsy, a little sleepy in the warm morning
and her flesh looked like the deep center
of a honeycomb, where the nectar is dark.
At home, when our maples bloom,
their honey is a lighter gold.
Our mind forces our hands to remain
still in such mornings, not to touch.
But what about our eyes?

Jaroslav siefert

The sky was blue.
    Paris smiled,
and I listened as a piece of ice
clinked against her teeth.
And as she emptied her glass,
    as the ice fell abruptly to the bottom
she put two fingers to her wet lips,
lightly kissed them,
and quickly pressed them to my forehead.

She got up at once and ran to the Metro entrance,
where the train was sounding its horn.
In that morning air, her palm was the light pink
of wild hedge roses.
Yes, wild roses, somewhere at home
blooming over a small stone fence in early June.

This is what happened at the little cafe, under the canvas,
on the Boulevard Montparnasse.

wole soyinka

(1934–   )

Prize awarded 1986 to this author who, with "wide cultural perspective and with poetic overtones, fashions the drama of existence." ★ *Soyinka was born in Abeokuta, in western Nigeria. After preparatory studies in Ibadan, he attended the University of Leeds in England, where he took his doctorate. During his six years in England, he was a dramaturgist at London's Royal Court Theatre from 1958 to 1959. Returning to Nigeria, he taught drama and literature at Ibadan, Lagos, and Ife, where since 1975 he has been a professor of comparative literature. He has periodically been a visiting professor at the universities of Cambridge, Sheffield, and Yale. In 1960 he founded a theater group, The 1960 Masks, and in 1964 organized the Orisun Theater Company, in which he acted and produced some of his own plays.*

Soyinka has published more than twenty plays, novels, and poetry collections. His works, written in English, are distinguished by his rich, literary language. As a playwright, Soyinka has been influenced by, among others, the Irish writer J. M. Synge, but he has roots as well in traditional Yoruba culture and theater with its blending of dance, music, and action. He bases much of his writing on Yoruba mythology, especially Ogun, the god of iron and war, and often works around the conflict as well as the identity of creation and destruction. Some of his better-known works include The Swamp Dwellers *(1963),* Death and the King's Horsemen *(1975), and* Requiem for a Futurologist *(1985). In 1967, during the Nigerian civil war, he was arrested for advocating a cease-fire and spent two years in jail. The experience produced* The Man Died: Prison Notes *(an excerpt follows) and* A Shuttle in the Crypt *(1972), about mental survival, human contact, anger, and forgiveness.*

THE MAN DIED

I AM SEATED IN A SPARE OFFICE—ON THE FLOOR above the interrogation office. Mallam D., my interrogator, fusses nervously about: what I would like you to do for me, Mr. Soyinka, is simply set down all the things you have told me, everything about your activities to stop the war, how it all began, how much you have done, the people you have talked to or still plan to contact . . . you know, all the details and any other thing you may have overlooked. I am sure your case will be cleared up in no time at all, just help me by putting it all down, and then maybe we can take up one or two points in it. . . .

Can I have a typewriter? My handwriting is so bad. . . .

It was the first thought at that point, nothing in my handwriting. And no signatures on anything. Even without formulating clear possibilities of danger, the risks could be reduced by making it all machine clinical. A hurried flit to and from offices, and Mallam D. soon returned—no, he could not find a spare typewriter. Doesn't matter, I said, thinking, Like hell it doesn't. So much bulk handwriting would yield plenty of practice material for an expert forger. I am not even thinking remotely of forgery for public consumption but of that cheap police trick—show a piece of "confession" to some other unfortunate sod and break his morale that way—"Here, read it yourself, he has implicated you in his statement. Why don't you tell your own side of it."

Caution. Even breath is drawn cautiously, deliberately. From now on all is calculation. A quick glance round the room for hidden microphones, hidden spy-holes. Microphones! But you are by yourself, man! So? A "sympathetic" cell-mate might be added later. Well, time to look for microphones when that happens. In the meantime stick to composing your statement. Organize your thoughts, select what you want to say and set it down. No deletions after writing, that would only arouse suspicions. What did you delete? Why? The first session with Mallam D. is recognized for what it was—the preliminary skirmish. There is no such thing as an "enlightened" interrogator. Methods differ, that is all. Any system which allows for the machinery of secrecy against an individual is the method of the Gestapo. The Gestapo mind believes more in holding than releasing, in guilt than in justice. This building is Gestapo headquarters, there is no other term, no other point of view for survival. . . . I begin to write.

The reminder was timely. Three men had just entered the room. At first I thought they had missed their way because they had with them heavy manacles and chains the like of which I had seen only in museums of the slave-trade. They looked sheepish and embarrassed, and I half expected them to turn round and disappear with an apology for intruding. But they had halted and were looking at me. One of them coughed and stammered out the news. They have been instructed to chain my legs together.

"Are you sure? I was put here to write my statement."

There was no mistake. Yet it was not fifteen minutes since Mallam D. left me. Nothing, of course, had been said about chains. I held out my legs, the manacles were fastened, my legs went down of their new acquired weight.

Settling down again was not very easy. The feel of chains was a novelty of sensation to which I could not immediately adjust. I looked down on the odd objects with truly detached curiosity, raised the legs again to feel their weight, tried walking in them and performed a hundred other experiments. Walking was possible—or, more strictly, shuffling. Again a wave of unreality, I think I laughed aloud at this point. I bent down, picked up the loose chain and held it up. One foot six at the most.

I sensed a vivid contradiction in all this, a contradiction in my being, in my human self-awareness and self-definition. In fact, one might say that never until this moment did that self-definition become so clear as when I viewed these chains on my ankles. The definition was a negative one, I defined myself as a being for whom chains are *not*, as, finally, a human being. Insofar as one may say

313

wole soyinka

that the human essence does at times possess a tangible quality, I may say that I tasted and felt this essence within the contradiction of that moment. It was nothing new; vicariously, by ideology or from racial memory, this contradiction may be felt, is felt, with vivid sufficiency to make passionate revolutionaries of the most cosseted life. Abstract, intellectual fetters are rejected just as passionately. But in the experience of the physical thing the individual does not stand alone, most especially a black man. I had felt it, it seemed to me, hundreds of years before, as I believe I did experience the triggering of a surely reincarnated moment when at school I first encountered engravings of slave marches in history books. Even when I met my first lunatics under the care of traditional healers, chained at the ankles to curb their violence, the degree of nonacceptance of such therapy bordered, I often think, on racial memory. Surely it cannot be a strictly personal experience.

That moment when the key was turned in the locks often comes back to me—I, seated on a straight-backed chair, the two men stooped down at my feet fastening the locks, the third man watching the dangerous animal in case he attacked—and it occurred to me, not then, no, only now, with the scene of the chaining passing before my eyes, that we were all black, that Mallam D., another black man, had given the order and fled, that I was not a "convict" in a chain-gang in south Alabama or Johannesburg, but that this human antithesis had its enactment in the modern office of a modern skyscraper in cosmopolitan Lagos in the year 1967.

Well, just in case it *was* real, just in case other realities such as going to the toilet, stretching out my legs in the middle of sleep or jerking them involuntarily at night from a mosquito bite, just in case all these other hazards of existence would be manifested, would accentuate the feel of the pendants at my feet, I commenced without any internal debate a hunger strike. It was one obvious antidote to a mood which, half-mocking, half earnest, raged: Ogun, comrade, bear witness how your metal is travestied! Well, the early chirurgeons bled the choleric; I have learnt to starve my violence into calm.

It worked. The very act of taking the decision not to eat brought the futile spasm of rage and the trembling under control almost at once. My mind was working again, dispassionately. Immediate aim. Far-reaching aim. Contingency. What effect must be produced in the Gestapo mind. I began work on the statement, a new motif being now dominant—the anticipation of a trial and the classic reversal of roles. Visions of Castro's *Historia me Absolvera!* The statement was a dense affirmation of my role in organizing lobbies to stop the supply of arms to both belligerents. I wrote in a vein calculated to prod them into bringing me to trial on the premise that my activities were antigovernment, completed the essay in two or three hours, transferred to an armchair, took another look at the chains and tried to drop off to sleep.

A knock. The cook contracted out to the Gestapo for the feeding of the hundred inmates undergoing interrogation was on his rounds. Thank you, no. The guard outside the door thought that I would prefer a "European" diet, the supposed ultimate accolade of VIPism to a prisoner or detainee. No? Not even a tin of sardines? Bread? Milk? I said, It's dangerous to feed chained animals, you know. I might get power and snap these trinkets.

Evening. "E" Branch was overcrowded. Every office, the library, even some landings were used as interrogation rooms. All through the day Ibos and suspected sympathizers were brought in by the hundreds. Denunciation was easy, and old scores were settled by a whisper to the police. Some, mostly non-Ibos, came in already defeated by terror, prostrating, pleading for a chance to make a defence. All evening I heard voices of new arrivals, men and women. The words were monotonous, the protests and counteraccusations: "I never said so. Na lie. I no say dat kin' ting." It was enough to accuse a man for expressing Ibo sympathy or damning the army. Or telling the truth of a torture or murder which he had witnessed. It was sufficient to look disapproving on methods of terror.

Night. A weird, brief encounter. I had dozed off. Suddenly the door was flung open, and a woman catapulted in. "Stay there and shut up." The officer gave orders for some others to be shut away in different offices. From her accent I knew she was Ibo. I had never witnessed such terror in a woman. It was some time before she was even aware that there was another being in the room. The shock—she was at first convinced that it was an officer, perhaps her appointed torturer—the shock took her to the opposite corner of the room from where she stared with huge panicked eyes and a quivering throat which barely stopped short of a shriek. Then her eyes came downwards and she saw the chains. I saw her body go lax, sympathetic. She came forward, her hand patting the table as if to

315

engage some reassurance of concrete things. I watched her silently. She needed no further comforting from me; the sight of my chains had done more than words could have done for me, calmed her down. But then I saw yet a new change in her face. She stood suddenly still, unbelieving. Recognition. I saw it even before she spoke. Are you not . . . are you not Wole Soyinka? I nodded. From my face, to my legs, back to my face. A pause to take it in. Then she broke down in tears.

The guard—he must have gone off briefly to help with the new influx—looked in a minute and gasped. What is she doing here? He screamed down the corridor for the officer on duty. No one is supposed to go in the room with that suspect! When they all rushed in she had stopped crying. The duty officer was all regretful; he had not known there was anyone in there. They led the woman away, calmer, stronger. She turned round at the door, looked at me in a way to ensure that I saw it, that I knew she was no longer cowed, that nothing ever again would terrorize her. I acknowledged the gesture. I wondered if she knew what strength I drew from the encounter.

"Confession—foiled escape—wail of humiliation." A trilogy aimed at the most cynical or blindly loyal mind. A beautiful logic all its own. A masterpiece of credible fantasy calculated to shatter any lingering resistance to the omnipotence of the régime. If *he* could break and break so abjectly, then anyone can break. This army is a force that can break anyone. And will. The sequence was loaded with whispers, furtive betrayals soon to be followed by purges.

In a moment of enforced calm I moved out of the echoes of voices in the streets, of voices in the markets, out of whispers in corridors, glances in gatherings, out of the rain of spittle and contempt, moved out from the target of pointed fingers, the giggle in the dark, out from the wise nods of geriatric consciences, out of the mockery, the assuaged envy and jubilation of the self-deluded. Slowly, tortuously, I commenced an exploration into the mind of the enemy and the future dangers. What are they doing now? Toasting each other in champagne, yes. What else? Backslapping one another for the masterstroke, heaving sighs of relief. Yes, yes, but what else? Place yourself in their position, what would you do now? This moment! What would be the next step?

Press the advantage. No rest. No quarter for the dissidents. Make

316

a clean sweep of every particle of opposition. Arrest. Purge! A little mysterious announcement, a little hint that, thanks to other revelations made by that new-converted pillar of the régime, it is now possible to cleanse the nation once and for all of all fifth columnists. Settle all the old scores! As for you . . .

Yes, come on. After all, you are the writer, the student of human nature. Let us have some creative identification. What is the worst thing you would do to the last possible danger, the sole witness to the foundation of falsehood laid for the superstructure of violent repression?

For this danger remains, even when I have filled the gaols to overflowing and built new concentration camps to house other "confessed" saboteurs, the danger of a leak in the bubble remains with you living. When the secret graves have been filled up and the agonies of the tortured have sated even the public lust for vengeance, what would I do? What can I do to destroy you thoroughly, leaving no loopholes?

The answer came with paralysing clarity: Set you free. Yes. In the one gesture that cannot but be interpreted as fulfilment of a despicable bargain, open the gates and set you free. Your teeth are pulled, your claws pared, your voice broken. Simply by opening the gates and releasing you out to public gaze.

Tell me, what would you say? Denials? My friend, your comrades are dead, locked up, cowed and broken. Even if they are no comrades, even if you never set eyes on them or known of their existence, the truth, yes, truth—recognize the malleable word?—truth, the truth is *that* truth of their arrest following upon hints of your generous confession. That is the Truth. We have re-created truth and truth is now defined in our image. Each man who loses liberty or life is added to the score of your betrayal. What will you say? How will you say it? Who will believe you? Who, above all, will dare believe you? Who will *want* to believe you? Who will *think* of believing? Truth, my dear friend, is the thousands who have vanished since we fixed your interfering little mind!

In an animal cage, in the spiritual isolation of the first few days the prospect became real and horrifying. It began as an exercise to arm myself against the worst, it plunged into horrors of the imagination. I had begun to lose sane distinction between the supposition and the reality. Even long after I had reestablished contact with the outside world, had been assured that the truth was known where

317

it mattered most it took only a little trigger of recollection to plunge back into that cauldron of racing pulses and nervous stress. Yet there was the strange fact, contradicting all logical expectation—my mind continued to function. If anything it had developed a sharp reckless cunning. Transferred to the Maximum Security Prison with lines of contact abruptly cut, realizing and near panicking from the thought that I was more than ever at the mercy of the state propaganda machine I became obsessed with finding a means of renewing that contact. I could think only of a scribbled denial of the fabrication handed in advance to that very inmate whose nerve had given at the critical moment. By now I realized he had probably chewed and swallowed it before the search which would inevitably follow.

It was a wild, all-consuming ambition—to get out a statement at all costs, to foil the plan of other denunciations which was surely building up on the cornerstone of cumulative forgery. The dual condition of my mind, the duality of its numbed despair and the weird instinctive cunning of those days struck me only long afterwards.

I watched, waited and schemed. My mind revolved a hundred schemes, scanned each warder, anatomized the trustee who came to feed the animal, delved into the soul of each inmate looking for that flash of collaborative recognition. A prisoner knows at once just who will aid him and who will not. And I was ready to take chances, there being nothing left to lose. My mind was racing when the chance finally came, a mere tantalizing flash of opportunity. I managed to arrest that flash and make it serve.

It was a chance in a thousand, a coincidence such as nearly makes one a convert to Providence, a combination of circumstances that came about ironically by virtue of the iron ring in which I was surrounded. Too much of the same precaution, one cancelled out another—my message was waiting.

I knew even in the headlong rush that I must phrase my statement to make it appear that it came from the other prison. It placed intolerable restraint on me, but it was better than to be moved at once from this imagined insulation which I had breached. A breach is worth all in confinement. My note took wings and flew into hope-famished hands. A newspaper or two inside the country found the courage to print my words; a vicious witch-hunt was begun in the wrong prison.

That small victory had to console me in the abysmal existence of the following days. The horror of the picture I had conjured up had become a haunting reality. While I waited for confirming news I knew the corrosion of anxiety. It ate into areas of the invisible being, in corners where I could not reach.

They were blank days, days of impenetrable darkness and pulses that ran out of all control. There were tranquilizers, sleeping pills, visits from the prison doctor. A faint rally from sources of will cautioned against reliance on pills, warned me to reject all artificial help. After two days I forced myself to throw them in the lavatory bucket. Two days later I asked the doctor again for their replacement, admitting what I had done with the first supply. I kept the pills on the box which served for a table, invented a drill of picking them up during bad spells, counting them carefully, patterning them and putting them back again. I lay flat, sat cross-legged, stood on my head, underwent a repertory of practised and improvised positions in the battle to rule my pulse, quiet noises in the head. I begged me to permit one pill, one pill, only this once and never again, moved quickly to take them again in my hands, count, then make patterns on the box with them. The taste of food or water vanished entirely. Cigarettes merely created dizziness.

Response to my surroundings came slowly, the recognition of passing inmates as human beings, as individuals with unique features. That crisis was over. If it returned I would find the strength to rule it. Knowing at last that my refutation had escaped the iron ring and had even been published helped. Even more uplifting was the confirmation of my fears, when Dan and Sojo finally made contact, that a programme of purges had been planned but was now forcibly abandoned. Or postponed. They would wreak vengence on those who lay within their power, but that source of pleasure could not now be expanded nor could it be based on a fantasy of betrayal.

Dreams. More strictly, variations on one dream. I would be on the scaffolding of a building in construction, high up. Cold. Mists. The mist barely reveals the outlines of my co-workers on other parts of the building. They are shadowy forms in blurred contours. A relay of hands pass the bricks on to me from the ground. When the last brick is set in place I signal, and a new brick flies through the mists, invisible until the last yard or two. But the aim each time is perfect. I catch it with barely a glance, literally by stretching my

319

hand out for the brick to fall into. I place the brick in position, fill the gaps with mortar and slice off the excess. It is hardly work; every movement is leisurely, slowed-down motion, ritualistic. The mists swirl all about us; from time to time a face passes close, balancing on the narrow catwalk, trundling a barrow to another part of the edifice.

It is a long while before I know that everyone else is gone. I did not hear the lunch gong. I could not have suspected it had rung since the bricks continue to drop into my outstretched hands. It is the silence that strikes me first, and slowly I realize that work has ceased. The work has proceeded till now in virtual silence, but now that silence has grown even deeper. I lean over to ask my own relay if they wish to stop or to continue until that line of the wall is completed. Only seven bricks left, I say; the figure is always seven. There is no response from them, and I notice now that they are also gone. A brick comes flying slowly through the mist, though there is no one below. I hold out my hand for it. It slips, I lunge for it and fall over. I am a long time falling in the void.

Later I recognize the physical landscape. It is one of the threads that have gone into the weaving of that metaphysical web which holds men dead in their tracks with the frightening certainty of having returned to a point in a cycle. The landscape of Shaki conjured up long-buried images of the Dutch lowlands where years ago, as a student, I once joined in building new houses for victims of a flood disaster. I recall the pure, uncomplicated giving and camaraderie, and I know what gave birth to the earlier nostalgic sadness. The rest is horror, the long fall in the abyss, night after night, the awful silence . . .

Through the bars I could see across the rooftops of other buildings in the yard. Acres of desolation between the buildings, huge swathes of space inside the walls. These manmade hives seemed feeble pockmarks on the authentic face of emptiness. The clumps of ferns, the potholes and the swamps spoke of recent reclamation from a sea that still promised a fight for repossession. I could, I imagined, hear its soft, near-stagnant wash over the crowded palm crowns just visible over the walls. Voices of the idling, gossiping, hoping prisoners drifted up towards me like echoes from another world. From some dim region of memory I was nudged by a voice, a touch, a thread of cobweb from the dark. It was that harrowing moment of reach, touch, slip, reach again but utterly fail to grasp. I was not capable even of the effort to reach my mind, a woolly receptacle floating in ether while this drop of dew from distant past settled gently on its rim and turned again to vapour in a fever that had just begun.

Time vanished. I turned to stone. The world retreated into fumes of swampland.

I have been here before. I have passed through this present point again and again. My head is filled with the smells and senses of that other time, and with recognition comes the added pain of a repeated leavetaking. I try hard to stay the moment, to come to terms with it and if possible, mark it in a place, a time. Desolation increases with my acute certainty that the sensation is deeper than the mere located place or event. It is closer to a phase of being. A self taken for granted in terms of humanity, faith, honour, justice, ideals. It resolves itself, insofar as anything has resolved itself today, lightly, on the rims of consciousness. A knowledge of where I have been till this moment, knowing it for a phase to which I will never return, yet aware also that this ritual of transition is a perpetual one and that the acquisition of experience in fording the pass does not lessen its overwhelming sadness.

Again and again I recognize this territory of existence. I know that I have come to this point of the cycle more than once, and now the memories are so acute that I wonder if it has not been truly in a mere prophetic expectation of it all, in the waiting upon it in captive attendance, wondering merely, when? What meaning then shall I attach to it, what name, what definition give to the monstrosity of this birth? I try to feed some muscularity into the marshmallow of sensations.

A private quest? Stuff for the tragic stage and the ritual rounds of Passion? A brave quest that diverges from, with never a backward glance at history's tramp of feet along the communal road? Is this then the long-threatened moment for jettisoning, for instance, notions of individual responsibility and the struggle it imposes? Must I now reject Kant? Karl Jaspers? "However minute a quantity the individual may be in the factors that make up history, he is a factor." Must I now say to him, Yes, a dead factor? About as effective as flotsam on ocean currents? Hang instead on to the ambiguity of the other face of fulfilment?—"Man can only grasp his authentic being through confrontation with the vicissitudes of life." I have quarrelled too often with the ego-centred interpretations to which the existentialist self gives rise. Any faith that places the *conscious* quest for the inner self as goal, for which the context of forces are mere battle aids is ultimately destructive of the social potential of that self. Except as source of strength and vision keep inner self out of all expectation, let it remain unconscious beneficiary from experience. Suspect all conscious search for the self's authentic being; that is favourite fodder for the enervating tragic Muse. *I do not seek; I find.* Let actions alone be the manifestations of the authentic being in defence of its authentic visions. History is too full of failed Prometheans bathing their wounded spirits in the tragic stream.

Destroy the tragic lure! Tragedy is possibly solely because of the limitations of the human spirit. There are levels of despair from which, it rightly seems, the human spirit should not recover. To plunge to such a level is to be overwhelmed by the debris of all those antihuman barriers which are erected by jealous gods. The power of recovery is close to acquisition of superhuman energies, and the stagnation-loving human society must for self-preserving interest divert these colossal energies into relatively quiescent channels, for they constitute a force which, used as part of an individual's equipment in the normal human struggle cannot be resisted by the normal human weapons. Thus the historic conspiracy, the literal brainwashing that elevates tragedy far and above a regenerative continuance of the Promethean struggle.

To survive, but to survive in a transmuted form, full of nebulous wisdoms, corrupted and seduced by sagehood homage, carefully insulated from intimacy with the affairs of men, that kind of bribery which Oedipus at first snatched at, blinding himself physically to eradicate in entirety the route to socially redemptive action—this is the preference of all establishment. Against all questioning and change, against concrete redress of the causative factors of any crisis, society protects itself by this diversion of regenerative energies into spiritual in-locked egotism. To ensure that there is no reassertion of will the poetic snare of tragic loftiness is spread before him—what greater sublimity than the blind oracular figure, what greater end to the quest for self than graceful acceptance, quiescence and senescence!

Do I or do I not recognize the trap? I summon history to my aid, but more than history, kindred knowledge, kindred findings, kindred rebellions against the lure of tragi-existentialism; for rage is no longer enough to combat the temptations to subside into unproductive, will-sapping wisdoms. I seek only the combative voices, and I hunt them down from remotest antiquity to the latest incidental reencounters on casual forums. "Tragedy is merely a way of retrieving human unhappiness, of subsuming it and thus of justifying it in the form of necessity, wisdom or purification. The rejection of this process and the search for the technical means of avoiding the insidious trap it lays is a necessary undertaking today." When? Where? I neither remember nor care. I recall only that I once made a note of it to use in what a student called my special antiliterature seminars. But the words hammer strident opposition to the waves of negations that engulf me, to the mob hatred that I distinctly hear even in this barred wilderness. It nerves me to mutter—Brainwashed, gullible fools, many-headed multitudes, why should your voices raised in ignorance affect my peace?

But they do. I cannot deny it.

From this pit of anguish, dug by human hands, from this cauldron stoked by human hands, from this deafening clamour of human hate, the being that emerges is literally an "anjonnu." He will return neither understanding nor tolerating as before. He will no longer weigh or measure in mundane terms. Reality for him is forever tinged in the flames of a terrible passage, his thoughts can no longer be contained by experiences. You, outside of these walls, whose hysteria I confess penetrates my proud defences, I know you sense this menace of a future revenge and must, in self-defence, redouble your efforts of annihilation—spiritual, psychic, physical and symbolic. And this is why I must dig into my being and understand why at this moment you have the power to affect me. Why, even when I have rationally rejected the tragic snare I am still overcome by depressive fumes in my capsule of individualist totality.

Said Hermias of Aternias, with his body broken and in a breath that barely held, "Tell my friends and companions that I have done nothing unworthy of philosophy." That longing in all human beings that will sooner expend last breath on words of affirmation than conserve it on behalf of life, believing that life is justified if only at the moment of quitting it, the remnant spittle of a parched tongue is launched against the enemy in one defiant gesture of contempt, supplying a final action of hope, of encouragement for the living, validating one's entire being in that last gesture or in a word of affirmation. Overcoming pain, physical degradation and even defeat of ideals to sum up, to send a reprise of faith to the comrades one leaves behind, and make even dying a triumph, an ultimate affirmation.

I know why you reach me, you mindless mob. I see myself consigned to a living death, denied that affirmation. And worse, not merely denied it but with my living corpse displayed to the world in the rank embalming fluid of its antithesis: recantation! Issuing as if from my catatonic body, the ventriloquist progaganda of frightened, desperate yet powerful criminals devoid of the vaguest notions of decency, justice or fair play! I race through catalogues of totalitarian situations where such "self-villifications" have issued forth even long after real or living deaths from victims of power insanity, but find there little consolation. I caution in vain against the acceptance of power morality by listing the lies and holding them up to fundamental lights. I grind them in the crucible of permanent truths demanding as a start: Let us assume you did try to escape, just whose ethics are affronted except those whom you have proved morally debased? Must this charade, the sudden "moral" awakening of millions whose moral sense lay heavily dead over the mass murder which has created your individual persecution—must this comedy be reckoned sane or wholesome? *That* moral sense? That putrid cadaver of abdicated will that resurrects only at the scent of a voiceless, powerless victim, and is activated by the kick of booted power?

And yet it is not enough. Not even the procession of past and living wraiths who float into vision in parallel trials, reinforcing a faith of individual decisions. From within my lifetime absorption in the fate of the individual in confrontation with bigotry and repression they emerge: Abraham Fischer; Nicodemus Frischlin (earliest recorded instance of the formula "killed while trying to escape"?); Cardinal Mindszenty (who chose his own prison); a bullet-crippled figure in a wheelchair, Dr. Arias, fleeing the Dominican dictator; John Wilkes moving just within and out of parliamentary immunity; even the Apostle Paul, with the repetitive aid of the "miraculous" . . .

With St. Paul I am brought to a sudden halt. An effort at self-mockery creates a hurtful grimace, yet it unwinds a little the self-strangulating knot that has formed within my guts. Ah, yes, you fancied yourself quite an Epistolatian, didn't you? Epistle of St.

You-know-whom from Kiri-kiri to the Ibadanians . . . be of good cheer, the Lord is with you, but beware of those wolves in sheep's clothing who roam among you, rooting up the corpse of yesteryear . . .

The effort at humour salvages yet another ghost, this time from the local pages of irony: Tony Enahoro, megaphone of official falsehoods. The irony is one of those belly jokes that history plays on men. When he fled from the scene after the abortive coup and was obligingly held by the British government on behalf of their feudal favourites, I flew to London, urged by a simple conviction. It was the conviction also of a small unpartisan and largely anonymous group which alone of the many movements has preserved an undeviating vision of future society. Our belief was: the repatriation of Enahoro would be too great a loss in the thinning ranks of the radicals. Perhaps Enahoro's friends had already begun private pressures to prevent his return; I know only that the public campaign did not begin until after my work in London. I enlisted the aid of the only two politicians I knew, Tom Driberg and Wayland Young (Lord Kennet), and recruited the more politically aware students into an active lobbying programme.

Prison projects scenes of vivid, total recall. Wayland's face I can almost touch, saying: "I don't really know much of your political situation—is he a good man, this Enahoro?"

I replied, "We need him, and in circulation." I had not then ever met Enahoro face to face.

At home the "intellectuals" said, Coward, let him return home and face the music. To which there was and remains only one reply: the soul of the revolutionary dance is in the hands of the flutist.

What was his name, that other Wurtenburg professor, a compatriot of Frischlin, perhaps also his contemporary? The worthy doctor who, in spite of his conviction of the superstitious, untenable injustice of witch trials, nevertheless prepared over two hundred successful prosecutions of witches who were duly roasted at the stake. A dichotomy of conviction and responsibility justified by seeking, in the meantime, ways and means of weaning his medieval society from its barbaric ways? So now the role of the intellectual is reduced to simply that! What exactly is the evaluation we must place on your doctorate dissertations, you boneless craniums whose tomes shall undoubtedly assail us titled with variations of *The Social Anomy of 1966, Its Roots and Consequences in the Nigerian Civil War*, etc., etc., with special reference to the role of the imperialist commercial interest, etc., etc.—two hundred witches? Two thousand? Two hundred thousand? Two million? Twenty? In presentation volumes bound in silence?

In my private realm of thoughts I seek keystones to shore my being against formless assaults that come in the wake of bouts of aggressive certainty. It is strange how that creative revelation of Picasso's has taken to haunting me: *I do not seek; I find.* It is like an incantation sneaked in the mind under hypnosis. I ask it finally, What is it? What are you saying to me? What are you trying to suggest that I did not know before? Some new twist to fit this situation, to reconcile me to this circle? For instance that, passive or provoking, protagonist or acquiescing, I was fated for this passage? That a visionary's course is one which, even with closed eyes and folded arms, finds? For example: every situation creates its own response? Antithetically, to vary the emphasis a little for that daily truism of abdications: eyes have they, but they *will not* see? It is strange and I do not really resolve it. The phrase beats time on my chest like an ambiguous talisman. Not in the least ambiguous, however, is another, a loud assertive chime, and I cannot even recall if the words are Japsers' or Kant's: *It is always our responsibility to decide critically whether or not it is immoral to obey a command of authority.* Yes, I allow only for this sole factor of decision; the physical power of choice.

Dreyfus. Dimitrov versus Goering. How much longer will it go on, this pattern of power-initiated crime and the political scapegoat? A hideous image looms from those Nazi mists, the bloodthirst of a bestiality of power, a rabid snarl and slavering model for the Yisa Adejos of the world, animalistic regressions which evoke a shudder even from the reconciled heart of carnage. Now in hindsight I wonder if it had been such a wise action to transmit from gaol a letter containing evidence of their guilt while I lay in the power of such men. (The liberal conscience even of Dimitrov's time knew better than to rest easy with the idea of those Bulgarian fall guys in the personal charge of Goering.) I fault myself now, accepting implicitly that Kantian imperative, recognizing that since I had settled within myself all doubts about the bankruptcy of Gowon's moral order from that moment of his release of the two murderers, it was not enough to send word to a band of emasculated intellectuals. I should have done then what I now stand accused of doing—

escaped. For there existed then, and exists even now in spite of its reverses, a truly national, moral *and* revolutionary alternative—Victor Banjo's Third Force. Morality and therefore actions which come from a moral inspiration create the only "authentic being," they constitute the continuing personality of the individual and cannot be substituted by absolving palliatives. The gap in my guts, the hurtful hiatus that threatens to suck my egoist essence into its own void, is the evasion of that moral imperative, the despair comes from a knowledge that I cannot now carry out this sole affirmation nor can I envisage, in this barren encirclement the possibility of a rational substitution. As for that wounded ego whose depredations on my peace of mind have been and will (I suspect) continue to be my worst enemy and friend in this place I pick on the words which have evoked in me the worst physical nausea. I force down the bilge that has welled even with their mere consideration and remind myself of the evil potency of the framers of those words and their knowledge of mass psychology. It is a cruel exercise but there is no help for it. I force the words through my lips and listen to the squelch—"he claimed he was protesting against government humiliation." I chew the phrasing as ratsbane and drink it down as hemlock—"he claimed he was protesting against government humiliation."

You criminals, you have imbued your cause with unlimited power. Your contemptuous insight into the minds of a hysteria-manipulated mob has rendered you immune to further confrontation—this is your purpose, and I acknowledge its present success. If doubts are created, even in one solitary example, if an acknowledged absolutist voice is polluted, if affirmation is turned into recantation in the mind of the mob, then you have established your race of serfs whose docility will be justified forever by "if he could break, then who are we to struggle?" For the few who are and have always been rulers in their own self-sufficiency there will be a grain of self-doubt implanted by the recollected instance.

I ought truly to have a contempt for this world of zombies. I shall, but you have yet to create them. I think that finally, you cannot. True, the voices which I hear are not the voices that I seek to hear. They are not testimonies of that quasi-mystic bond which, even allowing for self-delusion, exists between the loneliest of all combatants and the people whose cause he ultimately espouses. I have not heard, for instance, the long-awaited cry of justice which de-

327

mands, Bring him out for judgement, not—Crucify him! Let us be witnesses at the unmasking. Instead I see hands thrown up in horror. I see furtive slinks of shame in the streets, in dark corners of homes. I smell hate, evil, fright and capitulation. But it is your smell, the smell of irredeemable corruption that travels with you and clings to all over whom your breath of lies has blown. And I hear a fresh wind coming up from beyond the boundaries of expediency.

Listen to what Adolfe Joffe wrote to Trotsky before his death by suicide. "Human life has meaning only to that degree and as long as it is lived in the service of humanity. For me humanity is infinite."

For me, justice is the first condition of humanity.

Afterword: Alfred Nobel's Literary Legacy

THAT ALFRED NOBEL WAS THE INVENTOR of dynamite is almost as widely recognized as the prestigious annual prizes given in the fields of physics, chemistry, medicine, economics, peace, and literature that bear his name. Less well known, however, is the fact that this successful munitions capitalist was also a pacifist who perceived in literature a means of raising universal consciousness to the devastation of war.

In fact, Nobel was himself something of a writer. Educated primarily at home by his creative and demanding mother, he wrote poetry, often in English, throughout his late teens and early twenties. During this period Nobel developed not only his literary talents, but also an affinity for the lone creative genius struggling to find a commercial forum for his ideas.So seriously and industriously did he work at this craft that scholars allege Nobel might indeed have pursued a literary career were it not for the influence of his chemical engineer–entrepreneur father. And though he did ultimately follow in his father's footsteps, Nobel remained deeply committed to the cause of world peace and to the power of literature.

Legend has it that the inspiration for the Nobel Foundation came in 1888, when Nobel read what he thought was to be his brother's obituary, but through journalistic error found himself reading his own. Distraught that he was fated to be remembered only as the inventor of dynamite and a munitions millionaire, he drew up his first will, expressing his philanthropic wishes in the form of an institute to be established on his death. This document, revised in 1893, charged the Swedish Academy of Science, the Caroline Medico-Surgical Institute, the Swedish Academy, and the Norwegian Parliament with the responsibility of administering annual prizes in their given fields.

It is interesting to note that the first draft of Nobel's will had confined the life of the Nobel Institute to thirty years, ". . . for if in thirty years [the world has] not succeeded in reforming the present system [it] will infallibly relapse into barbarism." Nor, for that matter, was there a provision for a literature award, or even for a peace prize. The later inclusion of these awards was no doubt the result of the influence of Nobel's friend and confidante, Baroness Berthe von Stutter, a popular writer and peace activist (who subsequently won the 1905 Peace Prize). It was to her that Nobel expressed his "wish to produce a substance or device of such frightful efficacy for a wholesale devastation that war should become altogether impossible." The Economics Prize was instituted in 1953 by the Bank of Sweden, which supplies the prize money, in Nobel's memory.

Nobel's last will calls for the interest from his estate to be distributed annually to ". . . those persons who shall have contributed most to the benefit of mankind during the year immediately following: . . . one share to the person who shall have produced in the field of literature the most distinguished work of an *idealistic tendency* [our emphasis]. I declare it to be my express desire that, in awarding prizes, no consideration whatever be paid to the nationalities of the candidates . . . the most deserving be awarded whether of Scandinavian origin or not."

However, not only was a literal interpretation and execution of Nobel's will inherently problematical but, surprisingly, its mandate was actively opposed by the Swedish crown, the Swedish legal establishment, Nobel's own family, the Swedish institutions named as the selecting bodies, and a generally skeptical public. Only the Norwegian Parliament, chosen as the sole designator of the Peace Prize, gave early approval.

The eventual validation and execution of the will took five years. And ambiguity (for example, "work of an idealistic tendency") was only one of the many problems that had to be overcome in launching the Nobel Prize.

First, there was the issue of determining the country of Nobel's residence, since although he had remained a Swedish citizen, he had ceased living in Sweden at the age of nine. Nobel, who was born in St. Petersburg, Russia, never held a passport, owned homes in many different places, and was residing in Italy at the time of his death. Had his French assets not been quickly liquidated (and smuggled dramatically across borders at night), the French legal authorities might well have invalidated the will, or at the very least subjected his estate to heavy taxation. Even more troublesome was the fact that the principal heir, the Nobel Foundation, did not yet legally exist, nor had any of the named executors been consulted about their roles in the prize giving.

After lengthy negotiations, the members of the Nobel family were allocated five thousand pounds each and given the option of retaining control over Nobel's extensive Russian ventures. The common-law-wife claims of Nobel's shopgirl mistress were satisfied by continuing the annuity Nobel had set up for her. (For her part she agreed to surrender his letters, which were then suppressed for fifty years by the Nobel committee. She also agreed to total silence about their affair.)

The Swedish crown was appeased by the administrative and ceremonial role created for the king as well as by the conversion of Nobel's assets to Swedish government securities (his will stipulated only that the monies were to be invested in "safe papers").

Individual credit for bringing the Nobel Institute into being must go to Carol David af Wirsen, Secretary of the Swedish Academy. Throughout the long struggle to put the prize in motion, Wirsen was a center of power, controversy, and criticism and singlehandedly overcame the Academy's reluctance to administer the Literature Prize. Established by Swedish King Gustavus III in 1776, the Swedish Academy was modeled after the French and Spanish Academies, to promote ". . . the arts of elocution and poetry . . . [and preserve] the purity, force, and elevation of diction in the Swedish language." But the Academy felt itself constrained by Nobel's internationalist injunction and his refusal to favor Swedes. The members also felt unqualified to judge a literary prize, since the membership was weighted heavily in favor of historians and philologists, with only one literary critic (Wirsen) and only one poet (Snoilsky).

However, the tide began to turn with the Norwegian Parliament's

331

acceptance of its duties, the acquiescence of the Crown and Courts and the Caroline Institute, and finally the Bank of Sweden's approval of the Nobel Institute's revised bylaws. Wirsen was able to prevail over the Academy membership in a vote of 12–2, arguing that if the Academy demurred ". . . for reasons of personal convenience, the prize would be forfeit to the detriment of men of letters and would precipitate a storm of indignation and reproach from future generations."

Allocating funds to encourage and empower maverick researchers and writers, freeing them from the yoke of financial pressures, was and is a noble, if difficult, goal. Even if the costs of modern research had not escalated logarithmically, rendering obsolete the notion of the lone visionary, the organizational nature of prize-giving institutions themselves is such that pioneers such as Charles Steinmetz and Nikola Tesla (neither of whom received Nobel awards) and Albert Einstein (who did in 1921) can be recognized only *after* the publication and proof of their contributions—and often long afterward. Thus, the Nobel awards, founded to encourage the creative isolate, can never fulfill that promise, though by recognizing and rewarding achievements and discoveries already accomplished, the Prize has reinvigorated many of its recipients.

With respect to interpreting Nobel's proviso that the literature award go to works that exhibit an "idealistic tendency," the complications worsen. Only by accepting the most elastic and liberal meanings of the term "idealistic tendency" can there be any consensus at all. Even reaching agreement on what constitutes *literature* has proved a subject for debate. Historical and philosophical writing is often acknowledged, and Sigmund Freud was a contender for the Literature Prize. (A list of eminent authors who did not win the Prize—and the reasons they did not—makes for interesting reading.)

At the turn of the century, as now, there was a plethora of well-established writers whose contributions and influence cried out for recognition, and whose elimination from the Prize would have been an indefensible insult. With the death of Swinburne—Wirsen's choice for many years—the impetus to honor these older writers was underscored, but the resultant trend toward older recipients fueled critics' justifiable claim that the Literature Prize was in danger of becoming a "tombstone memorial" rather than a stepping-stone encouragement. The selection in 1907 of Rudyard Kipling, who at the tender age of 42 had only recently gained considerable international popularity, was no doubt in reaction to this sentiment.

Nobel's choice of the term "idealistic" seems to have devolved from some very personal ideological tastes on the part of both Nobel and Wirsen, who apparently admired the literature of ideas but were obviously reluctant to award a prize to anything considered radical. Ibsen and Strindberg, both personal enemies of Wirsen, were excluded, probably for the same reasons as Zola, whose issue-oriented realism was considered unidealistic. Thomas Hardy was rejected as "nonidealistic" because of his fatalistic pessimism, a consideration that apparently did not affect the selection in later years of such bleak, despairing writers as Beckett, Sartre, Lagerkvist, or even O'Neill and the misanthropic Patrick White. It is interesting, too, that Henri Bergson, who like many philosophers showed little artistry in his writing, was chosen over Maxim Gorki, who was a masterful writer, because Bergson's philosophy was deemed to be more "idealistic" than Gorki's. But tastes do change, and so did the membership of the committee, which today is more in tune with international, cosmopolitan tastes. In addition, previous Nobel laureates are now invited to help select recipients, further tempering the Academy's biases.

Nevertheless, a certain continuity has persisted in the nominating committee's choices, reaching back more than eighty years to Alfred Nobel's original inclinations and ideals. The humanistic-idealistic tendency does not by itself guarantee great or even good literature, but it does carry with it a certain spirit—a sensitivity and passion, two of the building blocks of quality. It is not surprising that these qualities are hallmarks of the Nobel laureates.

Nobel was perhaps naive in his fervent hope that human technological prowess would put an end to war, but he was in a way hedging his bets by developing the Peace and Literature Prizes. In rewarding writers whose ideas would propel their readers toward greater self-realization, thereby improving the quality of social discourse and human interaction, he hoped that we might find our way beyond barbarity and chaos.

Many of the Nobel laureates share similar ideology, but regardless of their social philosophy, the fact remains that these writers have produced some of the most outstanding literature of our age.

Whether they are current favorites, or have been overlooked in the contemporary marketplace, it is not often that the Nobel committee has missed the mark. Nor has the committee strayed too far from Alfred Nobel's original intentions, recognizing works in which the humanist strain, though often deep and moving, is seldom overt or revolutionary. Still, the case can be made that over the years, the pacifist, compassionate, and optimistic side of Alfred Nobel has turned out to be the most revolutionary of all.

Acknowledgments

Grateful acknowledgment is given to the following for permission to reprint copyrighted material:

"The Appointment," from *Oeuvres de Sully-Prudhomme* by René F. A. Sully-Prudhomme, translated by Arthur O'Shaughnessy. Copyright 1920 by Boni & Liveright, Inc.

"Lispeth," from *Plain Tales from the Hills* by Rudyard Kipling. Copyright 1897 by Rudyard Kipling. "Mandalay," from *Verses, 1889–1896*. Copyright 1897 by Rudyard Kipling.

"The Peace of God" by Selma Lagerlöf, translated from the Swedish by Jessie Brochner, from *The American-Scandinavian Review*, January 1917. Copyright 1917 by Selma Lagerlöf.

"The Cabuliwallah," from *Broken Ties and Other Stories* by Rabindranath Tagore, translated by Sister Nivedita. First published January 1912 in *Modern Review*. Copyright 1912 by Rabindranath Tagore.

"Eagle's Flight" by Henrik Pontoppidan, translated by Lida Siboni Hanson, from *The American-Scandinavian Review*, September 1929. Copyright 1929 by The American-Scandinavian Foundation. Reprinted with the permission of The American-Scandinavian Foundation.

"The Rose of the World," from *Early Poems & Stories* by William Butler Yeats. Copyright 1925 by the Macmillan Company. "Stream and Sun at Glendaough" and "Quarrel in Old Age," from *Collected Poems* by William Butler Yeats. Copyright 1933 by the Macmillan Company, renewed 1961 by Bertha Georgie Yeats. Reprinted with the permission of the Macmillan Publishing Company.

"The Religion of the Future," from *Religious Speeches of George Bernard Shaw*. Copyright 1911 by George Bernard Shaw.

335

ACKNOWLEDGMENTS

"Song," "On a Portrait," "At Graduation 1905," and "Spleen" by Thomas Stearns Eliot. First published in *The Harvard Advocate*.

"Thrift" by William Faulkner. Copyright © 1979 by Random House, Inc. Reprinted with the permission of the publisher.

"Has Religion Made Useful Contributions to Civilization?" from *Why I Am Not a Christian and Other Essays on Religion and Related Subjects* by Bertrand Russell. Copyright 1957 by Bertrand Russell, renewed 1985 by George Allen and Unwin. Reprinted with the permission of Simon & Schuster, Inc.

"The Myth of Mankind," from *The Eternal Smile and Other Stories* by Pär Lagerkvist. Copyright 1954 by Pär Lagerkvist. All rights reserved. Used by permission of Alfred Bonniers Forlag AB.

"Indian Camp," from *In Our Time* by Ernest Hemingway. Copyright 1925 by Charles Scribner's Sons, renewed 1953 by Ernest Hemingway. Reprinted with the permission of Charles Scribner's Sons, a division of Macmillan Publishing Company, Inc.

"The Renegade," from *Exile in the Kingdom* by Albert Camus, translated by Justin O'Brien. Copyright © 1957, 1958 by Alfred A. Knopf, Inc. Reprinted with the permission of the publisher.

"The Nobel Prize," from *In the Interlude: Poems 1945–1960* by Boris Pasternak, translated by Henry Kamen. Copyright © 1962 by Oxford University Press. Reprinted with the permission of A. D. Peters & Company, Ltd.

"Thirst" by Ivo Andrić, from *Introduction to Yugoslav Literature*, edited by Branko Mikasinovich, Dragan Milivojevic, and Vasa D. Mihailovich.

"The Infant Prodigy," from *Children and Fools* by Thomas Mann, translated by Herman G. Scheffauer. Copyright 1936 and renewed 1964 by Alfred A. Knopf, Inc. Reprinted by permission of the publisher.

"A Letter from the Queen" by Sinclair Lewis. First published December 1929 in *Cosmopolitan Magazine*. Copyright 1929 by Sinclair Lewis. Reprinted with the permission of the Estate of Sinclair Lewis.

"The Consummation," from *A Motley* by John Galsworthy. Copyright 1910 by Charles Scribner's Sons.

"A Breath of Air," from *Short Stories by Pirandello* by Luigi Pirandello, translated by Lilt Duplaix. Copyright © 1959 by Gli Eredi Di Luigi Pirandello. Reprinted with the permission of Simon & Schuster, Inc.

"Ile," from *The Plays of Eugene O'Neill* by Eugene O'Neill. Copyright 1919, renewed 1947 by Eugene O'Neill. Reprinted with the permission of Random House, Inc.

"The Good Deed," from *The Good Deed and Other Stories* by Pearl S. Buck. Copyright 1953 by Pearl S. Buck. Reprinted with the permission of Harper & Row, Publishers, Inc.

"Drops of Gall" and "Rodin's Thinker" by Gabriela Mistral, translated by Jonathan Eisen and Stuart Troy. English translation copyright 1987 by Jonathan Eisen and Stuart Troy.

"Inside and Outside" by Herman Hesse, translated by Deanna Tidmore. English translation copyright © 1986 by Deanna Tidmore. Used by permission of the translator.

"The Return of the Prodigal Son" by André Gide. Copyright 1908 by André Gide. Published in English June 1929 in *The Yale Review*. Copyright © 1973 by Twayne Publishers. Reprinted with the permission of Twayne Publishers, a division of G. K. Hall & Company.

"The Chrysanthemums," from *The Long Valley* by John Steinbeck. Copyright 1937, renewed © 1965 by John Steinbeck. Reprinted by permission of Viking Penguin Inc.

"The Kerchief," from *Twenty-One Stories* by S. Y. Agnon, translated by I. M. Lask. Copyright © 1970 by Schocken Books, Inc. Reprinted with the permission of Schocken Books, Inc.

"The Calmative," from *Stories and Texts for Nothing* by Samuel Beckett. Copyright © 1969 by Samuel Beckett. All rights reserved. Reprinted with the permission of Grove Press, Inc.

"The Ashes of a Poet," "In Yesenin Country," "Reflections," "The Old Bucket," and "A Journey Along the Oka," from *Stories and Prose Poems* by Aleksandr Solzhenitsyn, translated by Michael Glenny. English translation copyright © 1971 by Michael Glenny. Reprinted with the permission of Farrar, Straus and Giroux, Inc.

"Gentleman Alone" by Pablo Neruda, from *Selected Poems of Pablo Neruda*. Copyright © 1961 by Grove Press, Inc. Reprinted with the permission of Grove Press, Inc.

"Short Friday," from *Short Friday and Other Stories* by Isaac Bashevis Singer, translated by Joseph Singer and Roger Klein. Copyright © 1961, 1962, 1963, 1964 by Isaac Bashevis Singer. Reprinted with the permission of Farrar, Straus and Giroux, Inc.

"Eva Is Inside Her Cat," from *Innocent Erendira and Other Stories* by Gabriel García Márquez, translated by Gregory Rabassa. English

337

translation copyright © 1978 by Harper & Row, Publishers, Inc. Reprinted with the permission of Harper & Row, Publishers, Inc.

"You Are Asking" by Jaroslav Siefert, translated by Paul Jagasich and Tom O'Grady, from *The Hampden-Sydney Poetry Review*. English translation copyright © 1985 by Tom O'Grady. All rights reserved. Reprinted with the permission of Tom O'Grady.

"The Man Died," from *The Man Died* by Wole Soyinka. Copyright © 1972 by Wole Soyinka. All rights reserved. Reprinted with the permission of Rex Collings, Publisher.

We would like to thank the library staff of Fordham University for their assistance in helping us decipher some of the more arcane aspects of the Dewey Decimal System. Our thanks go also to Dean Ully Hirsch and Professor Bernard Gilligan for their unflagging commitment to worthy projects such as this. Nor do we want to overlook the kindness and help of the staff of the Swedish Consulate in New York. Also thanks to Jane Frances Troy, Missy Schueneman, Bill Shannon, and Miriam Eisen who may suspect why their names are here.